D1199452

Breaking
BREADS

Breaking
BREADS

Uri Scheft
with Raquel Pelzel

ARTISAN
NEW YORK

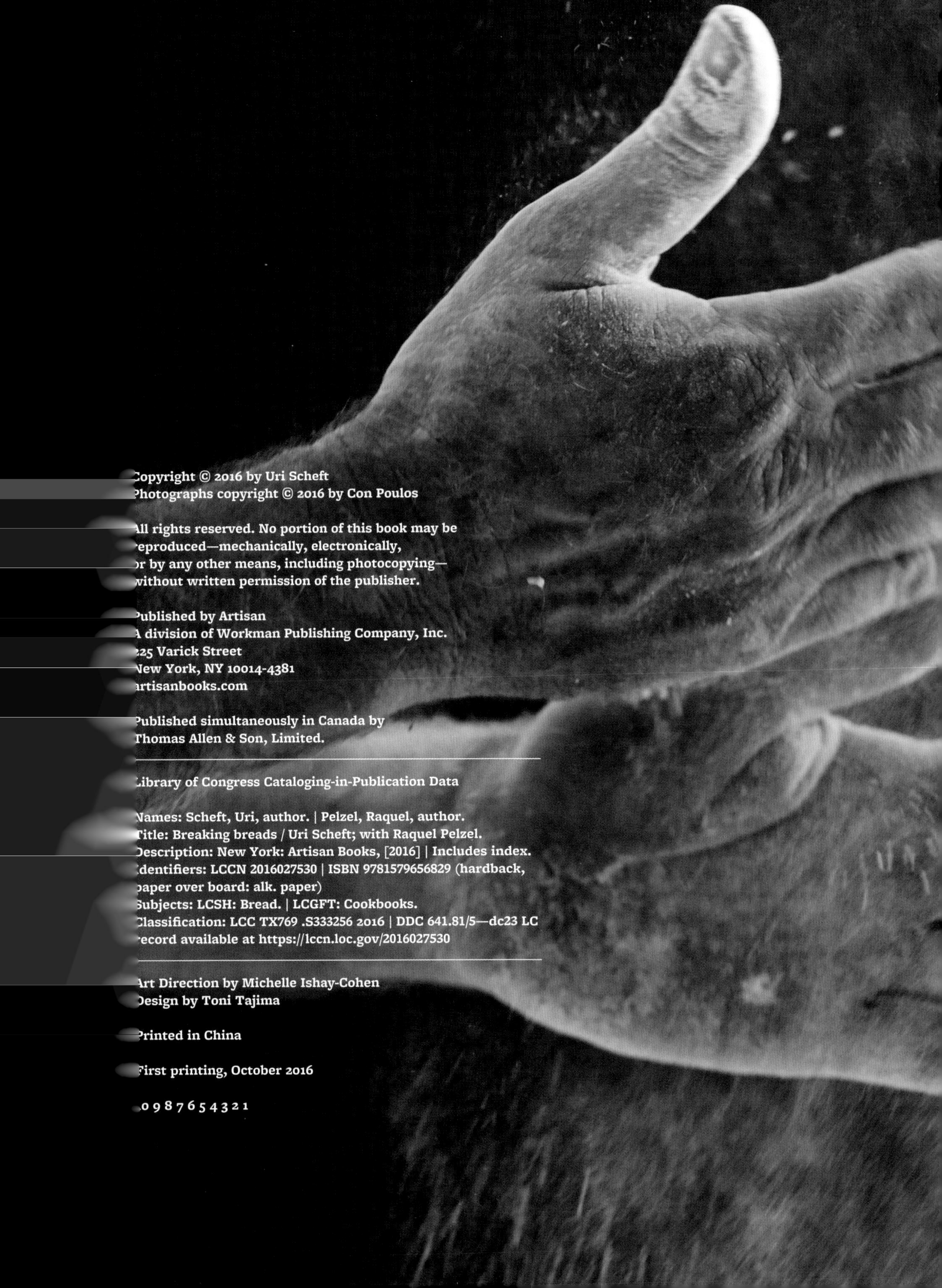

Copyright © 2016 by Uri Scheft
Photographs copyright © 2016 by Con Poulos

All rights reserved. No portion of this book may be
reproduced—mechanically, electronically,
or by any other means, including photocopying—
without written permission of the publisher.

Published by Artisan
A division of Workman Publishing Company, Inc.
225 Varick Street
New York, NY 10014-4381
artisanbooks.com

Published simultaneously in Canada by
Thomas Allen & Son, Limited.

Library of Congress Cataloging-in-Publication Data

Names: Scheft, Uri, author. | Pelzel, Raquel, author.
Title: Breaking breads / Uri Scheft; with Raquel Pelzel.
Description: New York: Artisan Books, [2016] | Includes index.
Identifiers: LCCN 2016027530 | ISBN 9781579656829 (hardback,
paper over board: alk. paper)
Subjects: LCSH: Bread. | LCGFT: Cookbooks.
Classification: LCC TX769 .S333256 2016 | DDC 641.81/5—dc23 LC
record available at https://lccn.loc.gov/2016027530

Art Direction by Michelle Ishay-Cohen
Design by Toni Tajima

Printed in China

First printing, October 2016

10 9 8 7 6 5 4 3 2 1

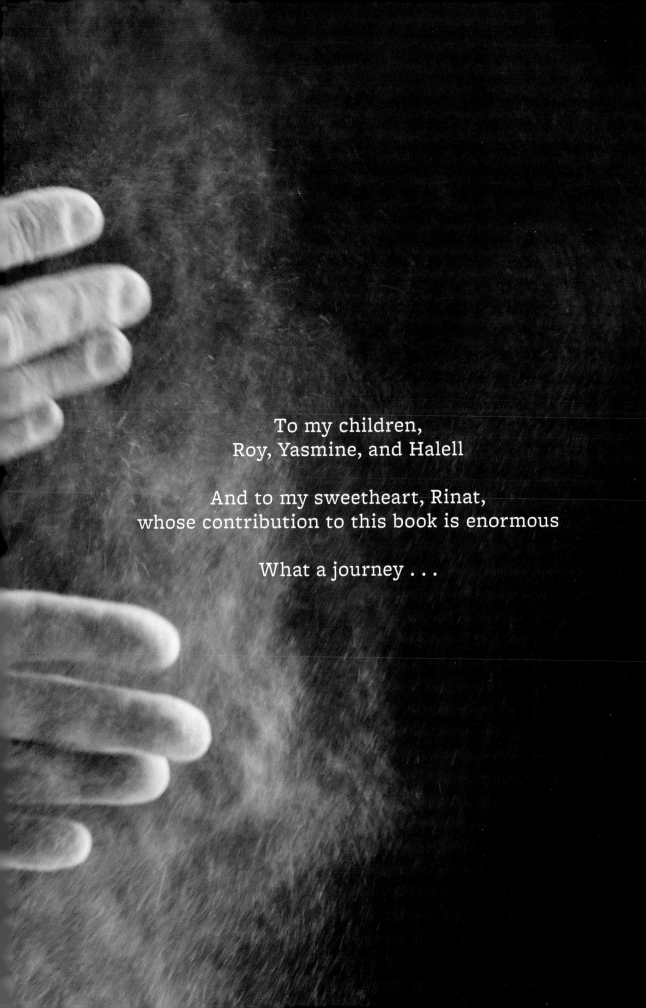

To my children,
Roy, Yasmine, and Halell

And to my sweetheart, Rinat,
whose contribution to this book is enormous

What a journey . . .

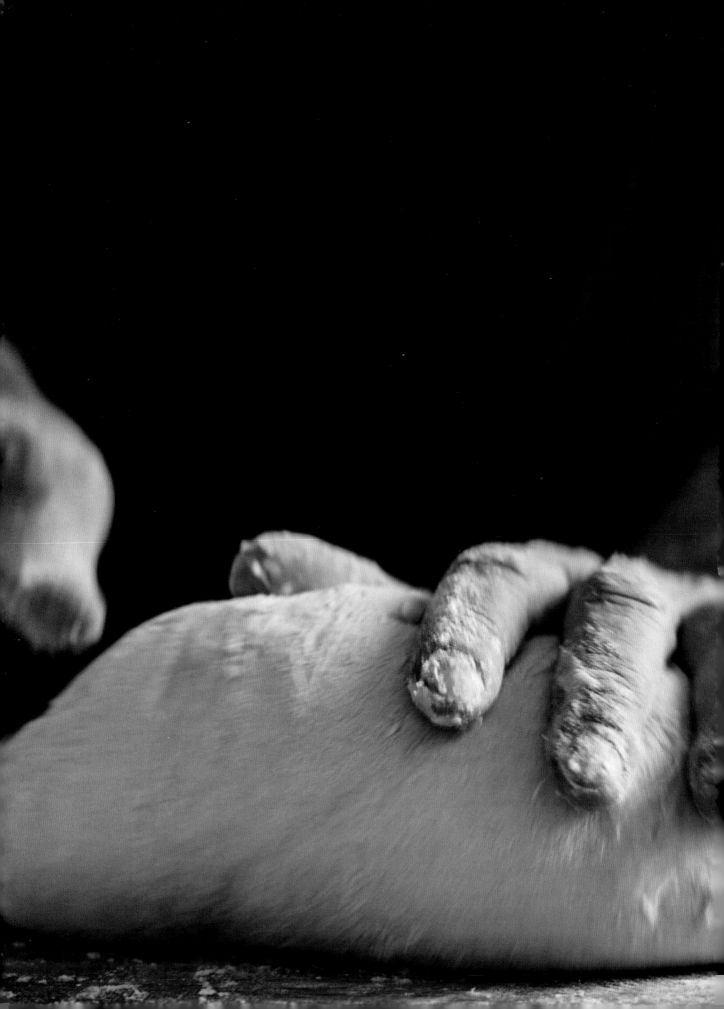

CONTENTS

INTRODUCTION

MY FIRST LOVE WAS BREAD. Or more specifically, the *smell* of bread. The smell of bread baking in the oven, the promise of its warmth, its sweetness, its supple crumb that contrasts to the browned, sometimes shiny-tender, sometimes rough and sharp-edged crust. My mother baked often—not every day, but enough for me to connect the smell of baking bread with a feeling of pure happiness. The idea of this beautiful and nourishing loaf made by hand and bringing people together around a table or even gathered at a kitchen counter to rip off a piece and eat it with such great enjoyment—to me, this is true love. And so it has become my life's work to re-create this feeling of anticipation and pleasure with every loaf and pastry I bake and sell in my bakeries—and this is the essence of *Breaking Breads*.

My passion for bread extends to a constant desire both to discover new breads and to revitalize traditional recipes to suit modern tastes with better-quality ingredients, new fillings, or different shapes. Some of these breads are ones I have grown up with—like challah and pita. Others, such as kubaneh and lachmajun, have been introduced to me through love, marriage, friendship, and travel. In turn, I want to introduce you to concepts, techniques, flavors, and breads that will become your new favorites.

I am Israeli, so there is, of course, a strong Middle Eastern inflection to the recipes in *Breaking Breads*. Others are recipes I picked up during my studies as a young baker working in Denmark, Italy, and France. Still other recipes come from my wife's family members, who are Moroccan and Yemenite, from Turkish friends, from a Druze woman who was generous enough to teach me her family's secrets for a traditional stuffed flatbread, and from the bakers I've worked with. But all the recipes are filtered through my experiences, and so the result is something that is close to the original but that is ultimately a reflection of my tastes and my cultural heritage, which is Jewish, Israeli, and Danish.

This is not a book about the true origins of kubaneh or the history that associates challah with the Jewish people. Many of the breads in this book—the Jerusalem bagel, burekas, babka, and pita—originated in a region that has been in flux for thousands upon thousands of years. People have been settling in the region of Israel for millennia, and now through marriage and travel, it's not uncommon to have someone like me, a mishmash of cultures and influences, who is married to a woman, also born in Israel, with Yemenite and Moroccan parents—and we have a child who was born in the United States, so she is American, Danish, Israeli, Yemenite, and Moroccan! These are the recipes—a challah from Israel, a flatbread from Iraq, a cookie from Denmark, a pastry from Lebanon—that have become a part of our culture and identity as Israelis and as a new-world family. These breads and pastries reflect how we eat in our daily life.

NEW ISRAELI CUISINE AND MODERN ISRAELI BAKING

As much as New York City is a melting pot, so is Israel. Although more than three-quarters of the 8-million-plus population is Jewish (which is, incidentally, roughly the same as the population of New York City), we are also a mix of cultures and cuisines that rivals that of any metropolitan area. Israel is a demographic hodgepodge of people from Russia, Morocco, Ethiopia, Germany, South Africa, Lebanon, Yemen, Scandinavia, Bulgaria, Poland, and, of course, the United States, among many other near and far lands. So it makes sense that our cuisine is a blend of recipes from many cultures.

But something interesting is happening in Israel—and has been happening over the past twenty years or so. Today Israelis want the food of their mothers and grandmothers, but also food made with the best ingredients and perhaps reinterpreted to reflect trends happening in Los Angeles, New York, London, and Barcelona. Israelis have a deep-rooted hunger for exploration and discovery. We are a nomadic people, don't forget, and after serving in the Israeli army, which is mandatory for all eighteen-year-olds, many Israelis quench their wanderlust by heading to South America, India, Europe, Asia, Australia, and the United States, and not just for two weeks—sometimes for two years! When the young generation comes home, they bring with them a passion for new tastes and dishes—gooey American-style chocolate chip cookies, Sriracha, green juice. Israelis always want to know what's new and exciting, especially when it comes to good things to eat!

The fusion in much contemporary Israeli food extends to baking and mirrors my own approach in the kitchen. This book is not a comprehensive study on the breads of the Middle East. It does embrace the spirit of discovery, of trying new things and melding them with classic techniques. The spices and aromas of the Israeli kitchen combine to create dishes and flavors that have recently captured the attention and adoration of the food world. Yotam Ottolenghi and Sami Tamimi, of Ottolenghi and Nopi in London, helped to ignite the interest in Israeli food, and chefs like Michael Solomonov of Zahav in Philadelphia, Einat Admony of Balaboosta in New York City, and Alon Shaya of Shaya in New Orleans are constantly introducing new flavors and taking liberties with classic "Israeli" dishes in their restaurants. The result is expats who are shaping modern Israeli food as much as chefs in Israel are.

To me, *this* is modern Israeli food: It's taking the old and infusing it with the new. It's taking traditions and flavors from all of its people—from Denmark to Ethiopia, Morocco to Poland—and funneling them through the creative minds of cooks who are constantly trying to create and conceive of new compositions. It's dill and cumin, it's pomegranate and ricotta, it's Nutella and pistachios. It's the most ancient of flatbreads as well as apple-stuffed, cinnamon-laced strudel.

A MODERN ISRAELI BAKER

My devotion to bread began when I was a child. When I was ten years old, my parents decided it was important for us to better understand Danish culture and our Scandinavian roots. So we moved from Ra'anana in Israel to Copenhagen. For me, this was a *total* disaster. In Israel, where we had a large home with a garden and a swimming pool, surrounded by orange plantations and strawberry fields, I was free to roam and play. In Denmark we moved into a New York City–style flat where five of us lived together in a tiny space that didn't even have a shower. Because I didn't have many friends at first, I was home a lot and became interested in cooking and baking. My natural curiosity for creating began to grow, and I was intrigued by this very practical way to express myself creatively (and after I was finished, I could eat my experiments!).

Of course I eventually made friends, but I never stopped missing Israel—the warmth, the busy streets, the sounds, the smells, and the food. I returned for high school and served in the Israeli army, and afterward studied biology at Tel Aviv University. I earned my degree, but my heart was still drawn to the kitchen; and in fact, maybe it was my confidence in science that eventually drew me to baking in particular. There is true chemistry when you combine yeast with water, flour, and a little salt. There are variables like temperature, humidity, seasonality, ingredients, and human manipulation. Baking is a very old art, but a very scientific one too.

I returned to Denmark to study baking at Ringsted Tekniske Skole, then went on to apprentice in bakeries throughout the world: from the oldest and most highly regarded confectioneries in Copenhagen, Conditori La Glace and Kransekagehuset, where my love for all things marzipan blossomed, to Aurion Bakery in northern Denmark, where I learned about baking with biodynamic grains. I learned patisserie at Lenôtre, outside Paris, and I've been lucky enough to call Eric Kayser, of Maison Kayser, a mentor and colleague.

As I became a more experienced baker, I found out that the best way to learn about a bread made in, say, Italy was actually to *go* to Italy. To learn about focaccia, I worked alongside multigeneration Italian bakers from Camogli to discover their secrets. When I wanted to master Turkish flatbreads, I went to Istanbul to watch women cook them on giant flattops or heated domes (called a saj oven) outside their homes. Going straight to the source is an experience that can never be replicated in a book (even mine!). The air, the surroundings, the sounds, the unguarded and open conversation with local cooks . . . I am so lucky to have experienced these breads and pastries in their places of origin. I think that if you understand the beginnings and the evolution of a product, you can play with it in a way that makes sense and give it new life without losing what made it beautiful in the first place.

Eventually it was time for me to open my own place, where I could showcase the diaspora of breads and traditions that I cared most about: breads like challah and focaccia, Danish dark rye, and naturally leavened European sourdough. In 2002, Lehamim Bakery (*lehamim* means "breads" in Hebrew) was born. Located in the heart of Tel Aviv near an old greenmarket, the bakery was designed to be open and bright, so customers could walk in and feel the energy of baking, see the bakers, smell the bread as it came out of the oven—in some ways replicating the experience I had as a young boy coming home to my mother's from-scratch, fresh-baked loaves of challah on Fridays.

After several years during which Lehamim Bakery was growing, creating, and earning the title of Tel Aviv's favorite bakery, a regular customer said to me, "Uri, you have

to open in New York City!" It seemed a good fit and a natural city to branch out to (and, I admit, it was a bit of a life goal of mine, to open a bakery in New York)—a city that is, at its heart, as much of a global melting pot as Tel Aviv is. Breads Bakery opened just off Union Square in Manhattan in 2013. Strangely, while I have quite a following in New York for my naturally leavened sourdough, my challah, and my rye bread, what I've become most known for is the chocolate babka, a twist on a home-style "grandma" (that's what *babka* means) cake called a kugelhopf! How funny it is—and how perfect to reintroduce a very old-fashioned cake in a very new way (my version, on page 74, has more chocolate and lots of Nutella, and is made with a croissant-like dough). The babka very much captures the essence of what I do: make space for traditional baked goods in the modern world, introducing a whole new audience to their deliciousness.

The recipes in *Breaking Breads* are a celebration of so many traditions: Jewish and Muslim, Middle Eastern and Scandinavian, North African and Eastern European. These recipes come from me, from my friends and family, from my staff and team in the bakeries, and from people whose skill and spirit I respect and admire—whether they are professional bakers or grandmas who have been using the same recipe for fifty years because *that's the way it's done (and you don't f—k with tradition!)*. The breads and pastries reflect the hands of so many talented people who create love and beauty from the humblest ingredients. Each recipe has been created, baked, and tested in home kitchens. Some are new; others are recipes that were tucked into books or pockets when families moved across oceans and continents. I hope that throughout this book, you will find new incentives to get into the kitchen and to break bread with those around your table, to continue with the old ways and create new ones, too.

BAKING BREAD AT HOME: A SIMPLE EXPLANATION FROM START TO FINISH

Bread baking is an art that goes back millennia to ancient Egypt, to the first threshing of wheat and the first flatbreads cooked over an open fire. It's important to always remember its humble beginnings, at a time before electricity and stand mixers, when there were no oven thermometers or food processors.

I like to say that the only things you need to bake great bread are flour, yeast, water, salt, and your hands. There is no reason to allow baking to intimidate you, no reason to not make bread because you don't have a mixer or the right pan or a fancy oven. Bread is infinitely forgiving and versatile. As long as you pay attention to what is happening with the dough—its moisture, its warmth, its vitality—it will yield wonderful results and will never fail to make you happy when you pull this beautiful and living thing (Yes! Yeast is alive!) from your oven. You made that! With your hands! Bread is something to be proud of and to share.

Bread Basics

Baking bread can be as complicated or as simple as you choose to make it. We can talk temperatures and humidity levels and protein percentages until we turn blue in the face, but my goal is to empower you to just make bread and not to overthink it. So here is a very simple explanation of what happens when you make bread and a little bit about the basic building blocks of bread.

At its core, when flour is leavened (with yeast or chemical leaveners) and mixed with liquid (water or milk), what is created is bread. Of course there are an infinite number of variations within this loose definition, from pita to focaccia to naturally leavened boules, baguettes, white sandwich bread, doughnuts, injera . . . the list is endless. What happens with all of them is this: the yeast eats the sugar and starch in the bread dough, creating alcohol, which contributes flavor (the alcohol burns off during baking), and generating carbon dioxide, which is trapped in the web of gluten and gliadin (proteins in flour) and causes the bread to rise and hopefully have very nice holes throughout the loaf. The balance of protein in the flour, the strength of the flour, the amount of liquid in the dough, and how much the dough is kneaded all affect how much a dough will rise and how tight that inner crumb will be.

Ingredients and Flavor

Flour, water, yeast, and salt. These four simple ingredients are the foundation for most breads and flatbreads. I prefer a medium-protein bread flour (about 11.5% protein), but to test the recipes in this book, I used King Arthur all-purpose flour (11.7%), Heckers, and Ceresota—all available in most supermarkets.

In the bakeries we use fresh cake yeast for flavor and texture, but instant yeast and active dry yeast work, too. (Blooming ensures that yeast is active and alive. Instant yeast doesn't need to be bloomed in water before being used in making the dough, and it's not necessary to bloom newly purchased active dry yeast. But if you want to be sure, then bloom active dry yeast in a little portion of warm water—just subtract about 60 grams or ¼ cup of warm water from the total amount of water called for in the recipe.)

While most bread recipes call for mixing warm water (usually around 105° to 110°F) with the flour, I use cool room-temperature water (around 70° to 75°F) because it allows the dough to take a little longer to rise and thus develop more flavor.

Another way to introduce flavor to newly formed dough is to add an old piece of dough saved from a previous batch. To create this "starter," knead a 60-gram (2-ounce) piece of saved dough with 5 grams (1 teaspoon) of fresh yeast or ½ teaspoon of instant yeast and place it in an airtight container. It will keep in the refrigerator for up to 2 weeks.

Realistically, however, not many home bakers have access to an older, nicely soured piece of dough the way professional bakers do, so a more practical approach is to create a pre-ferment, also known as a poolish (in French) or a biga (in Italian), in which a small amount of yeast, water, and flour is mixed to create a very wet sponge and then fermented over 24 hours in the refrigerator (called "retardation" because the process of fermentation is being slowed down) before being added to the remaining ingredients. There is also a shorter pre-ferment process (that takes only 1 hour) in which yeast and water are covered with flour, and then once the flour cracks on top, the rest of the ingredients are added. For more information about pre-ferments, see page 174.

Mixing

I like to say that when you start mixing your dough, stay with it. Get to know the dough, get your hands in there—your hands will eventually remember the feel of the dough. It's almost like you are thinking with your hands rather than with your head. You will eventually know if the dough needs more water or more flour—every time you bake, you become more aware of any adjustments to the dough that need to be made.

Throughout this book, ingredients are added to the mixing bowl in a specific order. There is a reason for this: with bread dough, the yeast and water are always combined in the bowl first, with the flour, sugar, and finally salt added on top, followed by oil or butter. The dough is usually mixed in a stand mixer fitted with a bread hook until you can tell that it is coming together nicely—usually within 1½ to 2 minutes. I like to stop the mixer and get my hand in there, squeezing and feeling the dough from all angles to see if it is too wet or too dry. If, at the 2-minute mark, the dough hasn't come together or is too wet, this is the time to add a small drizzle of water or a few pinches of flour. (Add extra flour or water later in the process, and you risk those ingredients not being worked into the dough well enough.)

There are so many variables when it comes to making dough—if the flour is old, it could yield drier dough, so you may need to add water; if you use a locally milled stone-ground flour, it may react in a different way than a supermarket brand and you will have to respond to the difference by adjusting the water or flour as you go. Never walk away from your dough while it is mixing—there are so many changes and small details to notice . . . not to mention that you don't want your stand mixer to "walk" away!

Kneading

After the dough comes together in the mixer, the mixer speed is often increased and the dough is kneaded mechanically to develop the gluten. Be wary of overwarming the dough—while using a mixer is a great time- and energy-saver (human energy, not electricity), the process does tend to warm up the dough, risking "burning" the flour and disempowering the gluten. If you notice that the dough is becoming too warm during this process (perhaps your room is very warm or your water or flour was too warm), stop the mixer and lightly flour the top of the dough; then place the dough in a lightly floured bowl and let it rest, covered, for 30 minutes. During the resting time the yeast is still active and the gluten is being worked—just in a gentler, more time-consuming way.

After kneading the dough in the stand mixer, I always like to finish kneading it by hand. I knead dough the way I learned from my mother: by stretching, tearing, and pushing the dough away from me (see photos below), then folding it back on itself, giving it a quarter turn, and repeating.

This is a little different than the traditional method of kneading the dough from the top down and rocking it back and forth without actually tearing it. I find that tearing the dough actually develops the gluten more quickly without overheating the dough (or exhausting your arms), so you end up with better bread. Once the dough begins to resist, cup your hands around the base of the dough and push and pull it, using your hands to guide it into a nice round shape. You don't ever want to fight the dough if it resists and doesn't want to be kneaded anymore. If the flour over-oxygenates, the dough will begin to lose flavor and the bread will be tough.

To know when the dough is strong enough to stop kneading, do the windowpane test: Break off a small piece, dip it in a little flour (to prevent sticking), and slowly stretch it out paper-thin (see photo below). If it tears before you can see through it, the gluten isn't strong enough yet. (You want

Stretching and tearing the dough

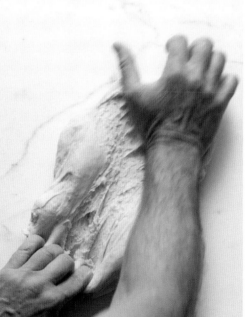

Pushing the dough away

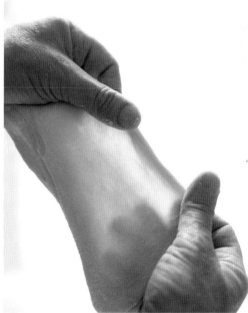

The windowpane test

an elastic dough, so the structure of the crumb is strong enough to hold the gas released by the yeast, creating air pockets and lightness. If I want volume in the bread, the gluten has to be strong enough to hold the air in.) If the windowpane test is successful and the dough can be stretched to a transparent sheet (see photo on page 15), then it's time to stop kneading and move on to the first rise.

Rising and Proofing

The dough develops most of its flavor during the first stage of rising. After the ingredients are mixed, the dough is kneaded and then set aside, covered, to rise until it has doubled (or nearly doubled). After this point, the dough is often divided into smaller pieces and shaped into buns, rounds, boules, braided loaves . . . whatever the recipe indicates. Then the dough goes into the proofing stage—anywhere from 40 minutes to a few hours, depending on the amount of yeast in the recipe, the warmth of the room, and the temperature of the dough. During proofing the dough truly opens up to develop lightness and to trap as much gas as possible in the interior. It is critical in this stage to proof the bread in a somewhat humid, air-sealed environment so it doesn't dry out. Take care to always cover rising dough so it doesn't develop a crust or dry out. If the dough becomes too dry, the yeast won't remain active. I like to lightly dust the top of the dough with flour, then drape a clean kitchen towel over the dough. Or use one of the methods outlined below.

Once you can press a finger gently into the dough and the depression fills in by about halfway, the dough is ready to be baked (if the depression fills in too quickly, then the dough needs more time to proof). Another way to tell when the dough is ready is to look at the side of the dough, between the bottom edge of the shaped loaf and the sheet pan or other surface it is proofing

The stages of proofing: an underproofed, proofed, and overproofed dough

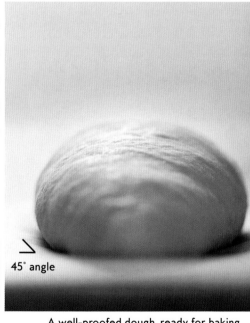

45° angle

A well-proofed dough, ready for baking

on. There should be about a 45-degree difference, an "air angle," if you will, between the side of the loaf and the board (see photo, opposite). If the dough hasn't relaxed enough during proofing, the angle will be greater; if the dough has overproofed, there will be hardly any air between the edge and the board.

In professional bakeries, we have walk-in proofers with controlled humidity and warm temperatures to encourage consistent rising. These are for professional kitchens—here are some of my favorite ways to build your own proof box:

Use a garbage bag: Place one or more overturned cups at each corner of the sheet pan holding the shaped dough, and then slide the sheet pan inside an unscented garbage bag. Tie the open end or tuck it under. The cups prevent the plastic from resting directly on top of the dough so that when the pan is removed, you don't risk the dough tearing.

Use a cardboard box: Use an X-acto knife to remove the top portion of a large cardboard box that is big enough to hold the sheet pan and a bowl of hot water to create humidity. Carefully lower the sheet pan into the box, set the bowl of hot water inside, and slide the entire contraption into an unscented garbage bag. Tie the bag closed or tuck the open end under the box, or simply cover the top of the box with another sheet pan or other tight-fitting "lid."

Use the oven: Just make sure to double-check and remove the dough from the oven before preheating to bake!

Baking

During baking the dough expands while the crust develops, caramelizes, and browns. Depending on the type of bread you are baking, you may choose to bake the bread with steam (see below) or without it. Baking with steam leads to a moister environment in the oven and produces a larger initial expansion of the dough when it first goes into the hot steamy oven. It also often contributes a crackly, crisp crust that shatters when you pull the bread apart.

A convection oven eliminates the problem of hot spots in an oven through the use of a fan that circulates the hot air around the item that is baking. If you want to use the convection option on your oven, decrease the baking temperature in the recipes by 25°F and the time by 20%. You can add steam when using a convection oven.

Color and timing are the main indicators of when a bread is finished baking. Some loaves (such as ciabatta) will sound hollow

---

CREATE YOUR OWN STEAM OVEN

To bake with steam at home, simply set a rimmed sheet pan on the bottom of the oven (or the bottom rack if the heating element of your oven is exposed on the floor of the oven) and let it preheat with the oven. Place the dough in the preheated oven, quickly pour about ¼ cup of ice water onto the sheet pan, and close the door. The ice water will create steam when it hits the hot pan.

when tapped, while other richer breads (challah, for example) won't. Since the tap test can be a bit confusing, I find that the most reliable method for checking doneness is to follow the visual cues described in the recipe, to look for even browning, and to keep the timing in mind (remember that some ovens run hot while others run cool, and this can affect your baking time). Another way to evaluate doneness is to press on the side of the loaf with your finger to see if it resists light pressure or gives in easily; but of course this depends on the loaf—a hearty muesli bun will feel firmer than a pain de mie roll. You can also take the bread's internal temperature with an instant-read thermometer—most breads are finished baking at 195°F. Remember that the loaf will continue baking once it is out of the oven, thanks to carryover heat—the heat trapped within the bread. At the end of the day, though, baking is about learning by doing, and after a bit of practice you'll know when your bread is done.

Storing

When storing bread, place it in a plastic bag and fold the open end under. If the bread has already been sliced, wrap the cut end in plastic wrap and then place the whole loaf in a plastic bag. To freeze bread, wrap the loaf in two layers of plastic wrap, then in a layer of aluminum foil. To defrost frozen bread, leave the loaf out at room temperature; when it has thawed, remove the foil and plastic wrap and rewrap in foil. If you don't have time to defrost the bread first, place the foil-wrapped loaf (remember to remove the plastic wrap!) in a warm oven for 8 to 10 minutes, removing the foil for the last minute or two to crisp the crust.

A Few Notes, Tips, and Tricks

These insider tips will help as you follow the recipes in this book.

BATCH SIZE AND INCREASING/DECREASING BATCHES LIKE A BAKER

You'll notice that many recipes yield two or three loaves, or even more (for example, the focaccia and lachmajun recipes). When making dough in a stand mixer, small amounts of ingredients don't get handled as efficiently as larger amounts. So for best results, make the bread as described and share it with your family and friends or freeze some for later.

If you need to increase a batch of dough, use the weight of the flour in the recipe as your 100% benchmark. So if a recipe calls for 800 grams of flour and you want to increase it to an even, simple 1 kilo (1,000 grams), multiply the amount you want to increase it to (1,000 grams) by 100, to yield 100,000. Then divide 100,000 by 800 grams (the original amount of flour, your 100% benchmark) to get 125. Finally, divide 125 by 100 to get 1.25— multiply all ingredients by 1.25 to get the new measurements. For example, if the recipe originally called for 25 grams of yeast, you multiply 25 grams by 1.25 to get 31.25 grams, which is the new amount of yeast (in grams) that you need to use in the enlarged recipe.

CALCULATION
based on 800 grams flour (100%)

800 grams = original amount
1,000 grams = amount you want to increase to
$100 \times \mathbf{1,000} = 100,000 \div \mathbf{800} = 125$
$125 \div 100 = \mathbf{1.25}$
multiply all ingredient quantities by 1.25 to get new amounts

---

BEFORE YOU BEGIN: READ, WEIGH, PREPARE

For me, this is a metaphor for living: *Read the recipe before you begin.* Read the ingredients list, reread the instructions, weigh all your ingredients, and get everything in order so you can follow the recipe exactly. I use a digital gram scale because it is more accurate than cup measures, meaning that your dough will be consistent from batch to batch.

I also like to have all my refrigerated ingredients at room temperature before beginning—room-temperature eggs beat with more volume; room-temperature butter creams more easily. For butter, you can microwave it in 10-second increments, checking it often, until it isn't cold but hasn't started to soften too much and become greasy.

WORK CLEAN

Invest in a bench scraper or dough scraper to remove excess flour and bits of dough from your work surface before sponging it off. If you start with a wet sponge, you'll end up with a floury, pasty mess. Keep a trash bag handy next to the counter or in the sink, or use a large bowl that you can wipe the garbage into. Keep everything clean and organized while you work.

FLOUR: SIFTING

When flour is oxygenated, it allows for better gluten development, and the gluten can trap more air in the loaf. I've taken the same ingredients and made the same bread, proofed and baked the same way, but used sifted flour in one loaf and unsifted flour in the other. In the sifted loaf I got 10 to 15% more volume compared to the unsifted one!

FLOUR: CONVERTING ALL-PURPOSE TO WHOLE WHEAT

You can also substitute up to 50% of the white flour in a recipe with whole wheat or spelt flour. You will have to add about 50 grams (3 tablespoons plus 1 teaspoon) more water to the dough to account for the heartier flour.

DON'T BE SHY WITH THE ADD-INS

My general rule of thumb when adding chocolate, seeds, nuts, dried fruits, or grains to bread is to weigh the dough, then add 20% of the weight in extra goodies. Now, for some goodies, you will need to add extra water to account for the absorbent properties of the add-ins—this is true for ingredients like quinoa and flaxseeds. Other extras, like sautéed onion and olives, actually add moisture to the dough, so you might need to reduce some liquid in the recipe. This is definitely a key point to consider when mixing the dough. In addition, always make sure you get all the extra ingredients out from the bowl or measuring cup. What is left in the cup could be 10% of the volume—the goodies really do matter! Get it all in there!

REMEMBER: YOU CONTROL THE DOUGH, NOT THE OTHER WAY AROUND

A good baker knows how to respond to a changing environment, whether that means reacting to a dry dough or slowing down or speeding up fermentation to develop more flavor or to bake off bread quicker. When dealing with yeast, remember that you are working with living creatures—similar to working with the bacteria in cheese or the yeast in wine. You are using these specific bacteria to create a chemical reaction in water and flour to make bread. These small microbes are greatly influenced by temperature, and learning how to control a dough by controlling the temperature of various ingredients or conditions is one of the best ways to manage your baking.

- If you want to prolong fermentation and create more flavor and aroma, use ice water instead of cool room-temperature water in the dough. This will slow down the activity of the yeast—slower fermentation creates more flavor nuance.
- You can also retard some doughs in the refrigerator to slow the process of rising and develop more flavor. Simply cover the bowl the dough is in with plastic wrap and refrigerate for up to 1 day.
- On the other hand, if you need to have a loaf of fresh bread fast, use warm water in the dough to speed up the rising process, and proof it in a warm environment.

How to Use *Breaking Breads*

Read the recipe through before baking, making sure you have not only all the ingredients you'll need but also the time that is required to complete it (some recipes take only an an hour while others stretch over several days). Measure out and get all of your ingredients assembled (this is called mise en place), and then follow the recipe exactly for at least the first few times you make it. Once you master a recipe and understand how the bread dough should look and feel during each step of the process, you can take creative license and make it your own by using different types of flours, substituting or adding ingredients, and shaping the dough the way you like. While the method of making the dough is strict, once you have the dough, you can play and manipulate.

CHALLAH

WHEN I WAS A BOY, every Friday for Shabbat my mother, who taught kindergarten from our home in Israel, baked challah with the schoolchildren. The rich and sweet smell of Friday challah is to Israelis what the smell of pumpkin pie is to Americans at Thanksgiving—except that our celebration of family and friendship comes together at the table each Friday before sunset, instead of just once a year.

This simple ritual of baking the challah and the pleasure that the children experienced upon holding the warm loaf fresh from the oven . . . well, it's a love story to me. I fell in love with the warm yeasty fragrance that filled our home. I fell in love with the feeling of excitement that each Friday brought, knowing that when I opened the door after coming home from school, this intoxicating, homey, beautiful smell would greet me. That fragrance was the marker of something delicious, as well as the human connection that is sparked when you share something made with love.

Challah is, at its essence, a bread meant for occasions: religious ones, holidays, weddings, and celebrations. In religious Jewish communities, it is the bread served on the dinner table for Shabbat. The head of the table says a blessing over the bread before ripping it by hand and passing each person his or her own piece. Made with what were once considered expensive ingredients like eggs and sugar, challah is a lightly sweet and very tender bread that pulls apart into long cottony strands. The way challah is shaped makes it special too. It is no ordinary loaf or boule: the dough is braided. The three-strand braided challah is an entry-level challah; shaping it is no more difficult than braiding a young girl's hair. Once you master that, try playing with the dough and see where you end up! I like to break with tradition and use challah dough as a way to express my creativity, which you'll see in the wide variety of shapes that can be made from this forgiving and easy-to-work-with dough. Even the ingredients you can add to it are limitless—from chocolate and candied orange peel to nuts, seeds, herbs, and marzipan; challah can be a canvas for expressing your creativity.

By nature I am a curious baker; I travel and take note of all the different ways of shaping and flavoring bread. Though challah is classically considered an Eastern European Jewish (Ashkenazi) bread, I have seen versions of challah baked on the island of Djerba in Tunisia and in Poland, Colombia, and different Jewish communities in Israel and Morocco. I have fashioned loaves inspired by ancient Roman art and texts depicting Jewish people baking a small tin to hold salt or honey into the center of the challah for dipping (see photos, pages 38–41). This inspired my festive challahs: I add hummus, chopped liver, or honey to the bowl, turning the challah into an edible serving vessel as well as a table centerpiece.

Challah can be a playground for your imagination as a baker. But follow the recipe first! Get to know the method. Like a musician who studies classical piano before exploring interpretive jazz, you will find that the fundamentals and techniques are important. Most people think of baking as a science that is all about precision—which it is, in part—but really, once you get to know a dough, you can break free from the structure to create new shapes and flavors that inspire you.

Challah

Makes 3 loaves, or 2 loaves and 10 rolls (1.75 kilos / 3½ pounds of dough)

Why make one challah when you can make three? Many of the recipes in this book produce more than one loaf of bread or babka because the result you get when mixing a large batch of dough is actually much better than what you get when making a small batch. With a good amount of dough in the bowl, it is easier for the mixer to do its job and properly knead it. Challah freezes beautifully—you can freeze a loaf whole, or slice it and then freeze it for toast or French toast. Or have one loaf for dinner or breakfast, and give the other loaf to a friend or someone close to your heart. The offer of fresh-baked bread is a beautiful gesture that is better than any bottle of wine or store-bought hostess gift.

DOUGH

Cool room-temperature water	400 grams (1²/₃ cups)
Fresh yeast	40 grams (3 tablespoons plus 2 teaspoons)
or active dry yeast	15 grams (1 tablespoon plus 1¾ teaspoons)
All-purpose flour (sifted, 11.7%)	1 kilo (7 cups), plus extra for shaping
Large eggs	2
Granulated sugar	100 grams (½ cup)
Fine salt	15 grams (1 tablespoon)
Sunflower oil or canola oil or unsalted butter (at room temperature)	75 grams (5 tablespoons)

EGG WASH AND TOPPING

Large egg	1
Water	1 tablespoon
Fine salt	Pinch
Nigella, poppy, or sesame seeds (or a combination)	90 grams (²/₃ cup)

1 Make the dough: Pour the cool water into the bowl of a stand mixer fitted with the bread hook. Crumble the yeast into the water and use your fingers to rub and dissolve it; if using active dry yeast, whisk the yeast into the water. Add the flour, eggs, sugar, salt, and oil.

2 Mix the dough on low speed to combine the ingredients, stopping the mixer if the dough climbs up the hook or if you need to work in dry ingredients that have settled on the bottom of the bowl. Scrape the bottom and sides of the bowl as needed. It should take about 2 minutes for the dough to come together (see photo on page 29). If there are lots of dry bits in the bottom of the bowl that just aren't getting worked in, add a tablespoon or two of water. On the other hand, if the dough looks softer than in the photo opposite, add a few pinches of flour.

NOTE: EVENTUALLY YOU'LL BE ABLE TO FEEL the dough and know if you need to add water or flour; it's always better to adjust the ratios when the dough is first coming together at the beginning of mixing rather than wait until the end of the kneading process, since it takes longer for ingredient additions to get worked into the dough mass at this later point and you risk overworking the dough.

3 Increase the speed to medium and knead until a smooth dough forms, about 4 minutes. You want the dough to be a bit firm.

4 **Stretch and fold the dough:** Lightly dust your work surface with a little flour, and use a dough scraper to transfer the dough from the mixing bowl to the floured surface. Use your palms to push and tear the top of the dough away from you in one stroke, and then fold that section onto the middle of the dough. Give the dough a quarter turn and repeat the push/tear/fold process for about 1 minute. Then push and pull the dough against the work surface to round it into a ball (see photos, opposite).

5 **Let the dough rise:** Lightly dust a bowl with flour, add the dough, sprinkle just a little flour on top of the dough, and cover the bowl with plastic wrap. Set the bowl aside at room temperature until the dough has risen by about 70%, about 40 minutes (this will depend on how warm your room is—when the dough proofs in a warmer room it will take less time than in a cooler room).

6 **Divide the dough:** Use a plastic dough scraper to gently lift the dough out of the bowl and transfer it to a lightly floured work surface (take care not to press out the trapped gas in the dough). Gently pull the dough into a rectangular shape. Use a bench scraper or a chef's knife to divide the dough into 3 equal horizontal strips (you can use a kitchen scale to weigh each piece if you want to be exact). Then divide each piece into 3 smaller equal parts crosswise so you end up with a total of 9 pieces. (If you plan on making 2 challah loaves and 10 rolls, leave 1 large piece intact and see page 35 for instructions on shaping rolls with that piece.)

NOTE: IT IS BEST NOT TO HAVE AN OVERLY floured work surface when rolling dough into cylinders, since the flour makes it hard for the dough to gain enough traction to be shaped into a rope.

7 **Shape the dough:** Set a piece of dough lengthwise on your work surface. Use the palm of your hand to flatten the dough into a flat rectangle; then fold the top portion over and use your palm to press the edge into the flat part of the dough. Fold and press 3 more times—the dough will end up as a cylinder about 7 inches long. Set this piece aside and repeat with the other 8 pieces.

8 Return to the first piece of dough and use both hands to roll the cylinder back and forth to form a long rope, pressing down lightly when you get to the ends of the rope so they are flattened. The rope should be about 14 inches long with tapered ends (see photo, opposite). Repeat with the remaining 8 cylinders. Lightly flour the long ropes (this allows for the strands of the braid to stay somewhat separate during baking; otherwise, they'd fuse together).

(continued)

STEP 2

STEP 4

STEP 5

STEP 6

STEP 8

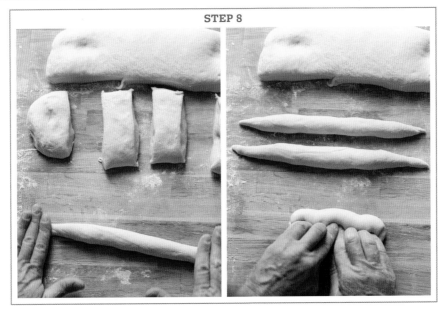

9 Pinch the ends of 3 ropes together at the top (you can place a weight on top of the ends to hold them in place) and lightly flour the dough. Braid the dough, lifting each piece up and over so the braid is more stacked than it is long; you also want it to be fatter and taller in the middle, and more tapered at the ends. When you get to the end of the ropes and there is nothing left to braid, use your palm to press and seal the ends together. Repeat with the remaining 6 ropes, creating 3 braided challahs. Place the challahs on parchment paper–lined rimmed sheet pans, cover them with a kitchen towel (or place them inside an unscented plastic bag), and set them aside in a warm, draft-free spot to rise until the loaves have doubled in volume, about 40 minutes (depending on how warm the room is).

10 Adjust the oven racks to the upper-middle and lower-middle positions and preheat the oven to 425°F.

11 Test the dough: Once the challah loaves have roughly doubled in size, do the press test: Press your finger lightly into the dough, remove it, and see if the depression fills in by half. If the depression fills back in quickly and completely, the dough needs more time to rise; if you press the dough and it slightly deflates, the dough has overproofed and will be heavier and less airy after baking.

12 Bake the loaves: Make the egg wash by mixing the egg, water, and salt together in a small bowl. Gently brush the entire surface of the loaves with egg wash, taking care not to let it pool in the creases of the braids. You want a nice thin coating. Generously sprinkle the loaves with the seeds.

NOTE: AT THE BAKERY, WE DIP THE EGG-washed dough facedown into a large tray of seeds and then roll it from side to side to heavily coat the bread. If you just sprinkle a few pinches over the top, it won't look very generous or appealing after the bread has expanded and baked, so be generous with the seeds whether sprinkling or rolling.

13 Bake for 15 minutes. Rotate the bottom sheet pan to the top and the top sheet pan to the bottom (turning each sheet around as you go), and bake until the loaves are golden brown, about 10 minutes longer. Remove the loaves from the oven and set them aside to cool completely on the sheet pans.

OIL OR BUTTER?

At both Lehamim Bakery in Tel Aviv and Breads Bakery in New York City, the challahs are made with vegetable or sunflower oil so that my kosher customers can bring home a loaf and serve it alongside meat. (In kosher tradition, you do not serve meat and dairy together.) You can also make challah with butter. I think the flavor is much richer and the crumb a little more tender—but really it's a personal preference, so choose what you like.

THREE IMPORTANT TIPS FOR CHALLAH

When you break into a loaf of challah, it should pull apart almost like cotton candy coming off the paper cone. There is a soft and tender threadlike quality to the crumb of well-kneaded challah. It is layered with sheets of tender gluten, so it can be almost unraveled rather than broken apart like a loaf of sandwich bread. There are three ways to achieve this:

1. **Underknead.** Slightly underknead the dough so it is not worked to the gluten's full potential. With most dough, you want to be able to stretch a small corner to a thin sheet without it tearing (this is called the windowpane test). With challah, you don't want the gluten to get that strong—so knead it only as instructed.

2. **Underproof.** Slightly underproof the challah, meaning that when you press a finger into the rising dough, the depression that's left fills in about halfway. If the depression remains after you remove your finger, the challah is overproofed.

3. **Use high heat to seal in moisture.** Bake the challah in a hot oven to get the crust to form fast. A nice crust seals in moisture so the interior crumb is delicate and supple and doesn't dry out. You don't want challah to have a hearty, thick, and crisp crust—you just want the crust to be substantial enough to lock in moisture during baking but soft enough to easily rip by hand when eating.

THE SYMBOLISM OF CHALLAH

There is a lot of folklore and symbolism behind challah, especially in the braiding (and let it be known that, stories aside, I think the braids make challah look beautiful and worthy of a holiday table). Some people say the braids mean unity and love because they look like arms intertwining. Three-strand braids also are said to symbolize truth, peace, and justice; round loaves that have no beginning or ending symbolize continuity or a complete year (which is why many people bake round loaves for Rosh Hashanah, the Jewish New Year). But mainly I think braided challah just looks special—it distinguishes challah from regular bread and marks it as special enough for the Shabbat table. There are many ways to make your challah stand out. Turn to pages 40 and 41 for ideas and inspiration.

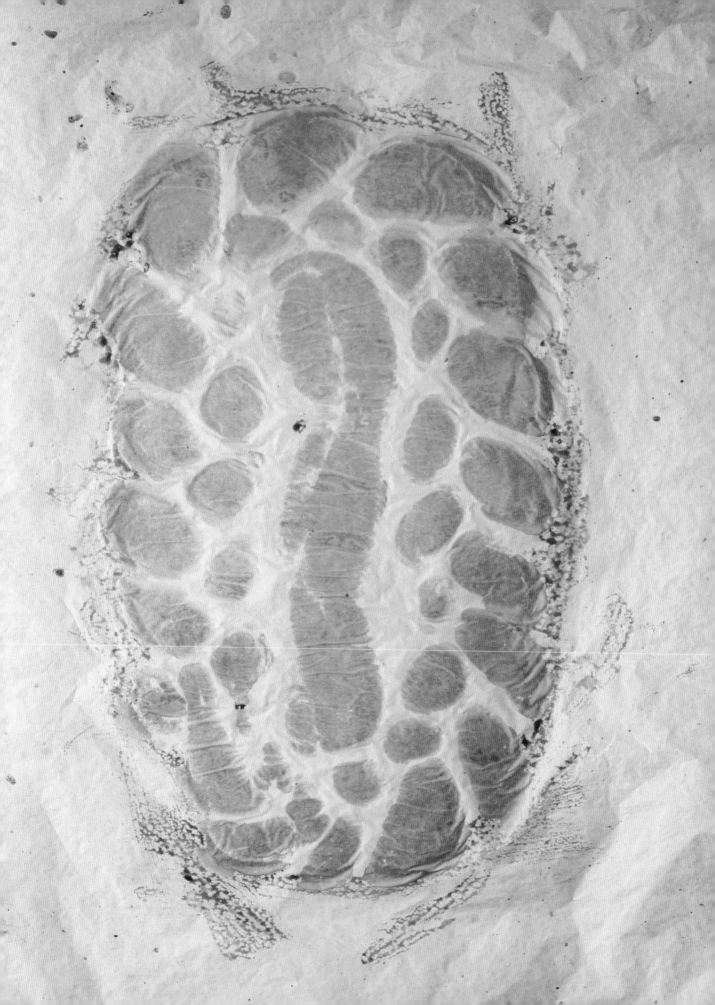

Challah Rolls

Makes 10 rolls (from 500 grams / 1 pound 1 ounce of dough)

As a child I found it impossible to smell the baking challah and then have to wait to eat it. So my mother took pity on me and would turn some of the dough into rolls—meaning I could rip into a roll right away without damaging her loaf of challah, which was destined for the dinner table. I keep the same tradition when I bake challah. Here, I take one-third of the challah dough from page 27 to turn into small rolls. You can shape them into traditional knots or form them into mini braids, leaving them long or pressing the ends of the braid together to create a circle.

1 As described in step 6 on page 28, the challah dough is divided into 3 large pieces. Use 2 of those pieces to make challah loaves. On a lightly floured surface, press the remaining piece into a rectangle with a long side facing you. Using a bench knife or a chef's knife, divide the dough vertically into 10 equal strips. Follow the instructions in step 7 on page 28 to flatten, fold, and press each piece into a cylinder shape (albeit a much smaller cylinder). Then roll each one into a long rope and tie it into a knot shape, knuckling the end through the center to create a little "button." Set the rolls on a parchment paper–lined sheet pan, cover them with a kitchen towel, and set aside in a warm, draft-free spot to rise until they have doubled in volume, 30 to 40 minutes (depending on how warm the room is).

2 Preheat the oven to 425°F.

3 Brush the rolls with the egg wash (see Note on page 40), sprinkle with seeds (if using), and bake until they are golden brown, 7 to 10 minutes. Transfer the baked challah rolls to a wire rack where they can cool (if you can stand to wait that long!).

Black Tie Challah

Makes 1 loaf (580 grams / 1 pound 4 ounces of dough)

This challah has a thin raised braid running lengthwise on top of the braided dough. My mother makes challah this way when she wants the bread to look extra special. Here I make it even more striking by coating the thin braid in nigella seeds (black sesame seeds work too); then I coat the sides of the challah loaf in white sesame seeds so the starkness of the black nigella braid stands out.

1 After dividing the challah dough into three 550-gram (1 pound 1 ounce) pieces as described in step 6 on page 28, take about 50 grams (1¾ ounces) from one piece of dough and set it aside. Divide the resulting 500-gram (17-ounce) piece of dough into 3 smaller pieces, and flatten, fold, and roll each piece into a rope with tapered edges, as described in steps 7 and 8 on page 28. Repeat this process with the 50-gram (1¾-ounce) piece of dough, dividing it into thirds, flattening, folding, and pressing each piece into a cylinder, and then rolling them into thin ropes about 12 inches in length. Set all the pieces aside, covered, to rest for a few minutes. Then stretch each of these thin ropes until it is about 20 inches long, lightly flour each piece, and braid them. Follow the instructions on page 30 to braid the 3 larger ropes of dough into a challah loaf.

2 Make the egg wash (see Note on page 40) and set it aside. On a piece of parchment paper, spread about 1 cup of nigella seeds in a long, thin strip. Brush the skinny braid with egg wash, then dip the braid, sticky-side down, in the nigella seeds to evenly coat it. Brush the larger braid with egg wash, and then set the long nigella-coated braid right down the middle of the larger loaf. You can pinch the ends together and then tuck them under, but I like to just gently press them onto the end of the loaf and leave them somewhat loose (the "loose ends" fan out as they bake, giving people something to talk about!). Generously coat the sides of the large challah with white sesame seeds. Follow the rising instructions in step 9 on page 30, and then bake.

(continued)

Épi Black Tie Challah

Épi is the word the French use to describe the flower of a wheat stalk. In a pain d'épi the shaped baguette dough is snipped or slashed at intervals and the resulting sections are turned left and right to create the classic "tear apart" loaf (I use the same technique in the cinnamon challah on page 56 and for the pistachio and marzipan rugelach on page 254). Essentially, each épi can be pulled off, producing a perfect dinner-roll piece—no slicing required. I turn a challah braid into an épi in the same way—however, when placed on top of the challah, it is purely decorative. (See page 343 for information on the bowls I use.)

(continued)

Crazy and Festive Challah

Making bread doesn't have to be serious or scary. Follow the recipe, weigh out the ingredients, learn the dough, then be like a jazz musician and take the bread on your journey, wherever that road leads. I am inspired by shapes and like to play with dough. Sometimes I leave the ends of the challah loose like fingers on a hand (like the hamsa, a famous good-luck symbol); sometimes I overlay other twists of challah on top of the dough to create an almost Medusa-like shape that is at once otherworldly and completely organic. Play with the dough. Leave the ends open, or twist instead of braid. Try different seeds—pumpkin seeds, nigella seeds, black sesame seeds, sunflower seeds. Bake a bowl into the bread (an oven-safe bowl, of course), or bake three bowls into it!

While you're shaping the bread, remember not to weave the strands or shapes too tightly—make sure you leave enough room for the dough to expand during the proofing stage. Also remember to flour all the individual pieces before braiding so the strands remain separate during baking. A fine dusting is all it takes. This really helps the final shape stand out.

> NOTE: WHEN EGG-WASHING THE CHALLAH, DO SO WITH A LIGHT HAND—
> no one wants a pocket of scrambled egg in their challah braid! I like to apply
> the egg wash from one direction and then turn the sheet pan around to brush
> in the other direction as well, so I am sure to evenly coat all of the surfaces.
> A spray bottle works fantastically too—it applies an even spritz without the
> risk of tearing or marring the dough (which has proofed, meaning there is air
> captured inside the loaf, so you do need to use a delicate touch).

Whole Wheat and Flax Challah

Makes 3 loaves (1.5 kilos / 3⅓ pounds of dough)

For this challah, some whole wheat flour is incorporated with the white flour, along with red quinoa, flaxseeds, and molasses-y brown sugar instead of white. Because the seeds and flour are moisture-hungry, there is 5 to 10% more water in this recipe than in others. Keep a little extra water next to the mixer bowl in case your dough needs it (it will depend on the kind of whole wheat flour you are using). Flour is alive, so every time you bake you need to be one with the dough: touch it, squeeze it, see if it is happy, and then adjust it to where it needs to be.

The coil shape of this challah is common during Rosh Hashanah, symbolizing the completeness and continuity of the year that has passed and the one that lies ahead. As with all the challahs in this chapter, you can shape the dough any way you'd like.

Whole flaxseeds	100 grams (½ cup plus 2 tablespoons)
Red quinoa	100 grams (⅔ cup)
Steaming-hot water	240 grams (1 cup)
Ice water	180 grams (¾ cup)
Fresh yeast	35 grams (¼ cup)
or active dry yeast	10 grams (2 teaspoons)
Whole wheat flour (sifted)	400 grams (3½ cups)
All-purpose flour (sifted, 11.7%)	320 grams (2½ cups), plus extra for shaping
Large eggs	2
Dark brown sugar	50 grams (¼ cup, packed, plus 1 tablespoon)
Fine salt	15 grams (1 tablespoon)
Sunflower oil or canola oil or unsalted butter (at room temperature)	60 grams (¼ cup)

EGG WASH AND TOPPING

Large egg	1
Water	1 tablespoon
Fine salt	Pinch
Millet seeds	50 grams (¼ cup)

1 Soak the flax and quinoa: Place the flaxseeds and the quinoa in a large heat-safe bowl or container and cover with the hot water. Stir, cover the bowl, and set aside for at least 30 minutes, or up to overnight, to soften.

(continued)

2 **Make the dough:** Fill a small bowl with ice and water and stir for a few seconds to allow the water to get icy cold. Measure out ¾ cup of the ice-cold water and pour it into the bowl of a stand mixer fitted with the bread hook. Crumble the yeast into the water and use your fingers to rub and dissolve it; if using active dry yeast, whisk the yeast into the water. Add the whole wheat flour, all-purpose flour, flaxseed mixture, eggs, brown sugar, salt, and oil.

> NOTE: IF YOU WANT TO USE WHOLE WHEAT flour in combination with white flour in a recipe, you will probably have to increase the liquid in the recipe by 5 to 10% because the whole wheat flour absorbs more water. The same is true for adding seeds: When adding seeds like flax or millet to a recipe, you will need to presoak them and increase the amount of liquid in the recipe since they will absorb a lot of liquid on their own.

3 Mix the dough on low speed to combine the ingredients, stopping the mixer if the dough climbs up the hook or if you need to work in dry ingredients that have settled on the bottom of the bowl. Scrape the bottom and sides of the bowl as needed. It should take about 2 minutes for the dough to come together.

4 Increase the speed to medium and knead until a smooth dough forms, about 4 minutes. You may need to add a little water if the dough is too stiff, or a little flour if it is too slack.

5 **Stretch and fold the dough:** Lightly dust your work surface with a little flour, and use a plastic dough scraper to transfer the dough from the mixing bowl to the floured surface. Use your palms to push and tear the top of the dough away from you in one stroke, and then fold that section onto the middle of the dough. Give the dough a quarter turn and repeat the push/tear/fold process for about 1 minute. Then push and pull the dough against the work surface to round it into a ball.

6 **Let the dough rise:** Lightly dust a bowl with flour, add the dough, sprinkle just a little flour on top of the dough, and cover the bowl with plastic wrap. Set the bowl aside at room temperature until the dough has risen by about 70%, about 40 minutes (this will depend on how warm your room is—when the dough proofs in a warmer room it will take less time than in a cooler room).

7 **Divide the dough:** Gently use a plastic dough scraper to help lift the dough out of the bowl and onto a lightly floured work surface (take care not to press out the trapped gas in the dough), and divide the dough into 3 equal parts (you can use a kitchen scale to weigh each piece if you want to be exact).

8 **Shape the dough:** Set the dough lengthwise on your work surface and use the palm of your hand to flatten 1 piece of the dough into a flat rectangle; then fold the top portion over and use your palm to press the edge into the flat part of the dough. Fold and press 3 more times—the dough will end up as a long cylinder, about 30 inches long and 2 inches thick. Repeat with the other pieces of dough.

9 Return to the first piece of dough, and use both hands to roll the cylinder back and forth to form a long rope, 4 to 4½ feet (48 to 54 inches) long, lifting one end in each hand and slapping the center of the rope against the table to elongate it if it gets tight and resists rolling. Repeat with the other two pieces of dough. Lightly flour the long ropes (this allows for the coils in the spiral to stay somewhat separate during baking; otherwise, they'd fuse together).

10 Line 2 rimmed sheet pans with parchment paper (you will probably bake two loaves on one sheet pan and one loaf on the other). Wind one rope into a spiral (see photo on page 44) on one of the prepared sheet pans, tucking the end up through the middle to make a little button. Repeat with the other two on the second lined sheet pan. Cover each sheet pan with a kitchen towel (or set an upturned cup in each corner of the sheet pan and then place the entire sheet pan inside an unscented plastic bag; the cups elevate the plastic bag so it doesn't touch the dough) and set it aside in a warm, draft-free spot to rise until the spirals have doubled in volume, about 1 hour (depending on how warm the room is).

11 Adjust the oven racks to the upper-middle and lower-middle positions and preheat the oven to 350°F.

12 **Test the dough:** Once the dough has roughly doubled in size, do the press test:

Press your finger lightly into the dough, remove it, and see if the depression fills in by half. If the depression fills back in, the dough needs more time to rise.

13 **Bake the loaves:** Make the egg wash by mixing the egg, water, and salt together in a small bowl. Gently brush the entire surface of the loaves with egg wash, taking care not to let it pool in the creases of the spirals. You want a nice thin coating. Sprinkle the top of each spiral with millet seeds.

> NOTE: I LIKE TO BAKE THIS LOAF WITH A little steam for an airy crumb. When preheating your oven, place a rimmed sheet pan on the floor of the oven (or if that is not possible, on the lowest oven rack). When you place the bread in the oven, add about ¼ cup of water to the sheet pan and quickly close the oven door. The water hitting the hot pan will create steam.

14 Bake the challah for 15 minutes. Then rotate the bottom challah to the top and the top challah to the bottom (turning the baking sheets too), and continue to bake until the loaves are golden brown, about 10 minutes longer. Remove the loaves from the oven and set them aside to cool.

Chocolate and Orange Confit Challah

Makes 3 loaves (2.1 kilos / 4½ pounds of dough)

Once upon a time, citrus plantations existed everywhere in Israel, and as a child I grew up with orange, mandarin, tangerine, grapefruit, lemon, lime, and blood orange trees just outside my backyard. I was absolutely spoiled. Pairing candied orange with good-quality chocolate chunks brings much of the pleasure of my childhood together into one happy marriage; it is a magical combination. This recipe replaces some of the water in the basic challah recipe (page 27) with sour cream to yield an even richer loaf. This is more of a cake than a bread—with a cup of coffee or tea, it's a satisfying snack.

ORANGE CONFIT

Room-temperature water	235 grams (1 cup)
Granulated sugar	235 grams (1 heaping cup)
Navel orange	1, thinly sliced into rounds, seeds removed

CHALLAH DOUGH

Cool room-temperature water	300 grams (1¼ cups)
Fresh yeast	40 grams (3 tablespoons plus 2 teaspoons)
or active dry yeast	15 grams (1 tablespoon plus 1¾ teaspoons)
All-purpose flour (sifted, 11.7%)	1 kilo (7 cups), plus extra for shaping
Large eggs	2
Sour cream	100 grams (scant ½ cup)
Granulated sugar	100 grams (½ cup)
Fine salt	15 grams (1 tablespoon)
Unsalted butter (at room temperature)	60 grams (4 tablespoons), plus extra for greasing the loaf pans
Best-quality bittersweet chocolate	340 grams (12 ounces), chopped into roughly ½-inch shards

EGG WASH

Large egg	1
Water	1 tablespoon
Fine salt	Pinch

1 Make the orange confit: Bring the water and sugar to a boil in a medium saucepan over high heat, stirring occasionally to dissolve the sugar. Once the sugar has dissolved, pour half the sugar syrup into a medium heat-safe bowl and set it aside.

Add the orange rounds to the syrup in the saucepan and return it to a boil. Then strain that syrup into a second bowl, leaving the orange slices in the pan, and discard the syrup (it will be bitter). Return the syrup from the first bowl to the saucepan and bring it to a simmer. Reduce the heat to medium-low and simmer gently, swirling the orange slices occasionally, until the mixture is as thick as marmalade, 10 to 12 minutes. Strain the confit through a fine-mesh sieve set over a small bowl; save any remaining syrup (see Note on page 51).

2 Make the dough: Pour the cool water into the bowl of a stand mixer fitted with the bread hook. Crumble the yeast into the water and use your fingers to rub and dissolve it; if using active dry yeast, whisk the yeast into the water. Add the flour, eggs, sour cream, sugar, salt, and butter.

3 Mix the dough on low speed to combine the ingredients, stopping the mixer if the dough climbs up the hook or if you need to work in dry ingredients that have settled on the bottom of the bowl. Scrape the bottom and sides of the bowl as needed. It should take about 2 minutes for the dough to come together.

4 Increase the speed to medium and knead until a smooth dough forms, about 4 minutes. You may need to add a little water if the dough is too stiff, or a little flour if it is too slack.

5 Stretch and fold the dough: Lightly dust your work surface with a spare amount of flour and use a plastic dough scraper to transfer the dough from the mixing bowl to the floured surface. Use your palms to

knead/push the dough away from you in one stroke; then pinch the front portion and stretch it toward you to rip the dough slightly, and fold it on top of itself. Give the dough a quarter turn and repeat the push/pinch/tear/fold process. After the fourth turn, the dough should be in a nice ball shape.

6 Chop 100 grams (about ½ cup) of the strained orange confit and set it aside (store the rest of the orange confit in the reserved syrup in an airtight container to use in other baked goods like muffins, cakes, or breads). Use a bench knife to press a checkerboard pattern into the ball of dough—don't cut all the way through the dough, just make deep depressions. Pile the orange confit and chocolate shards on top, and use the bench knife to completely chop through the dough and fold the dough over onto itself, continuing to chop and fold to mix in the ingredients. You don't really want it well mixed—you want a very chunky dough.

> NOTE: WHEN ADDING NUTS, DRIED FRUITS, chocolate, olives, cheese, roasted vegetables, or any "extras" to bread dough, I always finish mixing and folding the dough and *then*, once the dough is perfect, I add enough extras to measure 20% of the bread's total weight so you can really taste the added ingredients. Don't be cheap with the goodies!

7 Let the dough rise: Lightly dust a bowl with flour, add the dough, sprinkle just a little flour on top of the dough, and cover the bowl with a kitchen towel or plastic wrap. Set the bowl aside at room temperature until the dough has risen by about 70%, about 40 minutes (this will depend on how warm your room is—when the dough proofs in a warmer room, it will take less time to rise than in a cooler room).

(continued)

8 Divide the dough: Gently use a plastic dough scraper to help lift the dough out of the bowl and onto a lightly floured work surface (take care not to press out the trapped gas in the dough), and use a bench scraper or a chef's knife to divide the dough into 9 equal parts. (You can use a kitchen scale to weigh each piece if you want to be exact—they should be about 200 grams each for three 600-gram loaves plus a couple of small rolls; if you don't want rolls just make the loaves a little larger; you can also follow the method on page 28 to shape the remaining dough into a traditional braided challah if you only have 1 loaf pan.)

9 Shape the dough: Line three 9-by-5-inch loaf pans with parchment paper and grease with some butter. On your work surface, fold the corners of a piece of dough up and onto the middle, and then turn the dough over to create a roughly shaped ball. Repeat with the other pieces of dough. Return to the first piece and use a cupped hand to push and pull the dough in a circular motion to create a nicely shaped ball that is closed on the bottom. Repeat with the remaining pieces of dough (even the small ones, if making rolls). Set 3 balls into each loaf pan and cover them with plastic wrap. Set aside in a warm, draft-free spot to rise until the balls have nearly doubled in volume, 35 to 40 minutes.

10 Test the dough: Once the dough has risen, do the press test: Press your finger lightly into the dough, remove it, and see if the depression fills in by half. If the depression fills back in, the dough needs more time to rise.

11 Preheat the oven to 425°F.

12 Bake the loaves: Make the egg wash by whisking the egg, water, and salt together in a small bowl. Gently brush the entire surface of the loaves with the egg wash. Bake the loaves for 15 minutes, turn the pans, and then continue to bake until they are golden brown, about 10 minutes longer. Remove the pans from the oven and set aside to cool. Then use a paring knife to separate each loaf from the pan, turn the loaf out, slice into pieces, and serve.

NOTES: YOU WILL HAVE ENOUGH DOUGH FOR 3 loaves, so you will need 3 loaf pans. Or you can make 1 loaf and follow the instructions to make a braided challah (or two) and some rolls (see page 35).

RESERVE THE REMAINING HALF OF THE orange syrup for brushing over babka and other sweet breads to finish them after they come out of the oven. It's also delicious in hot tea.

FREEZING CHALLAH

If you freeze one (or more) of the baked loaves, double-wrap the baked challah in plastic wrap and then in aluminum foil and place the loaf in a resealable gallon-sized freezer bag. When you want to serve the challah, remove the plastic wrap layer, rewrap in foil, and heat it at 300°F until the bread is warmed throughout, removing the foil for the last 1 or 2 minutes to crisp the crust.

Marzipan Challah

Makes 3 loaves (1½ kilos / 3⅓ pounds of dough)

Think of marzipan challah as a cross between an almond croissant and a loaf of challah. It is also the marriage of my two worlds—my Danish heritage (marzipan) and my Israeli one (challah). Marzipan is a kind of almond paste; it is very important that you buy the best-quality marzipan you can find—and not the kind that comes in a can, which is too loose for any of the recipes in this book (see page 338 for more on marzipan). I have had luck buying marzipan "candy bars," or going to a professional pastry shop and buying marzipan there. See page 54 for instructions if you want to make just one marzipan challah loaf instead of the three called for here.

CHALLAH DOUGH

Cool room-temperature water	320 grams (1⅓ cups)
Fresh yeast	30 grams (3 tablespoons)
or active dry yeast	10 grams (2 teaspoons)
All-purpose flour (sifted, 11.7%)	800 grams (6¼ cups), plus extra for shaping
Large eggs	2
Granulated sugar	80 grams (⅓ cup)
Fine salt	10 grams (2 teaspoons)
Unsalted butter (at room temperature)	60 grams (4 tablespoons)

MARZIPAN FILLING

Best-quality marzipan (see page 338)	200 grams (7 ounces)
Granulated sugar	100 grams (½ cup)
Unsalted butter (at room temperature)	100 grams (7 tablespoons)
All-purpose flour	20 grams (3 tablespoons)

EGG WASH AND TOPPING

Large egg	1
Water	1 tablespoon
Fine salt	Pinch
Sliced almonds (preferably with skin) or chopped hazelnuts or chopped unsalted pistachios	100 grams (1¼ cups)
Granulated sugar	10 grams (2 teaspoons)

1 **Make the dough:** Pour the cool water into the bowl of a stand mixer fitted with the bread hook. Crumble the yeast into the water and use your fingers to rub and dissolve it; if using active dry yeast, whisk the yeast into the water. Add the flour, eggs, sugar, and salt. Then add the butter in 5 or 6 small pieces.

2 Mix the dough on low speed to combine the ingredients, stopping the mixer if the dough climbs up the hook or if you need to work in dry ingredients that have settled on the bottom of the bowl. Scrape the bottom and sides of the bowl as needed. It should take about 2 minutes for the dough to come together.

3 Increase the speed to medium and knead until a smooth dough forms, about 4 minutes. You may need to add a little water if the dough is too stiff, or a little flour if it is too slack.

4 **Stretch and fold the dough:** Lightly dust your work surface with flour and use a plastic dough scraper to transfer the dough from the mixing bowl to the floured surface. Use your palms to knead/push the dough away from you in one stroke; then stretch it toward you to rip the dough slightly. Fold it on top of itself. Give the dough a quarter turn and repeat the tear-and-fold process. After the fourth turn, the dough should be in a nice ball shape.

5 **Let the dough rise:** Lightly dust a bowl with flour, add the dough, sprinkle just a little flour on top of the dough, and cover the bowl with a kitchen towel or plastic wrap. Set the bowl aside at room temperature until the dough has risen by about 70%, about 40 minutes (this will depend on how warm your room is—when the dough proofs in a warmer room, it will take less time to rise than in a cooler room).

6 **While the dough rises, make the marzipan filling:** Place the marzipan and sugar in a large bowl and use your hands to work them together to combine. (Mixing the marzipan by hand ensures that the mixture will remain emulsified. If the mixture is overblended, which could happen if you mix the marzipan filling in a stand mixer, the fat could separate out.) Gradually add the butter, 1 tablespoon at a time, stirring between additions to fully incorporate it. Stir in the flour.

7 **Divide the dough:** Gently use a plastic dough scraper to help lift the dough out of the bowl and set it onto a lightly floured work surface (take care not to press out the trapped gas in the dough), and divide the dough into 3 equal parts (you can use a kitchen scale to weigh each piece if you want to be exact). Divide each piece into 3 smaller equal parts so you end up with a total of 9 pieces.

8 **Shape the dough:** Set a piece of dough lengthwise on a lightly floured work surface and lightly dust the top with flour. Use a rolling pin to roll the piece of dough into a 9-by-5-inch rectangle with the long side facing you. Spread a scant ¼ cup of the marzipan filling along the right-hand third of the dough. Roll the dough from right to left, enclosing the marzipan in a tight cylinder, and pinch the seam and ends shut. Repeat with the remaining pieces of dough and the remaining marzipan.

9 Return to the first cylinder of dough, and use both hands to roll it back and forth into

a long rope, pressing down lightly as you get to the ends of the rope so they are flattened (it is best not to have an overly floured work surface at this point since too much flour will make it hard to roll the dough into a rope). The rope should end up being 12 to 13 inches long. Repeat with the remaining cylinders of dough. Lightly flour the ropes (this allows for the strands of the braid to stay somewhat separate during baking; otherwise, they'd fuse together).

10 Pinch the ends of 3 ropes together at the top (you can place a weight on top of the ends to hold them in place) and braid the dough, lifting each piece up and over so the braid is more stacked than it is long; you also want it to be fatter and taller in the middle, and more tapered at the ends. When you get to the end of the ropes and there is nothing left to braid, use your palm to press and seal the ends together, then tuck them under the challah. Repeat with the remaining 6 ropes, creating 3 braided challahs. Place 2 challahs on a parchment paper–lined rimmed sheet pan and the other challah on a separate parchment-lined sheet pan, cover with a kitchen towel (or place inside an unscented plastic bag; see page 17), and set aside in a warm, draft-free spot to rise until doubled in volume, 1½ to 2 hours.

11 Adjust the oven racks to the upper-middle and lower-middle positions and preheat the oven to 350°F.

12 **Test the dough:** Once the loaves have roughly doubled in volume, do the press test: Press your finger lightly into the dough, remove it, and see if the depression fills in by half. If the depression fills back in, the dough needs more time to rise.

13 **Bake the loaves:** Make the egg wash by whisking the egg, water, and salt together in a small bowl. Gently brush the entire surface of each loaf with egg wash, taking care not to let it pool in the creases of the braids. You want a nice thin coating. Sprinkle each loaf generously with the sliced almonds and then with the sugar.

14 Set the sheet pans in the oven and bake for 15 minutes. Rotate the bottom sheet pan to the top and the top sheet pan to the bottom (turning each sheet around as you go), and bake until the loaves are golden brown, about 10 minutes longer. Remove the loaves from the oven and set them aside to cool completely on the sheet pans.

MAKING ONE MARZIPAN CHALLAH

Using your hands, mash together 100 grams (3½ ounces) of marzipan with 65 grams (⅓ cup) of granulated sugar. Once the mixture is smooth, use your hand or a spoon to stir in 60 grams (4 tablespoons) of room-temperature unsalted butter, 1 tablespoon at a time, and 15 grams (2 tablespoons) of all-purpose flour. Take 500 grams (1.1 pounds) of the dough and divide it into thirds. Continue the recipe from step 8 on page 53 to roll, fill, and shape the challah loaf.

Sticky Pull-Apart Cinnamon Challah Braid

Makes 2 loaves

You can either shape this challah like an épi (see page 39), as I have done here, or slice all the way through the rolled cylinder to create separate segments and then bake them like the stuffed brioche snails on page 223. The recipe calls for half a recipe of challah dough, so you can take the remaining dough to make 2 slightly smaller loaves or 1 full-size loaf plus a few rolls. You could also take a piece of challah dough, smear it with butter and sugar, and bake it off for a quick treat.

CHALLAH BREAD DOUGH

½ recipe (about 1¾ pounds) challah dough (see page 27), prepared through step 5

CINNAMON-SUGAR FILLING

Unsalted butter (at cool room temperature)	200 grams (1 stick plus 5 tablespoons)
Dark brown sugar	150 grams (¾ cup, packed)
Granulated sugar	100 grams (½ cup)
Ground cinnamon	5 grams (1 teaspoon)

EGG WASH

Large egg	1
Water	1 tablespoon
Fine salt	Pinch

SIMPLE SYRUP

Granulated sugar	160 grams (¾ plus 1 tablespoon)
Water	120 grams (½ cup)

1 Once the dough has risen by 70% (after about 40 minutes, depending on how warm your room is), divide the dough in half and gently press each piece into a square. Wrap them individually in plastic wrap and refrigerate for 1 hour.

2 **While the dough chills, make the filling:** Place the butter, brown sugar, granulated sugar, and cinnamon in the bowl of a stand mixer fitted with the paddle attachment, and cream the mixture on low speed until it is combined. Scrape down the bottom and sides of the bowl as needed and continue to beat until well combined without creating any volume, about 30 seconds.

3 **Fill the dough:** Remove 1 square of dough from the refrigerator and place it on a lightly floured work surface. Press or roll the dough into a 12-inch square, and then spread ½ cup of the cinnamon-sugar filling over the left half of the dough. Fold the right side of the dough over the left so the edges meet, and then use a rolling pin to roll and lightly flatten the dough. Wrap in plastic wrap and refrigerate while you repeat with the second piece of dough. Refrigerate the second piece.

4 Place the first piece of dough on the lightly floured work surface so the seam is at the top. Roll the dough to a 12-inch square. Use your hand to make 2 vertical indentations in the dough, dividing it into thirds. Spread ½ cup of the cinnamon-sugar filling over the left-hand third of the dough. Then create a simple fold by folding the left-hand side over the middle, then the right-hand side over the middle, so the dough is folded like a business letter. Wrap in plastic wrap and refrigerate for 1 hour. Repeat with the second piece.

5 Unwrap the first piece of dough and set it on a floured surface, seam at the top. Lightly flour the top of the dough and then roll it into a 12-inch square that is about ¼ inch thick. Spread half the remaining cinnamon-sugar filling over the dough (leave a ½-inch border at the top) and then, starting at the bottom, roll the dough into a cylinder, pressing down on the seam to seal it. Repeat with the second piece of dough.

6 **Shape the dough:** Place the cylinders onto a parchment paper–lined rimmed sheet pan. Starting at the top of one of the cylinders, use kitchen scissors to slice the dough on an angle and in 1-inch alternating intervals about three-quarters of the way through (so make your first snip on the left side on an angle, then the next snip on the right side on an angle, and leave the very bottom attached). Starting at the top, flip one piece over. Skip the next piece, then flip the next one over so it looks like the photo on page 58. Cover the sheet pan with plastic wrap and set aside in a warm, draft-free spot to rise until they have doubled in volume, 30 to 40 minutes.

7 Preheat the oven to 350°F.

8 **Bake the loaves:** Whisk the egg, water, and salt together in a small bowl, and brush the egg wash over the challah rolls. Bake until they are browned, 18 to 20 minutes.

9 **Meanwhile, make the simple syrup:** Combine the sugar and water in a small saucepan and bring to a boil over high heat. Reduce the heat to medium-low and simmer, stirring occasionally to dissolve the sugar. Turn off the heat and set aside to cool. Remove the rolls from the oven and immediately brush with the simple syrup. Cool completely on the sheet pan or serve warm.

Variation

Sticky Cinnamon Challah Snails

After step 5, slice the cylinders of dough crosswise into 1-inch-wide pieces. Stretch the end piece (the tail) of each slice across one of the open sides to seal it. Arrange the rolls in a buttered muffin pan, on a parchment paper–lined sheet pan (they can even be clustered in a design), or in a greased cake pan, tucked-side facing down. Proceed with proofing, egg-washing, baking, and glazing as described above.

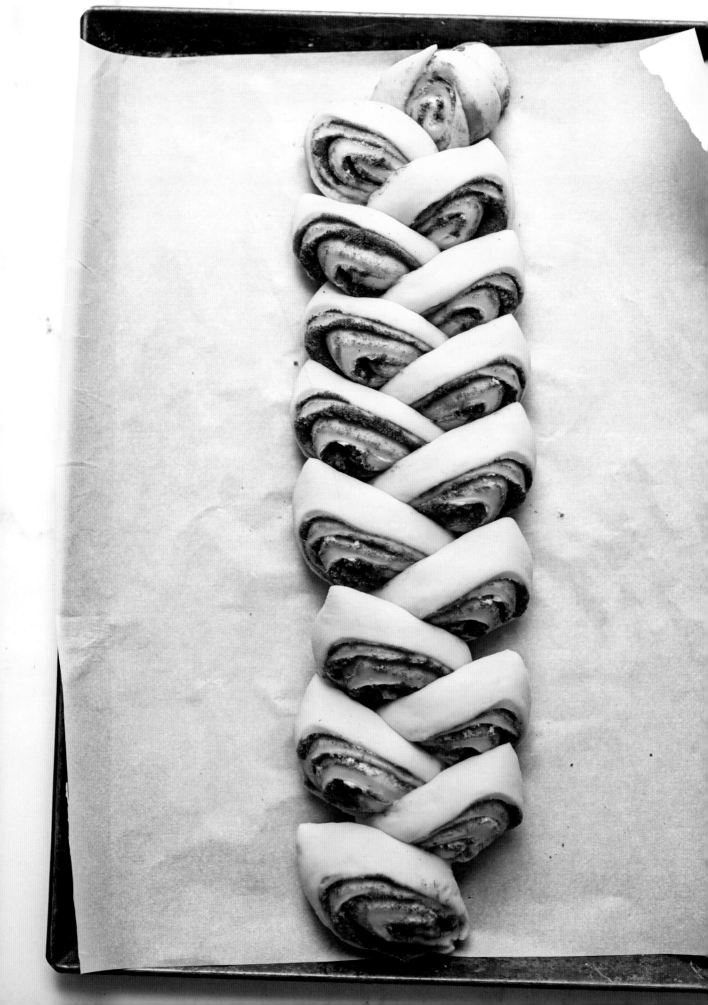

Challah Falafel Rolls

Makes 16 rolls

Rinat Tzadok, my life partner in and out of the kitchen, came up with this pure genius recipe. Just like Israel, it is a meld of cultures: challah meets falafel. Rinat was several months pregnant and working in the bakery making challah when she saw some cooked chickpeas and was inspired to make a challah roll that had all of the spices and magic of falafel. Eat it plain or slice it in half and add some lettuce, a few slices of tomato and hard-boiled egg, some z'hug (pages 318–319), and tahina (page 316) and be prepared to get hooked.

FALAFEL FILLING

Cumin seeds	1½ teaspoons, plus extra for sprinkling
Coriander seeds	1 teaspoon, crushed
Extra-virgin olive oil	30 grams (2 tablespoons)
Yellow onion	1 large, coarsely chopped
Garlic cloves	4, finely chopped
Jalapeño	½ large, coarsely chopped
Cooked chickpeas	250 grams (1½ cups, from about 130 grams dried chickpeas)
Cilantro leaves	1 bunch (about ½ cup), finely chopped

CHALLAH DOUGH

Cool room-temperature water	200 grams (½ cup plus ⅓ cup)
Fresh yeast	20 grams (1 tablespoon plus 2½ teaspoons)
or active dry yeast	7 grams (2¼ teaspoons)
All-purpose flour (sifted, 11.7%)	600 grams (3½ cups plus 6 tablespoons), plus extra for shaping
Large egg	1
Granulated sugar	50 grams (¼ cup)
Fine salt	8 grams (1½ teaspoons)
Extra-virgin olive oil or unsalted butter (at room temperature)	40 grams (2½ tablespoons)

EGG WASH AND TOPPING

Large egg	1
Water	1 tablespoon
Fine salt	Pinch
Caraway seeds	for sprinkling
Flaky salt	for sprinkling

1 **Make the falafel filling:** Place the cumin and coriander seeds in a medium skillet set over medium heat and toast them, shaking the pan often, until the seeds are golden brown and fragrant, about 2 minutes. Transfer the seeds to a cutting board and roughly chop (or lightly smash with the bottom of a heavy pot), and then place in a medium bowl. Add the olive oil to the same skillet, increase the heat to medium-high, and then add the onion. Once the onion begins to brown around the edges, about 3 minutes, reduce the heat to medium and cook the onion until it is very soft and golden, stirring occasionally, for about 10 minutes. Turn off the heat and stir in the garlic and jalapeño. Transfer the mixture to the bowl with the cumin and coriander and set aside.

2 **Make the dough:** Pour the cool water into the bowl of a stand mixer fitted with the bread hook. Crumble the yeast into the water and use your fingers to rub and dissolve it; if using active dry yeast, whisk the yeast into the water. Add the flour, egg, sugar, salt, and oil.

3 Mix the dough on low speed to combine the ingredients, stopping the mixer if the dough climbs up the hook or if you need to work in dry ingredients that have settled on the bottom of the bowl. Scrape the bottom and sides of the bowl as needed. It should take about 2 minutes for the dough to come together (see photo on page 29). If there are lots of dry bits in the bottom of the bowl that just aren't getting worked in, add a tablespoon or two of water. On the other hand, if the dough looks soft, add a few pinches of flour.

4 Add the onion mixture and the chickpeas. Increase the speed to medium and knead until a smooth dough forms (there will be small chunks from the chickpeas, spices, and onions), about 4 minutes. You may need to add a little water if the dough is too stiff, or a little flour if it is too slack.

5 **Stretch and fold the dough:** Lightly dust your work surface with a little flour and use a plastic dough scraper to transfer the dough from the mixing bowl to the floured surface. Sprinkle the cilantro over the dough. Use your palms to push and tear the top of the dough away from you in one stroke; then fold that section onto the middle of the dough. Give the dough a quarter turn and repeat the push/tear/fold process 8 times. Then push and pull the dough against the work surface to round it into a ball.

6 **Let the dough rise:** Lightly dust a bowl with flour, add the dough, sprinkle just a little flour on top of the dough, and cover the bowl with plastic wrap. Set the bowl aside at room temperature until the dough has risen by about 70%, about 40 minutes (this will depend on how warm your room is—when the dough proofs in a warmer room, it will take less time to rise than in a cooler room).

7 **Divide the dough:** Transfer the dough to a lightly floured work surface and lightly stretch it into a rectangle (try not to press out the trapped gas from the dough). Divide the dough into 4 equal pieces lengthwise, and then divide each strip crosswise into 4 equal pieces so you have 16 small pieces.

8 **Shape and proof the dough:** Line 2 sheet pans with parchment paper and set them aside. Use the palm of your hand to flatten a piece of dough; then fold the top portion up and over to meet the edge on the bottom and use your palm to press the edges

together. Flatten, fold, and press 3 more times. Repeat with the remaining pieces of dough. Lightly press and roll each piece to flatten and narrow the ends into a torpedo shape. Place the rolls on the prepared sheet pans, cover with plastic wrap, and set aside to proof until they have increased in volume by about 75%, 30 to 45 minutes (depending on how warm the room is).

9 Preheat the oven to 350°F.

10 **Bake the rolls:** Make the egg wash by whisking the egg, water, and salt together in a small bowl, then brush it evenly over each roll and sprinkle with the caraway seeds and flaky salt. Bake the rolls until they are golden brown, 7 to 10 minutes. Remove from the oven and transfer the rolls to a wire rack where they can cool.

BABKA

BREADS BAKERY PUT THE MODERN chocolate babka on the map. It's flaky. It's buttery. It's loaded with chocolate in the most craveable way. People travel from everywhere far and wide to try it—this is the babka that many consider to be the best in New York City and the country.

I'm always thinking of new ways to challenge myself and give my bakery customers something new to crave and covet. I've come up with lots of babka varieties, from apple babka to a labne and za'atar–filled babka "twist" and even a babka pie. As with challah—and with any bread, really—a babka can be tweaked in many ways to suit your tastes and mood. In this chapter you'll find lots of ideas to start with. I have also included two styles of dough for the babka: one is a basic babka dough; the other is advanced. I say "advanced" because it is laminated, much like making croissant dough, and it will take you about one day longer to make it (because of chilling and resting). To make the true Breads Bakery babka, you have to use the Advanced Babka Dough (page 70). The Basic Babka Dough (page 68) is very delicious, but not as flaky. Though I will bet that if you make either version for your family or friends, they won't be disappointed.

In Denmark, where I studied pastry, sweet yeasted cakes were called wienerbrød, "bread from Vienna," which traces back to kugelhopf and that kind of sweet enriched bread. Then, when I moved to France to study pastry there, of course I learned all about pain au chocolat, a pastry made with laminated dough. A laminated dough is a dough into which many layers of butter are folded (see photos on page 71); as the butter melts in the oven, moisture in the butter creates steam and flakiness. For comparison's sake, think of a regular yeasted dough made with butter, like brioche. Delicious and rich, yes, but compared to the flaky layers of a croissant that shatter into shards when you bite into it, the brioche can't compete for flakiness.

Germany is where I discovered the krantz cake, also called a chocolate kugelhopf. It is the melding of so many techniques into one yeasted cake—chocolate, swirls, yeast, dough—but the surprise here is that the chocolate kugelhopf isn't even made with hard chocolate but rather with cocoa powder. In Israel this cake also exists as a chocolate yeast cake.

It's in the States that I connected all these dots to create my award-winning chocolate babka: a laminated dough, not so unlike croissant dough or viennoiserie, but filled with Nutella and chocolate chips and twisted into loaves instead of cakes. At Breads Bakery, we bake new batches throughout the day, every day, so warm babkas fresh from the oven are always available. They're so fragrant that if you walked into Breads Bakery blindfolded, you could smell your way to the chocolate babka.

Basic Babka Dough

Makes about 900 grams (2 pounds) of dough, for two 9-by-5-inch babkas

This is the simpler of the two babka doughs—this dough will yield a very rich and delicious babka. And if you want an even richer, flakier version, try out the Advanced Babka Dough on page 70, which will produce a babka that tastes closer to the one we make at Breads Bakery. Making babka takes less than an hour of actual work—the rest of the time is the proofing and the baking. You can shape the cake into a twisted loaf, or bake it in smaller pieces in a muffin tin, or even try baking it free-form. The thing about babka is that even if it isn't perfect in your eyes, when it comes out of the oven hot and fragrant, I guarantee that your friends and family will devour it.

Vanilla extract	½ teaspoon
Whole milk (at room temperature)	120 grams (½ cup)
Fresh yeast	20 grams (2½ tablespoons)
or active dry yeast	6 grams (2 teaspoons)
All-purpose flour (sifted, 11.7%)	280 grams (2¼ cups), plus extra for dusting and kneading
Pastry or cake flour (sifted, 8.5 to 9%)	220 grams (2 cups plus 2 tablespoons)
Large eggs	2
Granulated sugar	75 grams (⅓ cup)
Fine salt	Large pinch
Unsalted butter (at room temperature)	80 grams (5 tablespoons plus 1 teaspoon)

1 Make the dough: Whisk the vanilla into the milk in the bowl of a stand mixer fitted with the dough hook. Use a fork or your fingers to lightly mix the yeast into the milk. Then, in this order, add the flours, eggs, sugar, salt, and finally the butter in small pinches.

2 Mix on the lowest speed, stopping the mixer to scrape down the sides and bottom of the bowl as needed, and to pull the dough off the hook as it accumulates there and break it apart so it mixes evenly, until the dough is well combined, about 2 minutes (it will not be smooth; see photo on page 29).

If the dough is very dry, add more milk, 1 tablespoon at a time; if the dough looks wet, add more all-purpose flour, 1 tablespoon at a time, until the dough comes together. Increase the mixer speed to medium, and mix until the dough is smooth and has good elasticity, 4 minutes.

3 Stretch and fold the dough: Lightly dust your work surface with flour and turn the dough out on top; lightly dust the top of the dough and the interior of a large bowl with flour. Grab the top portion of the dough and stretch it away from you, tearing the dough. Then fold it on top of the middle of the dough. Give the dough a quarter turn and repeat the stretch, tear, and fold. Continue to do this until you can stretch a small piece of dough very thin without it tearing, about 5 minutes. Then use your hands to push and pull the dough against the work surface and in a circular motion to create a nice round of dough. Set the ball in the floured bowl, cover the bowl with plastic wrap, and set it aside at room temperature for 30 minutes.

4 **Chill the dough:** Set the dough on a piece of plastic wrap and press it into a 1-inch-thick rectangle. Wrap the dough in plastic wrap and refrigerate it for at least 1 hour or up to 24 hours before proceeding with one of the recipes in this chapter.

NOTE: IF YOU CHOOSE TO MAKE A HALF recipe of the babka dough (to make only 1 babka—but why would you want to do such a thing?), you may need to scrape down the sides and bottom of the bowl quite often to make sure the dough mixes evenly. Sometimes, with a lesser quantity of ingredients in a mixer bowl, it takes more work to mix the dough. If the dough hook is not kneading the dough well (because the volume is too small), remove the dough from the bowl and stretch and fold it by hand until the dough is smooth.

Advanced Babka Dough

Makes about 1.1 kilos (2⅓ pounds) of dough, for three 9-by-2¾-by-2-inch babkas

The babka we make at Breads Bakery and Lehamim Bakery starts with the Advanced Babka Dough, which is a laminated dough, meaning it has very thin layers of butter sandwiched throughout (as you'll find in croissants and puff pastry). Making a laminated dough requires a lot of extra time, work, and patience, and for that reason I offer a simplified version of the babka dough (page 68). This advanced dough is for those who really want to take their babka to the next level. The dough recipes are exactly the same from the mixing through the first proofing and overnight refrigeration. From that point, however, in the advanced babka, you build in an extra day to fold in a hefty block of butter. And then you proceed to filling and twisting or rolling the babka however you like.

It is important to note that the Advanced Babka Dough requires a baking pan that measures 9 by 2¾ by 2 inches. At the bakery we use paper loaf pans; you can find these in some cooking stores and in professional baking supply stores (and online, of course). If you bake the Advanced Babka Dough in a standard-size loaf pan, the middle of the babka will sink. A pan that size is deep and wide, and because the dough doesn't get lift, it sinks in the middle. The babka will taste just as good, but it won't look like the babka we sell at the bakery.

1 recipe Basic Babka Dough (page 68)	
Unsalted butter (at cool room temperature)	200 grams (1 stick plus 5 tablespoons)
All-purpose flour	for rolling and shaping

1 Prepare the babka dough and refrigerate it as instructed on page 68. Rest the dough for 24 hours.

2 **Prepare the butter:** Set the butter on a large piece of parchment paper. Use a rolling pin (or your fist) to smack and whack it into a 7-by-8-inch rectangle that is between ⅛ inch and ¼ inch thick. Use a bench knife to square off the corners and then pound as needed to fit the measurements. Set the butter aside.

3 **Add the butter and make the first fold:** Place the dough on a lightly floured work surface, lightly dust the top, de-gas the dough by pressing down on it, and then roll the dough into a 7-by-16-inch rectangle with a short side facing you. Place the butter on the bottom half of the dough (see photo, opposite), leaving a ¼-inch border at the bottom. Fold the top of the dough over the butter to meet the bottom edge, pull the corners so they align perfectly, and use a pastry brush to brush away any excess flour from the surface.

(continued)

WHAT IS A SIMPLE FOLD?

When you fold a piece of dough into thirds like a business letter, it is called a simple fold. Bakers do this to create all the many flaky layers of butter and dough in a laminated dough, such as croissant, Danish, puff pastry, and babka dough. The simple fold is often repeated several times to increase the amount of delicate layers in the dough.

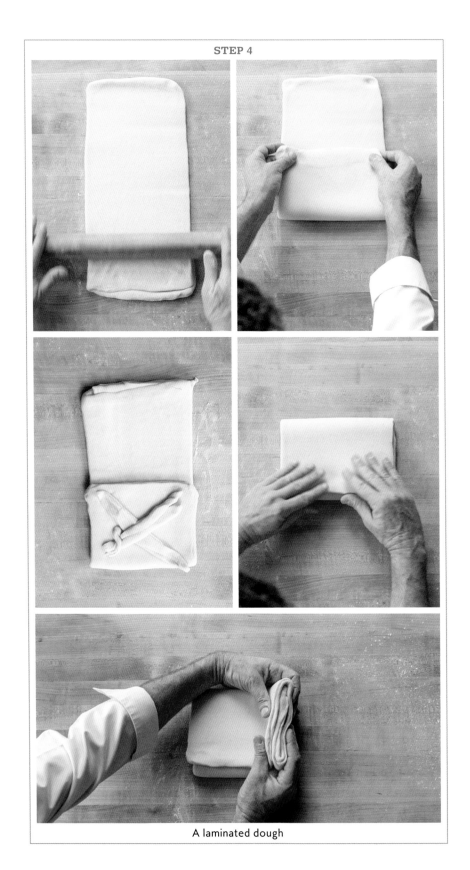

A laminated dough

NOTE: YOU WANT THE DOUGH TO BE ABOUT the same temperature as the butter. If the butter is too soft, it will seep out of the dough; if the butter is too cold, it will break into pieces rather than be pliable enough to spread into thin sheets. If the dough becomes too warm, it will begin to proof and become hard to roll out thin; if the dough is too cold, it will be too hard to roll. Work carefully and mindfully, and if either the butter or the dough starts to become too warm, cool them down in the refrigerator before continuing with the recipe.

4 Fold and chill the dough: Rotate the dough so the seam side (which was facing the bottom) is now facing to the right. Lightly flour the top and underside of the dough, and roll it into a 9-by-16-inch rectangle. Use a bench knife or a chef's knife to square off the edges (save the scraps to add to the dough). Then use your finger to mark the dough into equal thirds. Use a pastry brush to remove any excess flour from the dough. Fold the bottom up to the top mark and the top down and over to the bottom edge to create a simple fold (see photos, opposite). Try to keep the edges and corners as perfectly aligned as possible. Lightly dust the dough and the work surface again, and roll the dough just enough to flatten it slightly. At this point, the dough will probably bounce back when you roll it because you have been working the gluten a lot. Now is a good time to wrap it in plastic wrap and let it rest in the refrigerator for 30 minutes. Then repeat the simple fold two more times, refrigerating the dough between each time. Wrap the dough in plastic wrap and refrigerate it for at least 5 hours or overnight.

NOTE: IF, WHEN ROLLING, YOU GET A BUBBLE in the dough, don't force the rolling pin over the dough and risk tearing it. Instead, use the tip of a paring knife to pierce the bubble so that when you roll the dough, the air can escape.

5 Roll the dough as instructed in your choice of recipe: the Famous Chocolate Babka (page 74), Cinnamon-Raisin-Walnut Babka (page 82), Rum Raisin and Cheese Babka (page 87), Halvah Babka (page 91), Apple Babka (page 97), Za'atar Twists (page 100), or the Pistachio and Marzipan Pull-Apart Rugelach (page 254).

NOTE: BECAUSE THERE IS MORE BUTTER IN the Advanced Babka Dough, there is about 20% more weight of dough compared to the Basic Babka Dough. If you like, you can increase the quantity of any filling called for by 20% so the ratio of dough to filling remains in balance.

A WORD ABOUT PAN SIZES

If making the Advanced Babka Dough, be sure to source 9-by-2¾-by-2-inch loaf pans (visit bakedeco.com). A standard 8½-by-4½-inch pan is too deep and wide for delicate laminated Advanced Babka Dough, and your babka will sink in the middle. Of course, it will still taste good, but it might not look as pretty. If you can't find the narrow loaf pan, try using a straight-sided small Pullman-style loaf pan or shape the babka and bake it free-form on a sheet pan.

The Famous Chocolate Babka

*Makes 3 babkas using the Advanced Babka Dough in 9-by-2¾-by-2-inch loaf pans, or
2 babkas using the Basic Babka Dough in standard loaf pans (see the sidebar on page 73)*

When I create a new pastry, it is very important for me to make a psychological connection to the pleasures of childhood, and in Israel, just about every schoolchild eats a lunchtime sandwich made with a chocolate spread. To tap into that taste memory, I use Nutella to give this babka its intensely chocolate taste. The croissant-like babka dough is loaded with Nutella and chocolate chips and then twisted into a loaf shape.

I first called this chocolate krantz cake, but in all honesty, that name didn't effectively communicate the deep, ephemeral pleasure of biting into the wonderfully rich and deeply chocolaty pastry. We decided to call it chocolate babka instead, and within 3 months, our babka was selected by *New York Magazine* as the best in New York City. We went from selling a few dozen a day to a few *hundred* a day. It remains the most popular item at Breads Bakery, and we are very proud that our babka sparked a babka trend across the country.

1 recipe Advanced Babka Dough (page 70) or Basic Babka Dough (page 68), chilled 24 hours

Nutella	420 grams (1½ cups)
Semisweet chocolate chips	150 grams (1 cup)

SIMPLE SYRUP

Granulated sugar	160 grams (¾ cup plus 1 tablespoon)
Water	120 grams (½ cup)

1 Roll the chilled Advanced Babka Dough: Unwrap the cold babka dough and set it on a lightly floured work surface (or on a long dining room table—you need at least 4 feet of work space). Roll the dough into a 10-by-28-inch rectangle (it should be just a little shy of ¼ inch thick) with a long side facing you. Pull and shape the corners into a rectangle shape. (If you are using the Basic Babka Dough, see the sidebar on page 76 for shaping instructions.)

NOTE: ONLY ROLL GOING ALONG THE LENGTH of the dough (left to right) and not up and down the dough. The height will naturally increase as you roll the dough, and by rolling the dough in just one direction, you're not going to stress the gluten. If the dough starts to spring back, that means it's tired. Let it rest for 5 minutes before trying again.

2 Fill and roll the dough: Spread the Nutella in an even layer over the dough, all the way to the edges. Then sprinkle the chocolate chips in an even layer over the

Nutella, across the entire surface of the dough. Working from the top edge, roll the dough into a tight cylinder. As you roll it, push and pull the cylinder a little to make it even tighter. Then, holding the cylinder at the ends, lift and stretch it slightly to make it even tighter and longer.

3 Twist the strips into a babka: Use a bread knife to slice the cylinder in half lengthwise so you have 2 long pieces, and set them with the chocolate layers exposed. Divide the pieces crosswise into thirds, creating 6 equal-length strips. Match the strips into groups of two so a smaller strip is matched with a larger strip (so you end up with 3 equal-size babkas). Overlap one strip on top of another to make an X, making sure the exposed chocolate part of the dough faces up; then twist the ends together like the threads on a screw so you have at least 2 twists on each side of the X. Place the shaped babka in a 9-by-2¾-by-2-inch loaf pan, exposed chocolate–side up. The dough should fill the pan by two-thirds and fit the length perfectly. Cover the pan with plastic wrap and repeat with the other pieces of dough.

NOTE: EMBRACE THE MESS! TWISTING THE dough is a sticky process, but don't worry—after baking, even the messiest babka will still look beautiful and, more important, taste great.

IF YOU ARE USING BASIC BABKA DOUGH . . .

Lightly coat 2 standard loaf pans with room-temperature unsalted butter. Roll the babka dough into a 9-by-24-inch rectangle. Continue with filling and rolling the babka into a cylinder as instructed; then divide the dough in half lengthwise, and set the halves with the layers exposed. Then divide the 2 long strips in half crosswise (to get 4 strips). Continue with shaping, proofing, and baking as instructed.

(continued)

STEP 2

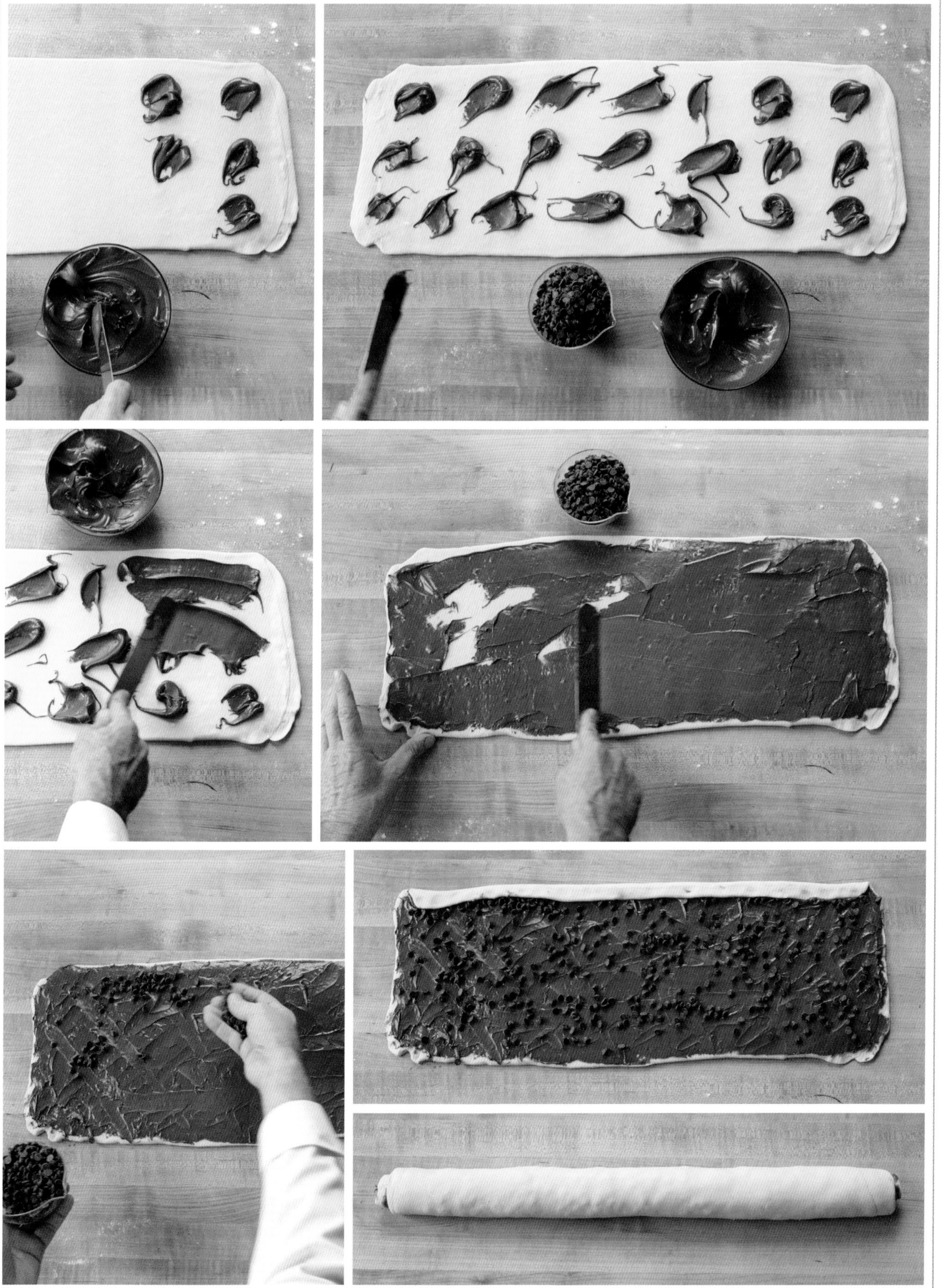

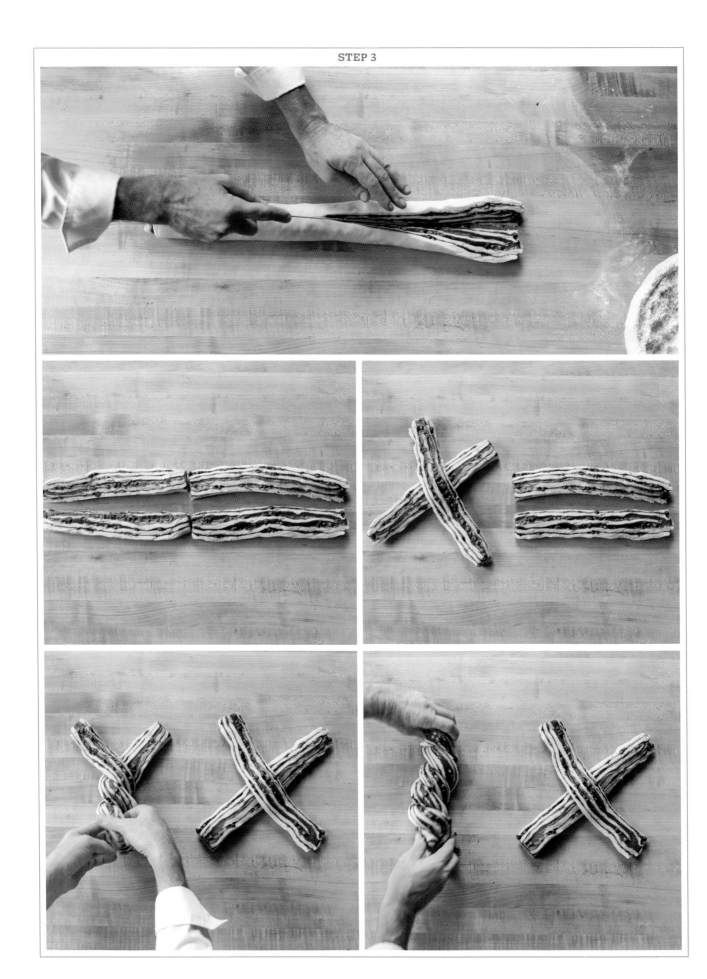

4 Let the dough rise: Set the loaf pans aside in a warm, draft-free spot until the dough rises 1 to 2 inches above the rim of the pan and is very soft and jiggly to the touch, 2 to 3 hours, depending on how warm your room is.

> NOTE: IF YOUR ROOM IS VERY COLD, YOU CAN speed up the rising process: Set a large bowl of hot water on the bottom of the oven, place the loaf pans on the middle oven rack, close the oven door, and let the dough rise in the oven. Just remember that your babka is in there before preheating the oven!

5 Preheat the oven to 350°F. (If you are letting the dough rise in the oven, as described in the Note, be sure to remove the loaf pans and bowl of water before preheating.)

6 Bake the babkas: Place the babkas in the oven and bake until they are dark brown and baked through, about 40 minutes; check them after 25 minutes, and if they are getting too dark, tent them loosely with a piece of parchment paper or aluminum foil.

7 Meanwhile, make the simple syrup: Combine the sugar and water in a small saucepan and bring to a boil over high heat. Reduce the heat to medium-low and simmer, stirring occasionally to dissolve the sugar. Turn off the heat and set aside the syrup to cool.

8 Brush with simple syrup: Remove the babkas from the oven, and while they are still hot, brush the surface generously with the cooled sugar syrup (the syrup makes the top of the babkas shiny and beautiful and also locks in the moisture so the cake doesn't dry out; you may not need to use all the syrup—save any extra for sweetening iced coffee or tea). Use a paring knife to separate the babkas from the pan edges, and turn them out from the pan. Slice and serve warm, or cool completely in the pans before unmolding and slicing.

FREEZING AND DEFROSTING BABKA

Babka dough can be frozen so a fresh-from-the-oven babka can be had anytime. To freeze the shaped dough, double-wrap it in plastic wrap, then in aluminum foil (and then in a resealable freezer bag if it fits). To defrost the dough, unwrap it and let it sit out at room temperature, loosely covered with a kitchen towel or in a homemade proofing box (see page 17), until it has proofed to about 1 inch above the lip of the loaf pan (the dough will take several hours to defrost, then extra time to proof depending on the warmth of your room). Then bake as instructed.

Baked babkas also freeze beautifully, so don't hesitate to wrap one or two from your batch in a double layer of plastic wrap and then aluminum foil and freeze them for up to 1 month. Leave the wrapped frozen babka at room temperature for a few hours to thaw, and then remove the plastic wrap and rewrap in foil and place it in a preheated 325°F oven for 8 to 10 minutes to warm through. For the last 5 minutes in the oven, open the foil to expose the surface of the cake so it dries out just a bit.

(continued)

Babka Pie

This is essentially a babka baked into a pie shape. It has a thin "crust" made of babka dough and is filled with a ring of chocolate babka. To make one pie, you'll need one 80-gram (just shy of 3-ounce) piece of Basic Babka Dough for the crust (if you are making this with the advanced dough, remove this much of the dough before laminating with the butter), one twisted and finished (but not proofed or baked) babka, and extra Nutella and chocolate chips.

Chill the 80-gram piece of dough for at least 30 minutes; then, on a lightly floured work surface, roll it as thin as possible. You want to get it as thin as possible without tearing. At the bakery we roll it to a 10-inch round that is 1 millimeter (about $\frac{1}{16}$ inch) thick—just get it as thin as possible.

Place the dough in a 9-inch pie plate, letting the excess hang over the edges. Use a fork to dock the dough, pricking holes all over the bottom. Spread 80 grams (a heaping $\frac{1}{4}$ cup) of Nutella over the bottom of the dough and sprinkle 20 grams (heaping 2 tablespoons) of chocolate chips over it. Stick the ends of the twisted babka together so it makes a ring shape and place it in the pie plate. Trim off the dough overhang and proof, bake, and glaze the babka as instructed on page 79. To serve it, slice it into wedges just like a pie.

Cinnamon-Raisin-Walnut Babka

Makes 3 babkas using the Advanced Babka Dough in 9-by-2¾-by-2-inch loaf pans, or
2 babkas using the Basic Babka Dough in standard loaf pans (see the sidebar on page 76)

Denser than the chocolate babka, this babka is loaded with chopped walnuts, raisins (or currants), and cinnamon and is what I consider a homey old-world babka cake. It's a little heavier and more traditional in flavor, but cinnamon-raisin aficionados adore it. The technique is mostly the same as for the chocolate babka (page 74) with a few differences in the filling. The shaping process is the same, so follow the photos on page 78 and your babka will turn out beautifully.

DOUGH

1 recipe Advanced Babka Dough (page 70) or Basic Babka Dough (page 68), chilled 24 hours

FILLING

Unsalted butter (at room temperature)	100 grams (7 tablespoons)
Granulated sugar	100 grams (½ cup)
Ground cinnamon	5 grams (1 teaspoon)
Walnuts	150 grams (1½ cups), coarsely chopped
Dried currants	150 grams (1 cup)

SIMPLE SYRUP

Granulated sugar	160 grams (¾ cup plus 1 tablespoon)
Water	120 grams (½ cup)

1 Roll the Advanced Babka Dough: Unwrap the cold babka dough and set it on a lightly floured work surface. Roll the dough into a 10-by-28-inch rectangle (it should be just a little shy of ¼ inch thick) with the long side facing you. Pull and shape the corners into a rectangle shape. (If you are using the Basic Babka Dough, see the sidebar on page 76 for shaping instructions.)

2 Fill the dough: Spread the butter evenly over the dough, all the way to the edges. Mix the sugar and cinnamon together, then sprinkle the cinnamon sugar over the butter, followed by the walnuts and currants. Use a rolling pin to roll the nuts and currants into the dough slightly, pressing down just enough to lock them into place.

3 Roll the dough from the top down, forming a tight cylinder. Turn the cylinder so it is seam-side down, gently pick it up by the ends, and stretch it slightly. Then use the rolling pin to flatten the cylinder (don't roll the cylinder—use the rolling pin to press down and flatten it).

4 Twist the strips into a babka: Use a bread knife to slice the dough in half lengthwise so you have 2 long pieces, and set them with the cinnamon layers exposed. Then divide the pieces crosswise into thirds, creating 6 equal-size strips. Match the segments into 3 sets with 2 pieces in each, matching small and large strips together to get 3 sets of equal-weight pairings of dough. Place one strip on top of another to make an X, keeping the exposed filling facing up; then twist the ends together like the threads on a screw so you have at least 2 twists on each side of the X. Place the shaped babka in the loaf pans, filling-side up. The dough should fill the pan by two-thirds and fit the length perfectly. Cover it with plastic wrap and repeat with the other pieces of dough.

5 Let the dough rise: Set the loaf pans aside in a warm, draft-free spot until the dough rises 1 to 2 inches above the rim of the pan and is very soft and jiggly to the touch, 1½ to 2 hours, depending on how warm your room is.

6 Preheat the oven to 350°F. (If you are letting the dough rise in the oven, as described in the Note on page 79, be sure to remove the loaf pans and bowl of water before preheating!)

7 Bake the babkas until they are dark brown and baked through, about 35 minutes; check them after 20 minutes and if they are getting too dark, tent them loosely with a piece of parchment paper or aluminum foil.

8 Meanwhile, make the simple syrup: Combine the sugar and water in a small saucepan and bring to a boil over high heat. Reduce the heat to medium-low and simmer, stirring occasionally to dissolve the sugar. Turn off the heat and set aside the syrup to cool.

9 Remove the babkas from the oven, and while they are still warm, brush the surface generously with the cooled sugar syrup (the syrup makes the top of the babkas shiny and beautiful and also locks in the moisture so the cake doesn't dry out). Use a paring knife to separate each babka from the loaf pan, and turn them out onto a cutting board. Slice and serve warm, or cool completely in the pans before unmolding and slicing.

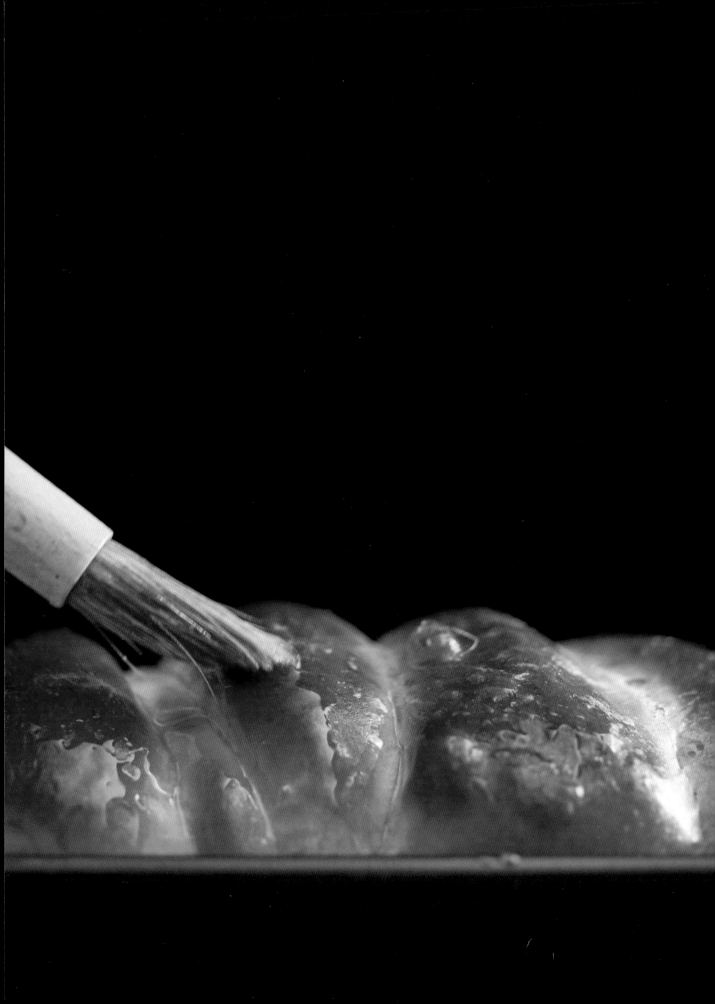

Rum Raisin and Cheese Babka

Makes 3 babkas using the Advanced Babka Dough in 9-by-2¾-by-2-inch loaf pans, or
2 babkas using the Basic Babka Dough in standard loaf pans (see the sidebar on page 76)

Filled with rum-soaked raisins and a combination of sour cream and ricotta, this babka is so tender and pillowy that it's easy to lose control and eat half the loaf in one sitting. The cheese bakes into the bread, making this babka a fantastic breakfast treat or not-too-sweet afternoon snack for tea. Note that you have to begin straining the sour cream the night before making the babka. Try to use the thickest and richest ricotta you can find.

Sour cream	120 grams (½ cup plus 1 tablespoon)
Raisins	60 grams (⅓ cup)
Dark rum	120 grams (½ cup)
Whole-milk ricotta cheese	300 grams (1¼ cups)
Large egg	1
Lemon zest	grated from ½ lemon
Vanilla bean	⅓, split, seeds scraped out and reserved
or vanilla paste	½ teaspoon
Confectioners' sugar	75 grams (½ cup plus 1 tablespoon)
Cornstarch	25 grams (3 tablespoons)
1 recipe Advanced Babka Dough (page 70) or Basic Babka Dough (page 68), chilled 24 hours	

SIMPLE SYRUP

Granulated sugar	160 grams (¾ cup plus 1 tablespoon)
Water	120 grams (½ cup)

1 The day before baking, drain the sour cream and soak the raisins: Line a fine-mesh sieve with a large piece of cheesecloth and set it over a medium bowl. Place the sour cream in the cheesecloth, gently drape the edges of the cheesecloth over the sour cream, and refrigerate overnight to drain. Combine the raisins and rum in a small bowl, cover the bowl with plastic wrap, and set aside overnight at room temperature.

2 The next day, make the ricotta filling: Transfer the strained sour cream to a medium bowl (discard the liquid in the bowl), and stir in the ricotta, egg, lemon zest, and vanilla. Sift the confectioners' sugar and cornstarch together into a small bowl, and then stir into the cheese mixture. Cover the bowl with plastic wrap and refrigerate for 1 hour.

(continued)

3 Roll the Advanced Babka Dough: Unwrap the cold babka dough and set it on a lightly floured work surface (or a long dining room table—you need at least 4 feet of work space). Roll the dough into a 12-by-28-inch rectangle (it should be just a little shy of ¼ inch thick) with a long side facing you. Divide the dough lengthwise into two 6-by-28-inch pieces. Pull and shape the corners into a rectangle shape. (If you are using the Basic Babka Dough, see the sidebar on page 76 for shaping instructions.) Separate the 2 strips so there is space between them.

4 Fill the dough: Spread the cheese mixture across the middle of each piece of the dough. Spread it out evenly, leaving at least a 1-inch border at the bottom. Squeeze the excess rum from the raisins and sprinkle them over the cheese.

5 Use a little water to dampen the bottom border of the dough (make sure there is no cheese there; otherwise, it won't seal) and then fold the top part of the dough over to meet the bottom, about 1 inch from the edge. Tuck it in, roll it to the edge, and press the dough to seal the edges. Turn the dough over, seam-side down, and gently lift and stretch it just to lengthen it a little bit. Repeat with the other piece of dough.

6 Twist the strips into a babka: Use a bench knife or a chef's knife to slice the dough crosswise into thirds (yielding 6 pieces of dough total). Then take 2 pieces of dough, overlap one over the other to form an X, and twist the ends together like the threads on a screw so you have at least 2 twists on each side of the X. Repeat with the remaining pieces.

Place each twisted babka into a loaf pan. The dough should fill the pan by two-thirds and fit the length perfectly.

7 Let the dough rise: Cover each pan with a kitchen towel and set them aside in a warm, draft-free spot until the dough rises 1 to 2 inches above the rim of the pan and is very soft and jiggly to the touch, 2 to 3 hours, depending on how warm your room is.

8 Preheat the oven to 350°F. (If you are letting the dough rise in the oven as described in the Note on page 79, be sure to remove the loaf pans and bowl of water before preheating!)

9 Bake the babkas until they are dark brown and baked through, about 40 minutes; check them after 25 minutes, and if they are getting too dark, tent them loosely with a piece of parchment paper or aluminum foil.

10 Meanwhile, make the simple syrup: Combine the sugar and water in a small saucepan and bring to a boil over high heat. Reduce the heat to medium-low and simmer, stirring occasionally to dissolve the sugar. Turn off the heat and set aside the syrup to cool.

11 Remove the babkas from the oven, and while they are still warm, brush the surface generously with the cooled sugar syrup (the syrup makes the top of the babka shiny and beautiful and also locks in the moisture so the cake doesn't dry out). Use a paring knife to separate each babka from the loaf pan, and turn them out onto a cutting board. Slice and serve warm, or cool completely in the pans before unmolding and slicing.

Halvah Babka

Makes 2 babkas

This babka is a cross-pollination of Yemenite kubaneh (page 160), traditional babka, and American monkey bread. Kubaneh tastes like brioche and is constructed of balls of dough stacked on top of one another. Monkey bread is a breakfast pastry in which bready cinnamon-bun-type rolls are shaped into balls and are also stacked one on top of the next in a heavily buttered and sugared tube pan. I combined the ideas here, using babka dough and stuffing it with a sweetened tahini paste, almost like a sesame version of Nutella, and even more halvah. After the babka is finished baking, it is inverted and a sugary syrup drips off the mound of pull-apart rolls. The texture is very buttery and rich, and the sesame flavor gives the babka even more depth and a sweet yet earthy flavor. Tahini glaze is drizzled over the finished babka for extra taste and shine and also to seal in moistness.

Unsalted butter (at room temperature)	65 grams (generous 4 tablespoons)
Large egg	1
Dark brown sugar	50 grams (⅓ cup, lightly packed)
Vanilla extract	¼ teaspoon
Honey	25 grams (1½ tablespoons)
All-purpose flour	20 grams (2½ tablespoons)
Fine salt	¼ teaspoon
Cornstarch	8 grams (1 tablespoon)
Tahini sesame paste	150 grams (¾ cup plus 1 tablespoon)
1 recipe Advanced Babka Dough (page 70) or Basic Babka Dough (page 68), chilled 24 hours	
Halvah	120 grams (¾ cup), finely crumbled
Granulated sugar	50 grams (¼ cup)
Water	50 grams (scant ¼ cup)

1 **Make the halvah filling:** Generously grease two small (6-cup) Bundt or tube pans with 30 grams (2 tablespoons) of the butter. In a medium bowl, whisk the egg, brown sugar, and vanilla together. Whisk in the honey; then add the flour and salt, and combine until the mixture is smooth. Add the remaining butter and whisk until well combined. Whisk in the cornstarch, followed by 100 grams (⅔ cup) of the tahini, and

whisk until the halvah filling is smooth. Chill in the refrigerator for at least 30 minutes before using.

2 **Roll the babka dough:** Unwrap the cold babka dough and set it on a lightly floured work surface with a long side facing you. Roll the dough into an 18-by-10-inch rectangle (it should be just a little shy of ¼ inch thick). Pull and shape the corners into a rectangle.

(continued)

3 Fill and roll the dough: Spread the halvah filling in an even layer over the dough all the way to the edges, and then sprinkle the crumbled halvah over it. Roll the dough up into a tight cylinder, working from the bottom to the top. Lift the cylinder, holding one end in each hand, and pull it to make the cylinder even tighter.

4 Divide the dough and let it proof: Use a bread knife to slice the cylinder crosswise into 1-inch-wide pieces (you will get about 24 pieces). Divide the pieces between the buttered Bundt pans, cut-side down, fitting them in tightly. Add another layer on top of the first and continue to stack the pieces in the pan until all the pieces are used. Place each pan in a plastic bag, tuck the open end under the pan, and set them aside in a warm, draft-free spot until the dough rises 1 to 2 inches above the rim of the pan or has doubled in volume and is very soft and jiggly to the touch, 1½ to 2 hours, depending on how warm your room is.

5 While the babkas rise, make the tahini glaze: Combine the granulated sugar and water in a small saucepan and bring to a simmer over medium-high heat, stirring occasionally. Once the sugar has dissolved, turn off the heat and let the syrup cool to room temperature. Whisk in the remaining tahini.

6 Preheat the oven to 350°F.

7 Bake the babkas until they are golden brown on top and the top sounds hollow when tapped, 25 to 30 minutes. Remove the babkas from the oven and let them rest for 5 minutes. Then turn each one out onto a parchment paper–lined sheet pan and brush with the tahini glaze. Serve once the babkas are cool enough to break apart into pieces.

Ricotta Streusel Babka

Makes one 9-by-13-inch sheet pan of babka

Babka dough is quite versatile—you can make it into a twist (page 100), form it into a traditional loaf (page 68), or roll the dough to make a pie crust (page 81) or rugelach (page 248). Here I roll the dough into a thin sheet to make a cakey cushion for lemony sweetened ricotta and streusel. This babka looks almost like a traditional cheese coffee cake, which it more or less is. These instructions will make a very small batch of dough (which is why it gets kneaded by hand and not using a stand mixer), but if you are making another type of babka, you can always just set aside one-third of the dough to make this cheese babka.

DOUGH

Whole milk (at room temperature)	45 grams (3 tablespoons)
Vanilla paste	¼ teaspoon
or vanilla extract	¼ teaspoon
Fresh yeast	10 grams (1 tablespoon)
or active dry yeast	3 grams (1 teaspoon)
Pastry flour or cake flour (sifted)	180 grams (1¾ cups), plus extra for dusting and kneading
Large egg	1
Granulated sugar	25 grams (2 tablespoons)
Fine salt	Pinch
Unsalted butter (at room temperature)	45 grams (3 tablespoons)

STREUSEL TOPPING

Granulated sugar	75 grams (⅓ cup)
Pastry flour or cake flour	170 grams (1⅔ cups)
Unsalted butter (cold)	120 grams (8 tablespoons)

RICOTTA FILLING

Ricotta cheese (preferably a thick ricotta)	300 grams (1¼ cups)
Sour cream	75 grams (⅓ cup)
Granulated sugar	35 grams (3 tablespoons)
Vanilla bean	½, split, seeds scraped out and reserved
or vanilla extract	1 teaspoon
Cornstarch	20 grams (3 tablespoons)
Lemon zest	grated from ½ lemon

Confectioners' sugar	for dusting

(continued)

1 Make the dough: Combine the milk and vanilla in a large bowl. Use a fork or your fingers to lightly mix the yeast into the milk. Then, in this order, add the flour, egg, sugar, salt, and finally 30 grams (2 tablespoons) of the butter in small pinches.

2 Begin to knead the dough in the bowl, pushing it up against the sides of the bowl and folding it over on top of itself. Once the dough comes together and there aren't any flour pockets, knead it on a lightly floured work surface until it is smooth and has good elasticity, 8 to 10 minutes.

3 Round the dough and let it rise: Round the dough into a ball. Lightly flour the bowl, add the dough, cover the bowl with plastic wrap, and set it aside at room temperature for 30 minutes.

4 Chill the dough: Remove the dough from the bowl, set it on a piece of plastic wrap, and press it into a 1-inch-thick rectangle. Wrap the dough in plastic wrap and refrigerate for at least 1 hour and up to 24 hours.

5 Make the streusel: Combine the sugar and flour in a medium bowl. Add the cold butter in very small slivers, and use your fingers or a dough cutter to work the butter into the dry ingredients, pressing the butter into thin bits and mixing until the mixture looks pebbly and all the butter bits are worked into the flour-sugar mixture. Cover the bowl with plastic wrap and refrigerate.

6 Make the ricotta filling: In a medium bowl, combine the ricotta, sour cream, sugar, vanilla, cornstarch, and lemon zest. Stir to combine, and refrigerate until you are ready to make the babka.

7 Build the babka and let the babka proof: Use the remaining 15 grams (1 tablespoon) soft butter to grease a 9-by-13-inch quarter sheet pan. Set the dough on a lightly floured work surface and lightly dust the top with flour. Roll the dough into a rectangle about the same size as your sheet pan, flouring the top and underside of the dough as needed. Place the dough in the pan, stretching it out to fit into the corners and using your fingertips to press the edges into the corners and edges of the pan. Use an offset spatula to cover the dough evenly with the ricotta filling, leaving a ¼-inch border around the edges. Cover the pan with plastic wrap (or insert the pan into a unscented plastic bag) and set it aside to rise in a warm, draft-free spot until the dough looks a little jiggly under the cheese layer, about 1 hour.

8 Preheat the oven to 325°F.

9 Sprinkle the streusel over the ricotta filling, and bake the babka until the cake layer is cooked through and the streusel is just evenly golden (you don't want it to be darkly browned), turning the pan midway through baking, 16 to 18 minutes total. Remove the pan from the oven and set it aside to cool completely before dusting the babka with the confectioners' sugar, cutting it into squares, and serving.

Apple Babka

Makes 3 babkas using the Advanced Babka Dough in 9-by-2¾-by-2-inch loaf pans, or
2 babkas using the Basic Babka Dough in standard loaf pans (see the sidebar on page 76)

In the fall, when apples are crisp and sweet, I turn them into the filling for an apple babka to celebrate the Jewish New Year, Rosh Hashanah. Seasonal fresh fruit always complements babka—so you can try plums or apricots in place of the apples and make this any time of the year.

Unsalted butter (at room temperature)	45 grams (3 tablespoons)
Granulated sugar	100 grams (½ cup)
Golden Delicious apples	4, peeled, halved, cored, and sliced ⅛ inch thick
Vanilla bean	½, halved lengthwise to expose the seeds
Lemon zest	grated from 1 lemon
Lemon juice	from 1 lemon
1 recipe Advanced Babka Dough (page 70) or Basic Babka Dough (page 68), chilled 24 hours	
All-purpose flour	for rolling and shaping

EGG WASH AND TOPPING

Large egg	1
Water	1 tablespoon
Fine salt	Pinch
Sliced almonds	275 grams (2¾ cups)

SIMPLE SYRUP

Granulated sugar	160 grams (¾ cup plus 1 tablespoon)
Water	120 grams (½ cup)

1 Cook the apples: Melt the butter in a large skillet over medium-high heat. Once the butter has melted, add the sugar and cook, stirring occasionally, until the sugar is dissolved and beginning to caramelize, 2 to 3 minutes. Add the apples and the vanilla bean and cook, stirring often, until the apples become juicy, their liquid cooks off, and the apples begin to caramelize, 8 to 10 minutes. Transfer the apples to a bowl, remove the vanilla bean, and stir in the lemon zest and juice. Set the bowl of apples aside to cool completely (if you can chill the apples for 30 minutes in the refrigerator, it's a good idea—in fact, the apple filling can be refrigerated for up to 5 days).

2 Roll the chilled Advanced Babka Dough: Unwrap the cold babka dough and set it on a lightly floured work surface. Divide the dough in half, return one piece to the refrigerator, and roll the other piece into a

5-by-28-inch rectangle (it should be just a little shy of ¼ inch thick) with a long side facing you. Pull and shape the corners into a rectangle.

> NOTE: AFTER SPRINKLING BABKA DOUGH with the filling (be it apples, Nutella, nuts, or whatever) and making the first roll to create the cylinder, push the dough back to tighten the roll. Roll the cylinder again and push back on the dough to tighten it. This way you are compacting the cylinder so you can get more turns in it, creating more layers when the babka is sliced.

3 Fill the dough and divide it into strips: Sprinkle half the apples evenly over the dough, leaving a 1-inch border at the bottom, and then roll the dough from the top down, forming a tight cylinder. Pick up the cylinder, holding one end in each hand, and gently stretch it. Using a bread knife, slice the cylinder crosswise into thirds. Repeat with the other piece of dough so you have a total of 6 filled segments.

4 Twist the strips to make the babkas: Take 2 pieces of dough, overlap one over the other to form an X, and twist the ends together like the threads on a screw so you have at least 2 twists on each side of the X. Repeat with the remaining pieces.

5 Let the babkas proof: Place each twisted babka in a prepared loaf pan. Cover the pans with a dry kitchen towel and set them aside in a warm, draft-free spot until the dough rises 1 to 2 inches above the rim of the pan and is very soft and jiggly to the touch, 1½ to 2 hours, depending on how warm your room is.

6 Preheat the oven to 350°F.

7 Bake the babkas: Make the egg wash by whisking the egg, water, and salt together in a small bowl. Brush each of the babkas with egg wash and then sprinkle them generously with the almonds. Bake until golden brown, 20 to 25 minutes, loosely tenting them with aluminum foil if they begin to get too dark.

8 Meanwhile, make the simple syrup: Combine the sugar and water in a small saucepan and bring to a boil over high heat. Reduce the heat to medium-low and simmer, stirring occasionally to dissolve the sugar. Turn off the heat and set aside the syrup to cool.

9 Remove the pans from the oven and, while the babkas are still hot, brush the tops with the simple syrup. Once the babkas are completely cooled, turn them out of the loaf pans, slice, and serve.

Za'atar Twists

Makes 14 twists

A savory babka? And why not? I got the idea to make a za'atar babka when I was making a za'atar-seasoned bread. To fill the babka, I use labne, which is ultra-rich strained yogurt that has a wonderfully creamy texture and tangy flavor—not unlike sour cream. Chiles, feta cheese, and pine nuts add to the savory appeal. Here you take the babka dough and instead of twisting it and placing it in a loaf pan, you bake it free-form for individual twists or sticks. (You can follow the twist-shaping method for just about any of the babkas—some of the filling may ooze out onto the sheet pan, but those crispy bits are often the best.)

Sesame seeds	30 grams (3 tablespoons)
1 recipe Advanced Babka Dough (page 70) or Basic Babka Dough (page 68), chilled 24 hours	
All-purpose flour	for rolling and shaping
Labne (see page 332)	400 grams (1⅓ cups)
Red jalapeño or Fresno chile	1, finely chopped (seeded for less heat)
Extra-virgin olive oil	20 grams (1 tablespoon plus 1 teaspoon), plus extra for finishing
Feta cheese	110 grams (1 cup), crumbled
Pine nuts	60 grams (½ cup)
Fresh oregano leaves	50 grams (1 cup)
Za'atar (see page 339)	25 grams (2½ tablespoons), plus extra for finishing

EGG WASH	
Large egg	1
Water	1 tablespoon
Fine salt	Pinch

1 **Toast the sesame seeds:** Place the sesame seeds in a small skillet over medium-high heat and toast them, shaking the pan often, until they are golden brown, 2 to 3 minutes. Transfer the seeds to a small plate and set aside.

2 **Roll the cold babka dough:** Unwrap the cold babka dough and set it on a lightly floured work surface. Roll the dough into a 12-by-28-inch rectangle (it should be just

a little shy of ¼ inch thick) with a long side facing you. Pull and shape the corners into a rectangle.

3 **Fill and roll the dough:** Spread the labne over the dough in a thin, even layer. Sprinkle it with the jalapeño, olive oil, feta, toasted sesame seeds, pine nuts, oregano, and za'atar. Divide the dough in half horizontally so you now have two 6-by-28-inch pieces. Working from the long bottom edge of one

of the pieces, roll the dough up into a tight cylinder, pushing back on the cylinder with each roll to make it even tighter. Lift the cylinder, holding one end in each hand, and gently stretch and pull to tighten it even more (it will stretch to about 35 inches long). Repeat with the second piece of dough.

4 **Divide the dough into strips and make the twists:** Use a bread knife to slice each cylinder in half lengthwise so you have 4 long pieces, and then slice those pieces crosswise into 7 equal sections (about 5 inches each) to make a total of 28 strips. Cross 2 equal-size pieces to create an X, keeping the exposed filling facing up. Twist the ends together like the threads on a screw so you have at least 1 twist on each side of the X (3 twists total). Repeat with the remaining pieces. Set 7 twists on one parchment paper–lined rimmed sheet pan and 7 twists on a second parchment paper–lined sheet pan.

5 **Let the twists proof:** Cover the sheet pans with plastic wrap and set aside in a warm, draft-free spot until the twists have doubled in volume and are very soft and jiggly to the touch, 2 to 3 hours, depending on how warm your room is.

6 Preheat the oven to 350°F (if you are letting the dough rise in the oven, as described in the Note on page 79, be sure to remove the sheet pans and bowl of water before preheating!).

7 **Bake the twists:** Make the egg wash by whisking the egg, water, and salt together in a small bowl. Brush egg wash over each twist, and bake until they are dark brown and baked through, about 20 minutes; check the twists after 15 minutes, and if they are getting too dark, tent them loosely with a piece of parchment paper. Remove the twists from the oven and, while they are still warm, brush with more olive oil and sprinkle with a little za'atar. Serve warm or at room temperature.

ZA'ATAR TWISTS AND . . .

Instead of making 14 twists, save half the dough and use it to make another loaf of your favorite babka, such as the Famous Chocolate Babka (page 74), Cinnamon-Raisin-Walnut Babka (page 82), or Apple Babka (page 97). This way you get a savory babka and a sweet one to satisfy both cravings!

Nechama's Poppy Seed Babka

Makes 3 babkas

Nechama means "comfort" in Hebrew, and it's also the name of my brother's mother-in-law, who is the creator of this wonderfully comforting poppy seed cake. Nechama Gafini was known for the very best poppy seed cake in all of Israel (at least according to our family). This is the recipe straight from the source—everyone loves it so much that I follow her instructions to the letter (self-rising flour included). Nechama baked her babka with the long cylinder-shaped cakes side by side on a sheet pan. The edges of the cakes stay soft and tender since they bake connected to one another, while the tops turn a deep amber color. Slice it open and you'll discover that the cake is *loaded* with poppy seeds. Note: It is best to make the dough the day before making this babka.

DOUGH

Lukewarm water	115 grams (½ cup)
Fresh yeast	45 grams (¼ cup plus 1 tablespoon)
or active dry yeast	15 grams (1 tablespoon)
All-purpose flour (sifted, 11.7%)	375 grams (3 cups), plus extra for dusting and kneading
Self-rising flour (sifted)	350 grams (2¾ cups)
Granulated sugar	200 grams (1 cup)
Unsalted butter (at cool room temperature)	200 grams (1 stick plus 5 tablespoons)
Sour cream	200 grams (¾ cup plus 2 tablespoons)
Large egg	1
Large egg yolks	2
Unsalted butter (at room temperature)	30 grams (2 tablespoons)

FILLING

Poppy seeds (see Note)	400 grams (3½ cups)
Whole milk	520 grams (2¼ cups)
Granulated sugar	200 grams (1 cup)
Apricot jam	30 grams (2 tablespoons)
Cookie or cake crumbs (if needed)	50 grams (¼ cup)

EGG WASH

Large egg	1
Water	1 tablespoon
Fine salt	Pinch

1 **Make the dough:** Pour the water into the bowl of a stand mixer fitted with the dough hook. If using fresh yeast, crumble the yeast into the bowl and use a fork or your fingers to lightly mix the yeast into the water. Sift the all-purpose flour and self-rising flour together into a bowl; if using active dry yeast, stir it into the sifted flour. Add the flour to the water, then add the sugar, cool butter, sour cream, whole egg, and egg yolks.

2 Mix the dough on low speed, scraping down the sides and bottom of the bowl as needed and pulling the dough off the hook as it accumulates there, until it is well combined, about 1 minute (it will be very sticky). Increase the speed to medium and continue to mix until the dough is soft and smooth, about 3 minutes.

3 **Stretch and fold the dough, then let it rise:** Generously flour your work surface (this is a very soft and sticky dough, and it's okay to use a good amount of flour to finish kneading). Use a plastic dough scraper to transfer the dough to the floured surface, and flour the top. Stretch and tear one corner of the dough, folding it on top of itself. Give the dough a quarter turn and repeat for 1 to 2 minutes, until the dough begins to resist tearing. Turn the dough over and round it into a ball. Take some flour from the work surface and use it to flour a large bowl. Add the dough to the bowl, lightly flour the top, cover the bowl with plastic wrap, and set it aside to rise until it has doubled in volume, about 1 hour. Then refrigerate at least 3 hours or, preferably, overnight.

4 **Make the filling:** Put the poppy seeds in a food processor or high-powered blender and grind them until they are finely ground,

stopping before they start to turn into a paste. Combine the milk and sugar in a medium saucepan, set it over medium heat, and stir often until the sugar dissolves, about 2 minutes; then stir in the ground poppy seeds. Reduce the heat to low and cook, stirring often (otherwise the poppy seeds could stick to the bottom of the pan and burn), until the mixture thickens and the poppy seeds have absorbed all the milk and the mixture begins to bubble, 6 to 7 minutes. Stir in the apricot jam, and transfer the filling to a shallow bowl or baking dish. Cover the surface directly with plastic wrap and set aside at room temperature to cool completely. If there is some moisture pooling in the bowl after the poppy seed filling has cooled, stir in about ¼ cup of neutral-flavored cookie or cake crumbs (crumbled muffins and biscuits work well too) to absorb some of the moisture and lighten the filling.

NOTE: ALWAYS TASTE POPPY SEEDS BEFORE using them. They should taste earthy and not exceedingly bitter. Poppy seeds have a high oil content and should be stored in the freezer to keep them at optimal freshness. From the moment the poppy seeds are ground, they should be held in the refrigerator because they get oxygenated and spoil very quickly. Some spice shops will actually grind the poppy seeds for you—ask if your spice shop (especially Indian markets or Middle Eastern shops) offers this service. The poppy seeds are crushed rather than ground, which creates a nicer consistency. If you don't use the ground poppy seeds immediately, freeze them.

5 **Divide the dough:** Grease a 13-by-9-inch baking dish or quarter sheet pan with the room-temperature butter. Transfer the dough to a floured work surface (the dough is quite soft, so don't be afraid to use enough flour so it doesn't stick), and use a bench scraper to divide the dough into 3 equal pieces. Use a rolling pin to roll

each piece into a 9-inch square, using your fingers to pull out the corners to create a nice square shape.

6 Fill and roll the dough, then let the babkas proof: Divide the poppy seed filling among the 3 dough squares, using a knife or offset spatula to spread the filling evenly over the dough and leaving a 1-inch border at the bottom edge. Roll the dough into a cylinder, starting at the top and rolling down toward the poppy-less bottom edge. Place the cylinders seam-side down in the prepared baking dish (there won't be much space between the logs, and that's fine). Cover the logs completely with a kitchen towel and set aside in a warm, draft-free spot until the dough has proofed and is jiggly, and when you press a finger into the side of the dough, the depression fills in by about halfway, about 1 hour.

7 Preheat the oven to 350°F.

8 Bake the babkas: Make the egg wash by whisking the egg, water, and salt together in a small bowl. Use a pastry brush to lightly coat the entire surface of each log with egg wash, making sure to coat the sides as well (take care not to let the egg wash pool between the logs or at the bottom of the pan). Bake until the babkas are golden brown all over and sound hollow when tapped, about 35 minutes. Remove from the oven and let cool completely in the pan before separating the babkas. Then slice and serve, or wrap in aluminum foil and freeze (either as a whole babka or halved crosswise) in a resealable freezer bag for up to 1 month. (See page 79 for full defrosting instructions.)

THE MAGIC OF CRUMBS

Cake crumbs are called for in the recipes for poppy seed babka here, for the hamantaschen on pages 258 and 261, and for the apple strudel on page 283. The purpose of cake crumbs is to absorb extra moisture that any ingredient might give off during the baking process so the dough doesn't become soggy. Adding cake crumbs is a very simple trick. Of course I realize not every baker has cake crumbs saved in a container in the freezer, and that's okay! You can use almost anything in place of cake crumbs, as long as it is somewhat neutral in flavor—for example, I wouldn't save the crumbs from a chocolate cake to add to apple strudel. But gingerbread? Or lemon pound cake? Sure, why not? Muffins, biscuits, cornbread, and finely processed white or challah-type bread all work quite well. You want the crumbs to be dry so they are extra absorbent, so you can either let the crumbs sit out overnight (uncovered) or dry them in a warm oven for a bit (but not long enough to actually toast them). Place the crumbs in a resealable freezer bag and store them in the freezer. Then use them to wick away the moisture in your chocolate or apples or poppy seeds the next time you're making something that could use a little help to achieve a nice, crisp bottom crust.

Chocolate Kugelhopf

Makes one 9-inch kugelhopf

Here is what many people consider to be the original or at least the classic babka. The texture of this cake, baked in a fluted mold, is finer-crumbed and is very different from the Famous Chocolate Babka (page 74). Within the deep chocolate swirls of this cake there is actually no hard chocolate. The filling follows the German and Austro-Hungarian cake tradition of being made solely from cocoa powder, sugar, and butter. Use the best-quality cocoa you can find. Great cocoa should smell rich and pungent and almost make you high with pleasure!

Bake this cake in a kugelhopf pan, which is narrower and a little taller than a Bundt pan. You can also bake it in a small Bundt pan, if you must. Note that the dough is chilled for at least 8 hours before you roll and fill it.

DOUGH

Whole milk	100 grams (⅓ cup)
Fresh yeast	20 grams (2 tablespoons)
or active dry yeast	6 grams (2 teaspoons)
All-purpose flour (sifted, 11.7%)	400 grams (3 cups plus 2 tablespoons), plus extra for dusting and kneading
Granulated sugar	75 grams (⅓ cup)
Dry milk powder	10 grams (2 teaspoons)
Fine salt	5 grams (1 teaspoon)
Large eggs	2
Unsalted butter (at cool room temperature)	150 grams (10 tablespoons), plus 45 grams (3 tablespoons) for greasing the pan

FILLING

Granulated sugar	200 grams (1 cup)
Dutch-process cocoa powder	30 grams (¼ cup)
Unsalted butter (at room temperature)	75 grams (5 tablespoons)
Boiling water	30 grams (2 tablespoons)

GLAZE

Unsalted butter (melted)	30 grams (2 tablespoons)
Granulated sugar	25 grams (2 tablespoons)

1 Make the dough: Pour the milk into the bowl of a stand mixer fitted with the dough hook. If using fresh yeast, crumble the yeast into the bowl and use a fork or your fingers to lightly mix the yeast into the milk; if using active dry yeast, stir the yeast into the

milk. Add the flour, sugar, milk powder, salt, and eggs. Mix on medium speed, stopping the mixer to scrape the bowl as needed, until the dough comes together in a well-mixed mass, about 2 minutes. With the mixer on medium speed, gradually add 60 grams (4 tablespoons) of the butter, a small pinch at a time, making sure each addition is incorporated before adding the next (this should take about 3 minutes). Cover the bowl with plastic wrap and set it aside at room temperature until the dough has nearly doubled in volume, about 30 minutes (depending on how warm the room is).

2 Return the bowl to the stand mixer, and while mixing on medium speed, add the remaining 90 grams (6 tablespoons) of unsalted butter, a pinch at a time. Use a plastic dough scraper to transfer the dough to a large sheet of plastic wrap. Gently shape the dough into a 1-inch-thick rectangle, wrap it in plastic wrap, and refrigerate for at least 8 hours and up to 24 hours.

3 Make the filling: In a medium bowl, stir together the sugar, cocoa powder, and butter. Add the boiling water and stir to combine.

4 Roll and fill the dough: Grease the kugelhopf pan with the remaining 45 grams (3 tablespoons) of butter. (The pan needs to be heavily buttered so the baked dough doesn't stick.) Place the chilled dough on a lightly floured work surface and sprinkle the top with flour. Roll the dough into a 12-inch square, lifting it and flouring as needed to ensure the dough doesn't stick, and making sure the square is very even (square off the edges and corners of the dough with a dough scraper or bench knife if necessary). Use an offset spatula or butter knife to spread the cocoa filling all the way to the top and left and right edges, leaving a 1-inch border at the bottom edge.

5 Shape and proof the kugelhopf: Roll the dough from the top to the bottom in a tight cylinder, pushing back on the cylinder after every roll to make it even tighter. Dab a little water along the bottom edge, roll the cylinder over onto the border, and press lightly to seal it at the seam. Open the center of one end of the roll and fit the other end inside, forming a circle; then pinch the seams shut. Carefully transfer the dough to the prepared pan, seam-side up (this is important—otherwise, the filling could leak out). Cover the pan with a dry kitchen towel and set it aside in a warm, draft-free spot until the dough has doubled in volume and is very soft and jiggly to the touch, 2 to 3 hours, depending on how warm your room is.

6 Preheat the oven to 325°F.

7 Uncover the pan and bake the kugelhopf until it is golden brown on top, 40 to 45 minutes. Remove the pan from the oven and set it aside for 10 minutes before turning the kugelhopf out onto a wire rack. Then immediately add the glaze: brush the kugelhopf with the melted butter and sprinkle the sugar over the top and sides. Let it cool completely before slicing.

FLATBREADS

IT IS ENDLESSLY FASCINATING TO me how a simple change in the amount of water or flour from one bread dough to the next can be a big enough difference to distinguish a pita from a focaccia, which are both made from very similar doughs, or how, with a slightly different shaping and baking technique, you can use pita dough to get the large and handkerchief-like pita called laffa or the thin, crêpe-like mofleta.

All the breads in this chapter can almost (almost!) be looked at as variations of one another. They all are, at their foundation, the same: flatbreads that originated in the Middle East, North and Northwest Africa, and the Mediterranean, where traditionally a softer, less "quality" wheat was available. The resulting breads didn't have the strength to capture air and develop gluten like their northern and western European cousins. They remained softer and flatter than boules, baguettes, and Pullman-style loaves, and since it is so warm in many of their locations of origin, they generally don't have long rises or call for pre-ferments to start the dough (you can always add a pre-ferment for more flavor; see page 174). These are simple, honest breads that people have been making on a daily basis for thousands of years.

My pita bread, which I developed specifically for home bakers to always get the pocket in the middle, is "baked" in a skillet. (It's a great summertime bread if you don't want to heat up the kitchen with baking.) Laffa is essentially the pita dough stretched even thinner, and za'atar pita is like a focaccia in the way the bread is shaped and baked. Lachmajun is the Turkish equivalent of focaccia or even pizza. And of course focaccia is a flatbread as well, but it is different from the Middle Eastern breads because of its spongier crumb.

When I wanted to learn how to make real Italian focaccia, the kind that is thin and tender, chewy yet with crisp edges and crust, and pocked with the telltale marks of a baker's fingers pressed into the dough, I enlisted two means of discovery: (1) I asked every Italian person I knew where he or she gets the best focaccia, and then (2) I traveled to Italy's most famous focaccerias and tasted for myself. In the end, I had two favorites, one from the north of Italy and one from the south, so I spent time in both places to learn the bakers' techniques and methods.

Malawach, jachnun, and mofleta are all breads I fell in love with thanks to my wife, Rinat, whose mother is Moroccan and father is Yemenite. There is something positively addictive about each of these breads—thin and chewy and very indulgent. These three breads may be somewhat unknown in the United States, but in Israel, they are beloved. Malawach is a Yemenite flatbread made by creating a dough with baking powder—not yeast—laminating it with butter like a puff pastry, then dividing the dough into small pieces, rolling each one very thin (almost like phyllo), wrapping the dough into a cylinder, winding it into a coil, then re-rolling the dough and pan-frying it. Cooked malawach separates into wonderfully flaky layers and is very delicious and rich.

Mofleta is a yeasted flatbread that lies somewhere between malawach and a crêpe and is served with honey and butter. The dough gets stretched very thin and then is browned in a skillet. After flipping the crêpe-like piece of dough, you lay another piece of dough on top, flip, brown, add another piece of dough, and repeat and repeat until you have a stack many sheets high. It's ingenious and addicting, but I could say that about each one of these flatbreads.

Pan Pita

Makes 8 pita breads (900 grams / 2 pounds of dough)

When I was a child in Israel, I would walk to a falafel stand run by a Yemenite man named Yefet. The falafel was so good—*the best*. For years I asked, "Yefet, what is your secret to the falafel?" He would never tell me. Years later, I asked him again, "Yefet, what is the secret to your falafel? Please tell me!" And he said to me, "Uri, the secret is not in the falafel . . . it is the pita!"

Think of the bread of the Middle East and you think of pita, but really this kind of flatbread is eaten throughout the region, from India's naan to pide in Turkey. In Israel the most common flatbread is pita, either made with a pocket, as in this recipe, or made without a pocket, like laffa (see page 121). Pita is a genius bread—eat it as a wrap or as a sandwich, or use it as a scoop. Or even toast it to make chips. The key to great pita is the right water-to-flour ratio and a very hot oven so the moisture in the dough evaporates, pushing the top crust up and creating an air bubble in the middle of the baking dough—what is known as the pocket. I developed this recipe specifically for home bakers to easily make pita—pocket guaranteed. The trick is making it in a skillet, which does as great a job as a bakery oven, clay oven, or wood-fired oven. Keep the skillet warm and covered so the steam doesn't escape while you bake the pita. After cooking, place the pita in a plastic bag so it stays soft and pliable while you cook the other pieces.

Cool room-temperature water	335 grams (1½ cups)
Fresh yeast	20 grams (2½ tablespoons)
or active dry yeast	8 grams (2¼ teaspoons)
All-purpose flour (sifted, 11.7%)	550 grams (4⅓ cups), plus extra for kneading and shaping
Granulated sugar	20 grams (1½ tablespoons)
Fine salt	15 grams (1 tablespoon)

1 Make the dough: Pour the water into the bowl of a stand mixer. Whisk in the yeast until dissolved, and then add the flour, sugar, and salt. Using the dough hook attachment and with the mixer set to low speed, mix the ingredients until they come together to make a shaggy-looking dough without any dry bits at the bottom of the bowl, about 1 minute.

If the dough looks dry, add more water, 1 tablespoon at a time; if it looks wet, add flour, 1 tablespoon at a time.

2 Knead, stretch, and fold the dough: Increase the speed to medium and knead until the dough cleans the sides of the bowl, about 3 minutes. Transfer the dough to a lightly floured work surface and lightly flour the top of the dough. Stretch one corner of the dough, lightly tearing the dough, then fold it back on top of itself. Give the dough a quarter turn and repeat about 12 times, until the dough has a nice round shape.

3 Let the dough rise: Lightly flour a large bowl, place the dough in the bowl, and lightly flour the dough. Cover the bowl with plastic wrap and set it aside at room temperature until the dough has increased in volume by about 50%, about 30 minutes.

4 Divide and round the dough, then proof it: Lightly flour the work surface, set the dough on top, and lightly flour the dough. Use your hands to pull the dough into a 1-inch-thick rectangle. Divide the dough in half crosswise and then cut each half into quarters. Very lightly shape each piece of dough into a ball by folding the 4 corners of the dough up on top of the center, turning the dough ball upside down, and then cupping your hand to push and pull the dough on the work surface into a taut round shape. Divide the dough balls between 2 floured sheet pans, lightly dust the top of the dough balls with flour, and cover the sheet pans with a kitchen towel (see page 17 for other homemade proof box ideas). Set it aside in a warm, draft-free spot until the dough springs back and fills in halfway when you lightly press a finger into it, about 40 minutes, depending on the warmth of the room.

5 Roll the dough: On a lightly floured work surface, roll each ball of dough into a ¼-inch-thick round, 5 to 6 inches in diameter.

6 Cook the pita: Heat an 8- to 12-inch nonstick or cast-iron skillet over high heat. Add 1 round of dough, reduce the heat to medium-high, cover the pan immediately, and cook until the first side is browned, 2 to 3 minutes (check the first pita often; once you know the pan is adequately heated, you'll have a better idea how long the pitas will take to brown and can check less often). Uncover the pan and quickly use a spatula to flip the pita over. Cover and cook until the second side is pale gold, 2 to 3 minutes. Transfer the pita to a plate, let it cool for a minute, and then place the plate inside a plastic bag, tucking the open end under the plate to lock in the moisture. Repeat with the remaining pieces of pita, stacking one on top of the next. Serve immediately, or let them cool completely and then wrap each piece in 2 layers of plastic wrap followed by a layer of aluminum foil and freeze until firm; place the wrapped frozen pitas in a gallon-size resealable plastic bag. The pitas can be frozen for up to 1 month. To reheat, let the pitas thaw at room temperature and warm them in an oven or even in a toaster.

(continued)

Laffa

Flat and chewy laffa bread is a pita without the pocket. You can rip off a piece to dip and scoop as you would with pita (although it's not quite as tender as pita), or, what's more common, use the whole laffa as a wrap for a kebab or falafel sandwich. Laffa is traditionally made in a very hot taboon, a wood-fired clay oven. While you can't turn your home oven into a taboon, you can get close by heating a pizza stone on an oven rack for 30 minutes at the highest temperature your oven will go to—either 500° or 550°F (if you don't have a pizza stone, heat an upside-down metal baking sheet for 15 minutes in the oven). After the bread comes out of the oven, it's critical to place it in a plastic bag so it semi-steams to stay soft and a little spongy.

To make laffa dough, follow the recipe for pita (page 116) through step 3. Set a baking stone (or upside-down sheet pan) in the oven and preheat the oven to 525°F or the highest setting.

Divide the dough into 8 pieces and round each piece into a ball as described in step 4. Set the balls on a floured surface, cover them with a kitchen towel, and let them rest until until the dough springs back and fills in halfway when you lightly press a finger into it, about 30 minutes, depending on the warmth of the room.

Set a ball of dough on a lightly floured work surface (or a floured pizza peel or piece of cardboard) and use a rolling pin to roll the dough to a 14-inch round or oval shape. Prick the dough all over with a fork or press your fingertips deep into the dough (this helps prevent the laffa from developing a pocket). Open the oven door and quickly place the laffa on the stone (or slide it off the peel or cardboard). Bake until browned, 4 to 5 minutes. Remove the laffa from the oven and immediately place it in a large plastic bag, tucking the open end underneath. Repeat with the remaining pieces of dough, stacking one piece of laffa on top of the next in the plastic bag. Once all the dough has been baked, serve it immediately or store the laffa in a fresh plastic bag (without condensation from the steam of the hot bread) for up to 2 days. Reheat in a warm oven before serving.

Za'atar Pita

Makes 8 pita breads

Sprinkle za'atar and olive oil over the pita dough to turn it into a more flavorful flatbread. First, press your fingers into the dough to create dimples; it's similar to the technique used to make focaccia (see page 125). These little crevices will catch the spices and olive oil. I like to drizzle more olive oil over the bread right after it comes out of the oven, or if it's tomato season, I'll squeeze a halved tomato right over the pita, just like a lemon.

1 recipe Pan Pita (page 116), prepared though step 5	
Za'atar (see page 339)	50 grams (heaping ¼ cup)
Sesame seeds	30 grams (3 tablespoons)
Extra-virgin olive oil	120 grams (½ cup), plus extra for drizzling (optional)

1 Adjust one oven rack to the upper-middle position and another to the lower-middle position, and preheat the oven to 400°F.

2 **Dimple and season the pita:** Press your fingers into the rounds of dough to create deep dimples (you can dip your fingers in flour first so the dough doesn't stick to them). Cover the sheet pans with kitchen towels and let the dough rest for 10 minutes. Then press your fingers into the dough again to further deepen the dimples. Sprinkle each round with za'atar and sesame seeds, and then drizzle each piece with 1 tablespoon of the olive oil.

3 Bake a sheet of pita on each oven rack for 4 minutes. Then switch the top sheet pan to the bottom and the bottom sheet to the top rack, and continue to bake until the breads are browned across the top and bottom, 2 to 4 minutes longer.

4 Remove the pita breads from the oven and transfer them to a wire rack to cool. Drizzle with more olive oil if you like, and serve warm or at room temperature.

STEP 1

STEP 2

STEP 3

STEP 5

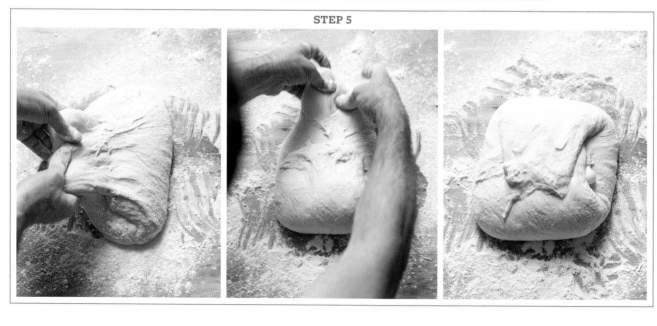

No-Knead Focaccia

Makes 8 focaccia (1.5 kilos / 3⅓ pounds of dough)

If you're familiar with Jim Lahey's no-knead bread technique, this focaccia lives in the same realm, which makes it a great "beginner" bread recipe. The recipe depends on the stretch-and-fold technique and time and yeast to work the dough from the inside out. This process activates the gluten naturally by turning sugar into carbon dioxide gas (the bubbles and air in the dough). That's why it's important to treat focaccia dough gently and not to mash and knead it with too much force, which would push out all the air.

Make a batch of dough and top it with your favorite ingredients. I use it to make Shakshuka Focaccia (page 136), Spinach Focaccia (page 133), and vegetable focaccia (pages 134 and 135). I've even finished focaccia sashimi-style with raw hamachi tuna and salmon! And there's no reason to stop at savory: top focaccia dough with fresh apricots or other stone fruits for dessert focaccia (drizzle with honey before serving). Let your imagination and creativity inspire you to come up with something original. And by the way, you can also use focaccia dough rolled very thin to make a really great pizza.

Cool room-temperature water	680 grams (3 cups)
Fresh yeast	10 grams (1¼ tablespoons)
or active dry yeast	3 grams (½ teaspoon)
All-purpose flour (sifted, 11.7%) or "00" pizza flour	850 grams (6¾ cups), plus lots of extra flour for dusting and kneading
Granulated sugar	10 grams (2 teaspoons)
Fine salt	10 grams (2 teaspoons)
Extra-virgin olive oil	as needed
Fresh oregano	as needed, finely chopped
Sesame seeds	as needed
Coarse salt	as needed

1 Make the dough: Pour the water into a large bowl. If you are using fresh yeast, crumble the yeast into the water and whisk until it is completely dissolved (since there is no kneading, it's very important that the yeast be completely dissolved). If you are using active dry yeast, mix the yeast into the flour. Then, in this order, add the flour, sugar, and salt to the water in the bowl. Use your hand to swirl the ingredients together; then use a plastic dough scraper to scrape down the sides and bottom of the bowl. Continue to mix the dough by hand in the bowl (it's very sticky, so you're really just scooping it away from the sides of the bowl with a cupped hand and folding it on top of itself) until there aren't any clumps, about 1 minute. Cover the bowl with plastic wrap and set it aside at room temperature until the dough has relaxed into the bowl and

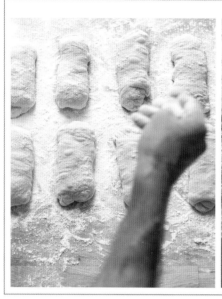

risen slightly (not a lot happens visually in this stage), about 30 minutes.

2 Stretch and fold the dough: Remove the plastic wrap and drizzle a little olive oil around the edges of the dough and over your hands. Use a dough scraper to help you grab one-quarter of the dough, stretch it up, and flop it over onto itself without pressing down on the dough. You're really just gently folding the edges onto the middle, giving the dough 4 folds without pressing on it, which would release the gas in the dough. Slide the dough scraper under the dough and turn it over. Cover the bowl with plastic wrap and set it aside for about 20 minutes, until, when you grab a small knob of the dough, you can see that there is a little gluten development, but if you stretch it too far, it rips easily.

3 Repeat the folding of 4 "corners" as you did in step 2. Turn the dough over again and let it rest for 20 minutes. After this rest, it will look a bit smoother, and when a small piece of dough is stretched, you should be able to feel and see a lot of gluten development.

4 While the dough rests, place a pizza stone in the oven and preheat the oven to 475°F. (If you have another sheet pan, you can use that instead of a pizza stone. If the sheet pan is rimmed, turn it upside down so you have a completely flat surface. The heat from the oven may cause the pan to warp slightly, but it will flatten out after it comes out of the oven.) You want the stone to be very hot when you put the bread in, so even after the oven is up to temperature, let the stone heat for at least 20 minutes before baking the focaccia.

5 Stretch and divide the dough: Heavily flour your work surface. Use the dough scraper to lift and transfer the dough to the floured surface, and flour the top of the dough (don't be cheap with the flour!). Gently lift, pull, and stretch the dough into a 14-by-8-inch rectangle. Use a bench scraper to divide the dough in half lengthwise so you have 2 long strips, and then divide the strips into 4 pieces each for a total of 8 pieces.

6 Shape and proof the dough: Place a piece of dough with a short edge facing you. Using your fingers and starting at the short edge, roll the dough over a quarter turn to start making a cylinder shape. Use your fingertips to firmly press the edge onto the dough, trying to only seal the edge and not press down on the body of the roll (you don't want to press out the trapped gas in the dough). Then roll the dough again and press the cylinder down to tack it onto the dough. Repeat twice, until you have a completed cylinder. Repeat with the remaining pieces of dough. Place the rolled pieces of dough on a heavily floured sheet pan (or leave them on your work surface) and cover it with a kitchen towel. Set it aside in a warm, draft-free spot until you see a few bubbles on the surface of the dough and each piece of dough has increased in volume by 50%, about 30 minutes (or a little less or a little longer depending on the temperature of the dough and the temperature of your kitchen).

7 Dimple and season the dough: Place a small bowl of flour on the work surface. Set a long sheet of parchment paper on a pizza peel, large cutting board, or upside-down sheet pan (a cool one, not the one in the oven!). You can also use a large piece of cardboard. Flour the parchment lightly and stretch 2 pieces of dough on top, creating two 8-by-4-inch rectangles. Dip your fingers into the flour and make deep depressions in the dough. Drizzle some olive oil over the dough, and then sprinkle the dough with a few generous pinches of oregano, sesame seeds, and coarse salt. Use your fingertips to further deepen the initial dimples in the dough.

8 Bake the focaccia: Open the oven door and quickly slide the dough-topped parchment onto the hot baking stone. Bake until the breads are nicely browned around the edges and golden brown everywhere else, 9 to 11 minutes. Slide the parchment onto a wire rack and drizzle the hot focaccia with more olive oil. Repeat with the remaining pieces of dough. Serve warm or at room temperature.

(continued)

HOT OVEN = GREAT FLATBREAD

Flatbreads are thin, so it's important that the dough doesn't dry out while it's developing its signature golden top and bottom crust. To keep the interior moist, you want to lock in that moisture by using a hot, hot oven to start creating a crust on the dough as quickly as possible. If the oven is not hot enough, it will take longer to brown the crusts, and during this time, your bread will lose moisture, and then it will continue to dry out as it cools when it comes out of the oven.

Heat a baking stone or upside-down sheet pan while you preheat the oven so both can get hot together. Once your oven reaches the temperature the recipe calls for (most likely in the 450° to 550°F range), don't put the bread in right away. Instead, let the oven continue to heat for at least another 10 minutes so it builds up heat; this means it will lose less heat when you open the oven door. Cooking the flatbreads hot and fast is part of the reason why the ones you bake, if wrapped and stored properly, will still be tender even a day or two after baking.

Variation
Focaccia with a Poolish (Pre-Ferment)

Focaccia made with a poolish has the most wonderful chewy texture and nuanced, tangy flavor (for more about pre-ferments, see page 174). If you have time to make a poolish for your focaccia, I recommend it.

To make the poolish, pour 100 grams (a scant ½ cup) of the water from the No-Knead Focaccia recipe into the bowl of a stand mixer. Add all the yeast and whisk to combine. Whisk in 60 grams (½ cup) of the flour called for in the focaccia recipe (so you are subtracting 60 grams from the 850 grams of total flour). The resulting mixture should look like pancake batter. Sprinkle another 60 grams (½ cup) of flour on top and do *not* stir it in (so now you will be adding 730 grams, not 850 grams, of flour to the final dough). Cover the bowl with plastic wrap and set it aside at room temperature until you see cracks in the flour, 1 to 2 hours.

Add the rest of the water (580 grams/2 cups), and the sugar and salt as indicated in the No-Knead Focaccia recipe. Fit the mixer with the dough hook and mix on low speed until the ingredients come together, 2 minutes. Stop the mixer and use a dough scraper to clear the sides and bottom of the bowl. Increase the mixer speed to medium-high and continue to knead until the dough becomes slightly elastic, about 4 minutes.

Cover the bowl with plastic wrap and set it aside at room temperature for 30 minutes. Proceed with stretching and folding the dough as described in step 2 of the No-Knead Focaccia recipe.

Spinach Focaccia

Makes 6 focaccia

When adding extra ingredients to bread dough—be they herbs, spinach, pitted olives, or cheese—there are a few things to keep in mind. First, you want to develop the dough before adding the extras so there is elasticity and gluten present when you add the goodies. Second, you want to make sure you add enough of the mix-ins to make a difference. I like to see lots of big pieces of olives and spinach and herbs—if you're going to bother with incorporating the additional ingredients, you might as well make them count!

Fresh baby spinach	200 grams (about ½ pound), coarsely chopped
Fresh oregano leaves	5 grams (about 1 tablespoon), finely chopped
Fresh rosemary leaves	5 grams (about 1 tablespoon), finely chopped
Fresh sage leaves	5 grams (about 1 tablespoon), finely chopped
Pitted Kalamata olives	50 grams (⅓ cup), coarsely chopped

After step 1 of the No-Knead Focaccia recipe on page 125, once the dough has risen for 30 minutes, add the spinach, herbs, and olives to the dough, folding them in following the instructions in step 2. Knead the dough by hand for 1 minute to combine. Let the dough rise for 20 minutes as instructed and proceed with the rest of the recipe, dividing the dough in step 5 into 6 pieces instead of 8.

FOCACCIA AS A CANVAS

Just the way you can top your pizza with whatever you feel like on a given day, the same is true for focaccia. I go to my local farmers' market and buy what is in season. Small tomatoes, peppers, leeks, scallions—they all make very good toppings. Get creative with your food styling, too: serving focaccia can be like serving edible art (see photos on pages 134 and 135).

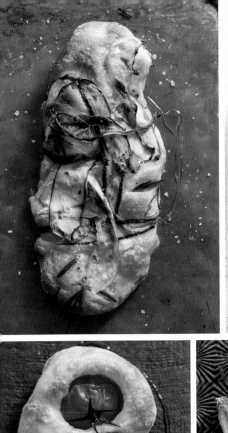

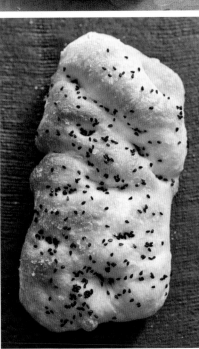

Shakshuka Focaccia

Makes 6 focaccia

One of Israel's most famous dishes is shakshuka, a humble meal of eggs poached in a concentration of sautéed tomatoes and onions. It is North African in origin—perhaps of Moroccan, Tunisian, or Libyan descent. Like hummus, shakshuka is an assemblage of ingredients common to many cultures that has been adopted by cooks because of its economy and pure tastiness. Here I use a round of focaccia as a plate, topping it with matbucha (tomatoes, onion, and garlic cooked until quite thick) and cracking the egg right into the center. Start the oven very hot. It will lose a bit of heat when you open the door to add the egg. If you start it at 500°F, it will still be around 475°F by the time you shut the door. For a soft and runny yolk, serve the focaccia immediately—as it cools, the yolk will harden.

All-purpose flour (sifted, 11.7%)	for shaping
1 recipe No-Knead Focaccia Dough (page 125), prepared through step 3	
Extra-virgin olive oil	as needed
1 recipe Matbucha (page 330)	
Sesame seeds or nigella seeds	40 grams (¼ cup)
Large eggs	6
Fine salt	as needed
Fresh flat-leaf parsley leaves	15 grams (¼ cup), finely chopped

1 **Stretch and divide the dough:** Heavily flour your work surface. Use a plastic dough scraper to lift and transfer the dough to the floured surface, and flour the top of the dough (don't be cheap with the flour!). Gently lift, pull, and stretch the dough into a 14-by-8-inch rectangle. Use a bench scraper to divide the dough in half lengthwise so you have 2 long strips, and then divide the strips into 3 pieces each for a total of 6 pieces. Fold the 4 corners of each piece of dough up and onto the center, creating a round shape; then flip the dough over.

2 **Proof the dough:** Place the balls of dough on a heavily floured pan (or leave them on your work surface) and cover with a

kitchen towel. Set aside in a warm, draft-free spot to rest until you see a few bubbles on the surface of the dough and each piece of dough has increased in volume by 50%, about 30 minutes (or a little less or a little longer depending on the temperature of the dough and the temperature of your kitchen).

3 While the dough is proofing, place a pizza stone in the oven and preheat the oven to 500°F. (If you have another sheet pan, you can use that instead. If the sheet pan is rimmed, turn it upside down so you have a completely flat surface. The heat from the oven may cause the pan to warp slightly, but it will flatten out after it comes out of the oven). You want the stone to be very hot

when you put the bread in, so even after the oven is up to temperature, continue to let the stone heat for at least 30 minutes longer before baking the focaccia.

> NOTE: IF YOUR KITCHEN IS VERY WARM, move the unbaked rounds of focaccia to a cool spot like a garage or even the refrigerator so they don't overproof while the first round or two of focaccia is baking in the oven.

4 Shape and season the focaccia: Place a long sheet of parchment paper on a pizza peel, flour the parchment lightly, and place 2 pieces of dough on top. If you don't have a pizza peel, you can place the parchment and dough rounds onto a large cutting board, an upside-down sheet pan, or even a large piece of cardboard. Slide the parchment (and dough) onto the hot stone just as you would do with a peel. Pour 1 tablespoon of olive oil into a small bowl and dip your fingertips in it; press your fingers into the center of the dough and press down, creating a flat depression in the center like a bowl. Widen the base of the depression until you stretch it into a circle,

leaving a 1-inch border around the edges of the dough (most of the dough will end up being flat, with a tall "wall" around the edges). Repeat with the other piece. Return to the first piece and re-flatten the well in the center, making it as thin as possible, then add about ⅓ cup of the matbucha sauce to the center, spreading it out slightly. Sprinkle the sesame seeds around the edges of the dough (try not to get them in the matbucha). Quickly make a little well in the center of the sauce, pressing down into the dough, and crack an egg into the depression. Sprinkle salt over the top.

5 Bake the focaccias: Slide the dough-topped sheet of parchment onto the hot baking stone. Bake until the breads are browned and the eggs are set, 9 to 10 minutes. Slide the parchment onto a wire rack and drizzle the breads with more olive oil. Repeat with the other pieces of dough, and then sprinkle the parsley over them all. Serve warm, while the yolks are runny, or at room temperature (the yolks will harden as they cool).

Potato Shakshuka Focaccia

Shakshuka is very much a seasonal dish in Israel, and in the old days, when tomatoes weren't available, potatoes were used instead. It's now quite common to serve a shakshuka with leeks, eggplant, spinach, potatoes, or whatever is plentiful. The inspiration for the seasoning in the potato topping comes from Dolly Haddad of Djerba, Tunisia. The Tunisian herb mixture is called Bzaa'r; every household in the region has its own blend. Hers has a warm, earthy flavor that works especially well with the hearty potatoes.

Freshly ground black pepper	1/8 teaspoon
Ground ginger	1/8 teaspoon
Licorice powder	1/8 teaspoon
Rose powder	1/8 teaspoon
Freshly grated nutmeg	Pinch
Ground white pepper	Pinch
Cinnamon	Pinch
Extra-virgin olive oil	80 grams (1/3 cup)
Yellow onion	1 large, halved and thinly sliced
Fine salt	10 grams (2 teaspoons)
Chile flakes	1 teaspoon
Water	60 grams (1/4 cup)
Yellow potatoes	4, peeled and chopped into 1/2-inch cubes
Garlic cloves	2 to 3, finely chopped
Red chile	1 large, halved, seeded, and finely chopped

During the rise in step 1 of the Shakshuka recipe, make the potato shakshuka topping: In a small bowl, stir together the black pepper, ginger, licorice powder, rose powder, nutmeg, white pepper, and cinnamon; set aside.

Heat the olive oil in a large pot over low heat. Add the onion and salt and cook, stirring often, until it browns around the edges, about 30 minutes. Add the chile flakes and the water, and once the pot is nicely deglazed (it should look like a paste), stir in the potatoes until they are well coated. Add the garlic, chile pepper, and the remaining olive oil, stir, and cook gently for 5 minutes. Stir in the spice mixture, cover the pot, and cook until the potatoes are tender but not falling apart or mushy, about 30 minutes. Transfer the potato mixture to a medium bowl to cool.

Follow the Shakshuka recipe through step 5 to shape, proof, fill, and bake the focaccias, using only the yolk of the egg and substituting the potato topping for the matbucha.

Lachmajun with Roasted Eggplant and Scallions

Makes 4 lachmajun (about 800 grams / 1½ pounds of dough)

Somewhere between a flatbread and a pizza, lachmajun is a Turkish flatbread I learned to make from my friend Hedai Offaim, who is a cheese maker and food writer in Israel. Lachmajun is classically topped with ground lamb, chiles, and spices, but in the summer you can top it with something lighter. I use goat's-milk yogurt with some dried mint (make sure it is very fresh) and eggplant in this version. There are probably as many variations, toppings, and shapes for lachmajun as there are for pizza. Top the dough with your favorite ingredients.

DOUGH

Cool room-temperature water	120 grams (½ cup)
Fresh yeast	15 grams (2 tablespoons)
or active dry yeast	5 grams (1 teaspoon)
All-purpose flour (sifted, 11.7%)	500 grams (4 cups), plus extra for kneading and shaping
Granulated sugar	15 grams (1 tablespoon)
Fine salt	10 grams (2 teaspoons)
Extra-virgin olive oil	75 grams (⅓ cup)
Goat's-milk yogurt	125 grams (½ cup)

TOPPINGS

Eggplants	3
Scallions	12 large, root ends removed
Extra-virgin olive oil	15 grams (1 tablespoon), plus extra for finishing
Goat's-milk yogurt	400 grams (1⅔ cups)
Dried mint	2 teaspoons, or more to taste
Fine salt	1 teaspoon
Freshly ground white pepper	½ teaspoon
Flaky salt	for finishing

1 **Make the dough:** Pour the water into the bowl of a stand mixer fitted with the dough hook. Crumble the yeast into the water and use your fingers to rub and dissolve it (if you are using dry yeast, whisk the yeast into the water). Add the flour, sugar, salt, olive oil, and yogurt, and mix on low speed until the dough comes together, about 1 minute. (If the dough looks dry, add more water, 1 tablespoon at a time. If it looks sticky and wet, add flour, 1 tablespoon at a time.)

(continued)

2 Knead the dough: Increase the speed to medium-high and mix until the dough is smooth and soft, about 2 minutes, stopping the mixer to scrape down the bowl and dough hook as needed.

3 Stretch and fold the dough: Transfer the dough to a lightly floured work surface and lightly dust the dough with more flour. Take the top corner of the dough and stretch it away from you until the dough rips, then fold it over the middle. Give the dough a quarter turn and repeat. Do this 4 times. Place the dough in a lightly floured bowl and dust the dough with more flour. Cover the bowl with plastic wrap and set it aside in a warm, draft-free spot until the dough has doubled in volume, about 1 hour.

4 Roast the eggplants: Preheat the oven to 375°F. Prick each eggplant a few times with a fork, place them on a rimmed sheet pan, and roast until they are tender and deflated, 40 to 50 minutes. Remove the eggplants from the oven and carefully use a paring knife to make an X in the bottom of each one. Stand the eggplants upright in a colander set in the sink and let the juices drain until the eggplants are cool enough to handle. Remove the stem ends of the eggplants and halve them lengthwise. Remove the flesh by pulling it out in long strands; set it aside on a plate.

5 Sauté the scallions: Separate the scallion green tops from the bases. Reserve the bottom 2 inches of the green tops, discarding the rest. Thinly slice the green tops and set aside. Heat the olive oil in a large skillet over medium-high heat. Reduce the heat to medium, add the scallion whites, and cook, stirring them occasionally, until they soften and become tender, 8 to 10 minutes (reduce the heat if they begin to darken too quickly).

Remove the scallions from the pan, let cool, and halve them lengthwise.

6 Divide the dough into 4 equal pieces. Pull and fold each corner of the dough up and onto the middle to create a ball, being careful not to press out all of the gas from the dough. You are not fully shaping the dough, so don't work the dough too much. Set the dough balls, smooth-side up, on a lightly floured work surface, cover with a clean kitchen towel, and let them rest for 5 minutes.

7 On a very lightly floured work surface, roll each ball of dough to a 5-by-11-inch oval and transfer them to 2 lightly floured rimmed sheet pans. Cover with a clean kitchen towel (see page 17 for other homemade proof box ideas) and set aside in a warm, draft-free spot until the dough has risen slightly, about 30 minutes.

8 Set one oven rack at the upper-middle position and one rack at the lower-middle position, and preheat the oven to 375°F.

9 Make the yogurt topping and bake: Whisk together the yogurt, mint, salt, and white pepper. Divide the yogurt among the pieces of dough, and top each with a few strands of the eggplant and 3 pieces of the cooked scallions. Bake one sheet of lachmajun on the upper rack and the other on the lower rack for 8 minutes; then rotate the pans from bottom to top and top to bottom and bake until golden brown around the edges, 4 to 6 minutes.

10 Remove the baking sheets from the oven and let the breads cool slightly before finishing them with olive oil, a few pinches of flaky salt, and a sprinkle of scallion greens.

Malawach

Makes 8 malawach (1.7 kilos / 3¾ pounds of dough)

What is the best way to describe malawach? Addictive? Delicious? Decadent? (Yes, yes, and yes!) Malawach is a thin round of buttery pan-fried dough that is so satisfying that even the mention of "homemade malawach" will make any Israeli drool. It is Yemenite-Jewish in origin, and like other Yemenite breads, it is served with grated tomato and z'hug, the fiery hot Yemenite chile paste (see pages 148 and 318). I learned to make malawach from Rachel Tzadok, Rinat's mother, who is Moroccan but makes it for her Yemenite husband. It isn't difficult—just time-consuming. You make the dough by using butter to stretch it very thin on a work surface; then layer it with more butter, fold it up, chill it, and finally roll it out with a rolling pin and pan-fry. As the dough fries in the skillet, the moisture from the butter in the layers evaporates and causes the dough to puff and become very flaky. I like to make a big stack and freeze some of the dough to fry another time (see page 148).

DOUGH

All-purpose flour (sifted, 11.7%)	1 kilo (8 cups), plus extra for rolling
Granulated sugar	50 grams (¼ cup)
Fine salt	20 grams (1 tablespoon plus 1 teaspoon)
Baking powder	4 grams (1 teaspoon)
Warm water	630 grams (2⅓ cups)
Unsalted butter (very soft—nearly melted)	270 grams (2 sticks plus 2 tablespoons)

FOR SERVING

Ripe tomatoes	2, grated on the large-hole side of a box grater (see page 148)
Fine salt	Pinch
Red or Green Z'hug (pages 318–319)	

1 **Make the dough:** Place the flour, sugar, salt, and baking powder in a medium bowl and mix with your hand to combine. Place your hand over the middle of the bowl and pour one-quarter (about 157 grams / ½ cup) of the water over your hand (this helps disperse the water evenly without flooding one section of the flour mixture), using your hand to stir the water in. Repeat until all the water is added, and continue to mix with your hand until the dough is well combined, scooping your hand from the perimeter and along the bottom of the bowl to get beneath the dough and pull it out. Continue this kneading process until the dough is smooth, 4 to 7 minutes. Cover the bowl with plastic wrap and let it rest at room temperature for 10 minutes.

(continued)

2 Divide the dough into balls: Lightly butter a large plate. Butter your hand and pat some butter under the dough and over the surface. Grab a corner of the dough, squeeze your forefinger and thumb around it, and push a ball of dough up through the circle made by your finger and thumb. Squeeze a ball about the size of an orange from the dough and break it off. Place your thumb in the center of the dough ball and use your other hand to fold the edges over your thumb, using your thumb to pinch down each of the edges as they get folded over. Pinch all the corners shut, and then set the dough on the buttered plate, smooth-side up. Repeat with the remaining pieces of dough to make 8 orange-size balls. Cover the balls loosely with a kitchen towel and let them rest at room temperature for 10 minutes.

3 Stretch, shape, and chill the dough: Lightly butter your work surface and place one of the dough balls on top. Use your hand to butter the top of the dough, and then start to push and stretch the dough into a very thin—paper-thin—square that is about 22 inches around. Add more butter as needed to prevent tearing (but don't worry if the dough tears). Fold the right side of the square over the center, lightly butter the top of the fold, and then fold the left side over (creating a simple fold) and lightly butter the top. Starting at the short edge of the narrow strip, fold the right corner up and over into a somewhat triangular shape, fold the left side up and to the right, and then fold and tuck the bottom up to create a ball at the base of the dough (see photos, opposite). Now, much as you would fold a flag, work the right side folded up to the left, then the left side folded up to the right, until you reach the top of the rectangle. Tuck the ends under and return the dough to the buttered plate. Repeat with the other pieces of dough; cover them with plastic wrap and refrigerate for 1 hour.

4 Roll and fry the dough: Remove the dough from the refrigerator. Lightly flour your work surface and roll each piece of dough to a 10- to 12-inch round. Heat a 10- or 12-inch skillet over medium-low heat and place a dough round in the pan. Press the dough down and stretch it a bit in the

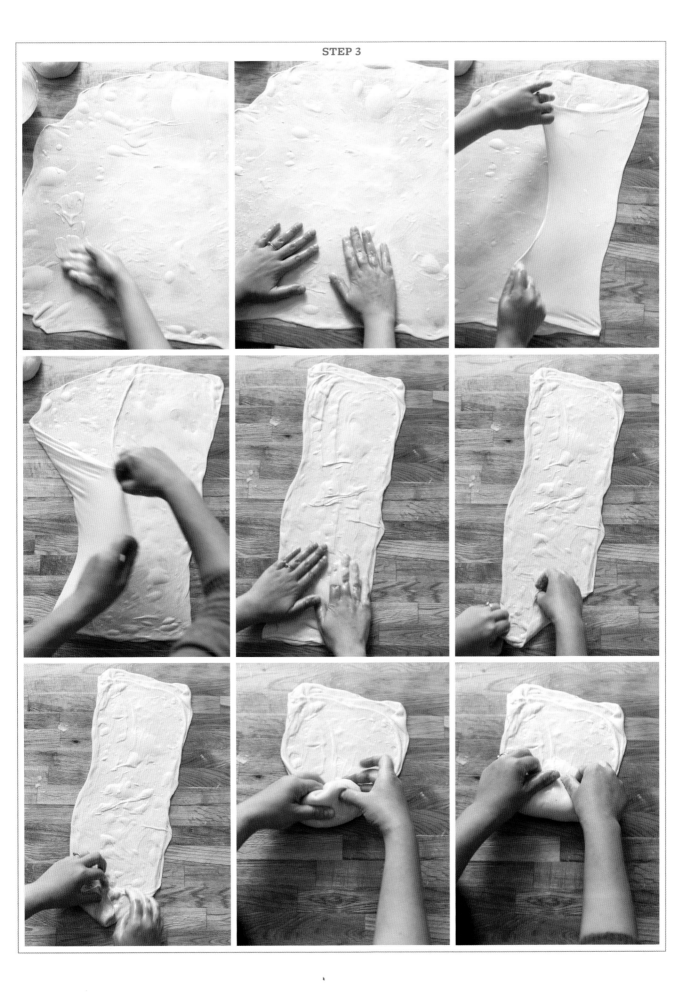

pan, cover the pan, and cook until it begins to brown, about 5 minutes. Flip the dough over, cover, and cook until the dough is nicely puffed and has deep brown spots on both sides, another 3 to 5 minutes. Slide the malawach onto a plate and repeat with the rest of the dough.

5 Place the grated tomato in a medium bowl and season it with a few pinches of salt. Serve the malawach hot, with the grated tomato and z'hug alongside.

MALAWACH NOW, MALAWACH LATER

Do what lots of Israeli families do and make enough malawach to serve a few pieces now, then freeze the rest for another time. To freeze, just place the rolled pieces of dough on a sheet pan in the freezer until they harden (an hour or two); then wrap each one individually in plastic wrap and freeze them in a stack in a large freezer bag. When you want to serve the malawach, remove it from the freezer and leave it at room temperature for an hour or so to defrost; then pan-fry as instructed.

YOU CAN NEVER HAVE ENOUGH GRATED TOMATO

The classic accompaniment to Yemenite dishes like malawach, jachnun, and kubaneh is a grated tomato and a little salt plus some z'hug on the side. The grated tomato is so simple—cut a ripe and juicy tomato in half and grate the cut side against the large-hole side of a box grater until you get to the skin. Discard the skin and grate the other half; then add a few pinches of salt for balance. Be sure to use the most flavorful tomatoes you can find—since only salt is being added, you want the taste of the tomato to be really present. Keep grating as many tomatoes as you have, because if there is one ever-constant truth to grated tomato salad, it's that you never, *ever* make enough of it! There's something about the sweet, fresh, and slightly acidic tomato that is so juicy against the buttery, flaky dough. The z'hug adds a necessary spice component, and the trio . . . well, I can hardly imagine a more perfect union.

Jachnun

Makes 10 pieces

Jachnun, a hearty, heavy, crêpe-like Yemenite bread, is most often served with grated tomato and spicy z'hug on Saturdays as part of the Sabbath brunch. Observant Jews who don't cook on Saturdays place a tightly covered pan of jachnun in a barely warm oven on Friday night (or drop the tin in the embers of the taboon) and slow-bake it until they pull it out Saturday and serve it for lunch. Traditionally one egg for each guest is baked on top of the dough within the sealed tin; when they are peeled and quartered the next day, the shell and the white are deeply browned. The egg makes the meal complete, while the grated tomato and z'hug add a light, fresh, peppery counterpoint.

This is hearty, heavy eating at its best—eat one or two pieces and you're happily satisfied for hours. Some people like the caramelized and chewy pieces from the bottom of the pan; others like the soft and dense pieces from the middle. Do remember that it bakes for 12 hours.

All-purpose flour (sifted, 11.7%)	1 kilo (8 cups)
Granulated sugar	50 grams (¼ cup)
Baking powder	2 grams (½ teaspoon)
Honey	35 grams (2 tablespoons)
Fine salt	20 grams (1 tablespoon plus 1 teaspoon)
Warm water	675 grams (2½ cups plus 1 tablespoon)
Vegetable oil	15 grams (1 tablespoon)
Unsalted butter (very soft—nearly melted)	200 grams (1 stick plus 5 tablespoons)
Large eggs	10
Ripe tomatoes	2 large, grated on the large-hole side of a box grater (see page 148)
Red or Green Z'hug (pages 318–319)	

1 Make the dough: Place the flour, sugar, baking powder, honey, and salt in a large bowl. Add the water to the bowl and stir until the dough is shaggy and the water has been absorbed. Knead the dough in the bowl for 2 minutes (it will be pretty wet and sticky). Set the dough aside at room temperature to rest for 5 minutes.

2 Knead the dough: Slide your hand beneath the dough toward the center so your fingers point up (beneath the dough). Lift the dough from the middle, moving your hand toward the edge of the bowl to stretch it. Release the dough, give the bowl a quarter turn, and repeat 7 times. Cover the bowl with plastic wrap and set the dough aside to rest at room temperature for 1 hour.

(continued)

3 Divide the dough and shape it: Lightly oil a large plate. Oil your hand and pat some oil under the dough and over the surface. Grab a corner of the dough and squeeze your forefinger and thumb around it, pushing a baseball-size ball of dough up through the circle made by your finger and thumb. Break off the ball, place your thumb in the center of the ball, and use your other hand to fold the edges over your thumb, using your thumb to pinch down each of the edges as they get folded over. Pinch all the corners shut and then set the dough on the oiled plate, smooth-side up. Repeat with the remaining pieces of dough to make 10 baseball-size balls. Cover the dough loosely with a kitchen towel and let it rest at room temperature for 5 minutes.

4 Adjust an oven rack to the lowest position and preheat the oven to 225°F.

5 Stretch and shape the dough: Fold a long piece of parchment paper in half lengthwise and place it across the bottom of an 8-inch springform pan or kubaneh pan so the edges of the parchment hang over the sides (like a sling). Heavily butter your work surface and set a ball of dough on top. Butter the top of the dough and use your hands to push and stretch the dough into a very thin—paper-thin—rectangle (stretch it as far as you can without the dough tearing, adding more butter as needed to prevent tearing—but don't worry if it tears). Fold the left side of the rectangle over the center, lightly butter the top of the fold, then fold the right side over (creating a simple fold; see pages 71 and 72) and lightly butter the top. Starting at a narrow edge, roll the dough into a tight cylinder. Set the cylinder in the parchment paper–lined pan, perpendicular to the length of the paper. Repeat with 3 more balls. Once the first layer of the pan is full, set the next layer on top of the first, across the first layer in a crosshatch pattern. Place the final 2 cylinders around the edges of the pan.

6 Bake the jachnun: Butter another doubled sheet of parchment paper and place it, buttered-side down, on top of the dough. Place the (unpeeled) eggs on top of the parchment, and then cover the pan with aluminum foil, crimping it around the edges to seal the pan (if you're using a kubaneh pan, you can skip that step and just put the lid in place). Place the pan in the oven and set a sheet pan on top of the foil (unless there is a kubaneh lid). Bake the jachnun overnight, for 12 hours.

7 The next morning, remove the jachnun from the oven. Uncover the pan, set the eggs aside, and discard the parchment paper. Place the jachnun on a platter. Peel the eggs and arrange them around the jachnun. Serve with the grated tomato and z'hug alongside.

Mofleta

Makes one 14-inch pan of mofleta (about 24 sheets)

In Morocco, at the end of Pesach, a sweet feast called Mimouna celebrates the return of the leavened foods and wheat that are forbidden during the eight days of Passover. In the earliest days of the tradition, at the end of the holiday, family, friends, and Muslim neighbors were invited to Jewish homes to enjoy cakes and cookies and pastries because families had been very insular during the holiday. Now this tradition is celebrated throughout Israel, too, and it is an excuse to have a wonderful dessert party at the end of the eight-day wheat fast! One of the classic dishes served is mofleta, a stack of thin yeasted crêpes that are smeared with butter, drizzled with honey, rolled like a cigar, and then eaten by hand. Sweet and chewy, it is a wonderful dessert.

Cool room-temperature water	300 grams (1 cup plus 3 tablespoons)
Fresh yeast	15 grams (2 tablespoons)
or active dry yeast	5 grams (1 teaspoon)
Cake flour or white pastry flour (sifted, 8 to 9%)	500 grams (4¾ cups), plus extra for kneading and shaping
Granulated sugar	5 grams (1 teaspoon)
Fine salt	½ teaspoon
Neutral oil	720 to 960 grams (3 to 4 cups)
Unsalted butter (at room temperature)	for serving
Honey	for serving

1 Make the dough: Combine the water and yeast in the bowl of a stand mixer and whisk until the yeast is mostly dissolved. Add the flour, sugar, and salt. Attach the dough hook and mix on low speed until the dough comes together into a semismooth ball, about 2 minutes.

2 Stretch and fold the dough: Transfer the dough to a lightly floured work surface. Stretch one corner of the dough out and fold it on top of the middle of the dough. Give the dough a quarter turn and repeat a few more times, until each corner has been stretched and folded twice to make a nicely shaped ball.

3 Let the dough rise: Lightly flour a large bowl and set the dough in the bowl; sprinkle the top with a little flour, cover the bowl with plastic wrap, and set aside at room temperature until nearly doubled in volume, about 30 minutes.

4 Divide the dough and shape into balls: Pour 3 cups of the oil into a large bowl and set it aside. Lightly flour the work surface and set the dough on top. Pat and stretch the dough into an 8-by-12-inch rectangle that is as even as possible. Use a bench knife to divide the dough lengthwise into 4 equal strips, and then into 6 strips crosswise, to yield 24 pieces. Holding a piece of dough in your hand, stretch one-quarter of the piece up and over onto the middle. Repeat with the other 3 sides to create a rough ball shape. Place the dough, seam-side down, on the work surface and repeat with the remaining pieces.

5 Wipe the excess flour from the work surface and cup your hand around a piece of dough. Push and pull the dough in a circular motion on the work surface until it is rounded into a tight ball with hardly a seam at the bottom, and drop the dough ball into the bowl of oil. Repeat with the other pieces of dough. Once all the dough has been shaped, let the balls rest in the oil for 10 minutes (add more oil as needed to make sure they are completely covered; you don't want them to dry out).

6 Stretch and cook the dough: Set a dough ball on the work surface. Using your hands, stretch and push it into a paper-thin sheet (try not to create holes, but if you get a few, it's okay). It should stretch very easily. Heat a large nonstick skillet over medium-high heat. Reduce the heat to medium and carefully lay the sheet in the pan. While the first piece of dough cooks, stretch another piece of dough. Once the dough in the skillet starts to become golden brown, after about 2 minutes, use a spatula to carefully flip it over. Lay the second sheet of stretched dough on top of the first in the skillet. Stretch your next piece of dough. When the underside of the dough in the pan is golden brown, after another 2 to 3 minutes (adjust the heat as needed so the dough doesn't get too dark), carefully flip the two layers over together and place the just-stretched piece on top of the stack. Repeat this process, stretching, flipping, and adding to the dough stack, until all the dough pieces are stacked in the skillet like a giant flatbread layer cake. Remove the stack from the skillet and place it on a large plate.

7 Serve the mofleta with lots of butter and honey. To eat, peel away a layer of mofleta, add a smear of butter and a drizzle of honey, and roll it into a cylinder. Mofleta is best eaten while hot.

A FEW CLASSICS & NEW DISCOVERIES

(WHAT HAPPENS WHEN CULTURES COLLIDE)

PERHAPS IN NO OTHER PLACE, aside from New York City, do people jump on new trends and flavors the way the people in Israel do. Israel is a multi-culti country by definition, with immigrants from around the world making it their home, bringing their traditions and recipes with them. And what happens when you have so many people all mixed up in a small country about the size of New Jersey? You get Yemenites marrying Russians and Moroccans marrying Danes—and all the cultures become a delicious balagan—a "big mess" of inspiration and cravings and new traditions.

The people of Israel have an unquenchable spirit and natural curiosity for travel and discovery, too. I'm not talking about spending just one week here or there, but a month or eight weeks or two years on another continent or in a different hemisphere. We travel and connect with others, experience the foods and customs, and then bring the discoveries back to Tel Aviv and beyond.

My own wanderlust has brought me to Poland, Italy, Tunisia, China, Colombia, India, Turkey, Morocco, France, and so many other influential places. Even the Greenmarket in New York City has provided inspiration to re-create the breads and pastries I have seen, sampled, and studied around the world. All these experiences contribute to the innovation and creative energy that get poured into Lehamim Bakery and Breads Bakery. I bring home the ideas, think about them, consider the possibilities—until one day, when there is a new bread (or pastry or cake).

Each of the breads in this chapter touches on a part of my life. The Spelt and Muesli Buns go back to my Danish roots; the Dill Bread reflects my experience traveling to Djerba, off the Tunisian coast. The Light Brioche and Everyday Loaf are distillations of my experience as a baker in Paris. The Jerusalem Bagel and Jerusalem Baguette both reflect on my time in Israel . . . but also in France and New York. The magic of Yemenite Kubaneh came into my life when I met Rinat. Each is important to me and is a relevant part of my history as a baker and as a citizen of this world that we share and live in together. Some are classics you are likely familiar with, while others are breads I hope you will get to know and make your own.

Kubaneh

Makes one 9-inch round loaf (860 grams / 1 pound 14 ounces of dough)

Kubaneh, a rich Yemenite bread, is a cross between a brioche and a flatbread. The bread is traditionally started on Friday, when the dough is prepared and shaped; the pieces of dough are stacked in a special lidded tin, almost as you would arrange pieces of dough for monkey bread, and baked overnight (similar to jachnun, another Yemenite flatbread made without yeast; see page 149). The tin is pulled from the oven on Saturday and served for lunch with grated tomato and z'hug, with everyone at the table ripping the bread apart to get their own treasured piece. Some people go for the crusts and edges, while others want the soft and spongy interior.

Classic kubaneh is baked in a covered pan that holds in all the steam. This is essential to create the bread's pillowy, tender texture and ensures that the bread doesn't totally dry out as it bakes overnight. The slow bake also allows butter in the dough to deepen and even caramelize, creating a beautiful deep brown crust. This version doesn't require you to bake the kubaneh overnight (see page 163), but instead in a moderately warm oven, making the cover unnecessary. As the bread grows and expands, you can see all the layers created during the shaping.

Cool room-temperature water	290 grams (1¼ cups)
Fresh yeast	20 grams (2½ tablespoons)
or active dry yeast	8 grams (2¼ teaspoons)
All-purpose flour (sifted, 11.7%)	500 grams (4 cups), plus extra for shaping
Granulated sugar	60 grams (¼ cup)
Fine salt	20 grams (1 tablespoon plus 1 teaspoon)
Unsalted butter	150 grams (1¼ sticks), cut into small pieces
Ripe tomatoes	2, grated on the large-hole side of a box grater (see page 148)

1 **Make the dough:** Pour the water into the bowl of a stand mixer fitted with the dough hook. Crumble the yeast into the water and use your fingers to rub and dissolve it; if using active dry yeast, whisk the yeast into the water. Add the flour, sugar, and lastly the salt.

2 Mix the dough on low speed to combine the ingredients, stopping the mixer if the dough climbs up the hook or if you need to work in dry ingredients that have settled on the bottom of the bowl. Scrape the bottom and sides of the bowl as needed. Once the dough comes together, increase the speed to medium-high and continue to knead until the dough cleans the bottom and sides of the bowl, about 3 minutes.

3 **Stretch and fold the dough:** Lightly dust your work surface with a little flour and use a plastic dough scraper to transfer the

dough from the mixing bowl to the floured surface. Use your palms to stretch a corner of the dough away from you in one stroke, and then fold the front portion over and on top of itself. Give the dough a quarter turn and repeat. Do this about 10 times, until the dough is shaped into a nice smooth round.

4 Let the dough rise: Lightly flour a large bowl, set the dough in the bowl, lightly flour the top of the dough, and cover the bowl with plastic wrap. Set it aside at room temperature until it has just about doubled in volume, about 30 minutes (depending on the warmth of the room).

5 Divide and shape the dough: Place the butter in a microwave-safe dish and heat it in the microwave just until it is very soft and perhaps 25% melted, 10 seconds or so. Lightly grease a large plate with a little bit of the butter. Lightly flour your work surface and set the dough on top. Divide it into 8 equal pieces. Cup your hand around a piece of dough, and then push and pull it, rolling it against the work surface, to gently shape it into a ball. Set the ball on the buttered plate and repeat with the remaining pieces of dough. Cover the plate with plastic wrap and set it aside at room temperature for 30 minutes.

6 Stretch the dough: Use about 2 tablespoons of the softened butter to generously grease a 9-inch springform pan (or use a smaller springform pan or a kubaneh pan). Take about a tablespoon of the butter and use it to grease a clean, nonfloured work surface. Take a ball of dough from the plate, smear another tablespoon of butter on top of it, and gently press and spread it out to form a paper-thin 12- to 13-inch square (see

the malawach photos on pages 146 and 147). Use more butter as needed—you want to use a lot! The butter helps spread the dough very thin without tearing (but don't worry if it tears).

7 Shape the dough: Fold the left side of the dough over the center, then the right side over the left to create a simple fold. Starting at the bottom of the strip, roll the dough into a tight cylinder. Slice the cylinder in half crosswise, and then place the halves in the prepared springform pan, with the cut side facing up. Repeat with the remaining balls of dough (reserve 1 tablespoon of butter to use in step 10), arranging the pieces in a circle in the pan with a few pieces in the center. If you're using a smaller springform or a kubaneh pan, stack the dough (as you would for monkey bread). If you are using a springform pan, wrap the bottom of the pan in a large sheet of aluminum foil just in case any butter drips out (this will prevent the butter from burning and smoking up the oven). If you are using a kubaneh pan, you can skip this step.

8 Let the kubaneh proof: Cover the pan with plastic wrap and set it aside in a warm, draft-free place until a finger gently pressed into the dough leaves a depression that quickly fills in by three-quarters, about 40 minutes (depending on how warm the room is).

9 Preheat the oven to 350°F.

10 Bake the kubaneh: Melt the remaining 1 tablespoon butter, brush it over the top of the dough, and place the pan in the oven. After 15 minutes, reduce the oven temperature to 325°F and bake until the top is deeply golden, 30 to 40 minutes. Remove the pan from the oven and set it aside to cool for at least 20 minutes before turning the bread out of the pan.

11 To serve, invert the bread onto a platter so the pretty side faces up. Let people rip the kubaneh apart, separating the bread into small rolls. Serve the grated tomato on the side.

Variation

Traditional "Overnight" Kubaneh

Follow the Kubaneh recipe through step 8. Preheat the oven to 225°F. Set a sheet of aluminum foil on your work surface and smear some of the butter in the center of the foil to make a 9-inch round. Remove the plastic wrap from the pan and invert the aluminum foil over the pan so the buttered area is centered over the dough; then tightly crimp the foil around the top of the pan.

Place the pan in the oven and set a heavy baking sheet on top of it to ensure that no steam escapes (if using a kubaneh pan, just place the lid on the pan). Bake for 4½ hours. Turn the oven off and leave the bread in the oven until you're ready to serve it.

To serve, remove the foil (or kubaneh pan lid) and turn out the bread; then invert it onto a platter so the pretty side faces up. Let people rip the kubaneh apart, separating the clusters into small rolls. I like to warm the bread before serving.

DO YOU NEED A KUBANEH PAN?

Traditionally, kubaneh is baked in a kubaneh pan—a round aluminum cake-style tin that is between 5 and 7 inches in diameter and about 4 inches deep, with a lid that fits on top. The lid traps the steam, which is essential to steam-baking the bread for its signature light and spongy texture. But you can make kubaneh in a springform pan, which is wider and shallower than a kubaneh pan. While you'll fit only one layer of rolls in the springform, the kubaneh will still achieve a nice rise in the oven. If you're baking the kubaneh the traditional way (see page 163) overnight, cover the springform pan tightly with buttered aluminum foil, then place a baking sheet on top of the pan to trap moisture and steam. If you're following my method, you don't need to cover the pan. People have been making kubaneh for centuries—don't let not having the traditional pan stop you from making it. I've even seen creative chefs bake it in terra-cotta flower pots with great results.

THE YEMENITE-ISRAELI CONNECTION

In the United States, not many people know about Yemenite food—the wonderfully rich and soulful beef soups, the variety of yeasted and non-yeasted breads like malawach (page 145) and kubaneh (page 160). Spices, too, can be uniquely Yemenite in flavor profile, like hawaij. Hawaij is made two different ways—one with sweeter spices and one with more pungent, savory spices. For example, to "season" coffee, hawaij is made with sweet baking spices, such as cardamom, cinnamon, ginger, cloves, nutmeg, and sometimes caraway. The hawaij used to season sauces and stews, however, is made with strong and earthy coriander, turmeric, cardamom, cumin, black pepper, and fenugreek. Fenugreek—the spice that gives traditional curry powder its signature musky, heady aroma—is also the base of a foamy sauce called hilbeh that is used as a dip for a spongy injera-like bread made from sorghum, known as lachuch.

Because of religious persecution, nearly fifty thousand Yemenite Jews relocated to Israel in 1949 and 1950, bringing their recipes and cooking techniques (like baking in a taboon oven) with them. Yemenites have bettered the cuisine of Israel in so many ways—the most prominent and absolutely vital addition being z'hug (pages 318–319), a cilantro- and chile-heavy spicy paste that Israelis eat with everything at nearly every meal (but, most important, with falafel), but also with malawach, jachnun, and kubaneh.

Light Brioche

Makes 2 loaves or 20 rolls (900 grams / about 2 pounds of dough)

French brioche bread is fluffy and rich thanks to lots of eggs and butter; the dough actually has no water in it whatsoever. It can be a bit time-consuming and tricky to make, so I decided to take a different enriched dough—my challah dough—and change the recipe slightly to create a simplified version that is easier to make at home. Now, this is not traditional brioche—there is water in the dough, and that, by definition, disqualifies it from the "brioche" title—but I like to think of it as a "light" brioche. The lightness refers to the lesser amount of butter and eggs added, but rest assured, there's nothing light in fat about this version! It is wonderfully rich.

You can bake light brioche as a loaf or as individual rolls (see page 35 for shaping ideas) or stuff the rolls to make buns and snails (see pages 216 to 225). Using great-quality butter with a low water content makes a big difference to the final product. I am Danish, so of course I like to use a nice cultured Danish butter, but any cultured European-style butter will work well in this bread.

DOUGH

Unsalted butter (at room temperature)	135 grams (9 tablespoons—only 6 tablespoons need to be at room temperature), plus extra for greasing the pans
Cool room-temperature water	150 grams (½ cup plus 2 tablespoons)
Fresh yeast	20 grams (1 tablespoon plus 2½ teaspoons)
or active dry yeast	7.5 grams (2½ teaspoons)
All-purpose flour (sifted, 11.7%)	500 grams (4 cups), plus extra for shaping
Large egg (at room temperature)	1
Granulated sugar	50 grams (¼ cup)
Fine salt	10 grams (2 teaspoons)

EGG WASH

Large egg	1
Water	1 tablespoon
Fine salt	Pinch

1 **Make the dough:** Freeze 45 grams (3 tablespoons) of the unsalted butter on a plate for 20 minutes, then grate it on the large-hole side of a box grater. Return the grated butter to the freezer. Pour the water into the bowl of a stand mixer fitted with the dough hook. Crumble the yeast into the water and use your fingers to rub and dissolve it;

if using active dry yeast, whisk the yeast into the water. Add the flour, egg, sugar, salt, and the remaining 90 grams (6 tablespoons) room-temperature butter.

2 Mix the dough on low speed to combine the ingredients, stopping the mixer if the dough climbs up the hook or if you need to work in dry ingredients that have settled on the bottom of the bowl. Scrape the bottom and sides of the bowl as needed. It should take about 2 minutes for the dough to come together.

3 **Knead the dough:** Increase the speed to medium and knead until a smooth dough forms, about 4 minutes. You may need to add a little water if the dough is too stiff, or a little flour if it is too slack. (Eventually you'll be able to feel the dough and know if you need to add water or flour. It's always better to adjust the ratios when the dough is first coming together rather than during the kneading process, since it takes longer for ingredient additions to get worked into the dough mass at this later point.)

4 Reduce the mixer speed to low and begin adding the grated butter, a little bit at a time, until it is all added; this shouldn't take more than 30 seconds (you don't want to overknead the dough or the grated butter will melt). If the dough starts to ride up the dough hook, stop the mixer to push it off.

> NOTE: FROZEN BUTTER WILL REMAIN IN THIN sheets after the dough is kneaded. When it comes time to bake, the little pockets of butter melt and create steam within the interior of the loaf, adding height, tenderness, and lots of flavor. That's why I like to freeze the butter for about 20 minutes before grating it on the large-hole side of a box grater, then return it to the freezer to make sure it stays nice and cold until you add it to the dough.

5 **Shape the dough into a ball and let it rise:** Lightly dust your work surface and a bowl with a little flour, loosely shape the dough into a ball, and transfer it to the bowl. Lightly flour the top of the dough and cover the bowl with plastic wrap. Set it aside in a draft-free spot at room temperature until the dough has nearly doubled in volume and a finger pressed into the dough leaves a depression that quickly fills in about halfway, 40 minutes to 1 hour.

6 **Divide the dough:** Gently use a plastic dough scraper to help lift the dough out of the bowl and onto a lightly floured work surface (take care not to press the trapped gas out of the dough), and divide the dough into 2 pieces.

7 **Shape and proof the dough:** Stretch each piece gently into a rectangular shape, then fold the top down to just above the middle and lightly press (trying not to de-gas the dough) the top edge into the dough. Fold 2 more times to make a cylinder, set the dough on a lightly floured work surface, cover with a kitchen towel, and let it rest for 15 minutes. Firmly press down on each piece of dough to de-gas it, and pull it to make a 9-by-5-inch rectangle. Fold the left side over to meet the middle, then fold the right side to meet the middle. Use your fingers to fold the top edge down by one-quarter, and use the heel of your palm to seal the edge to the bottom part of the dough. Repeat 3 more times to make a cylinder; then lay the dough horizontally and roll, lightly pressing down on the edges. Repeat with the other piece of dough.

8 Grease 2 standard loaf pans with butter and set the shaped dough in the pans. Cover with a clean kitchen towel and set them aside to rise in a draft-free spot at room temperature until a finger pressed into the dough leaves only a slight depression, about 1 hour. (If you are making rolls, divide each half into 10 pieces to yield 20 rolls and follow the instructions on page 35 to shape the rolls. Place the rolls on a parchment paper–lined sheet pan, cover with a kitchen towel, and set aside to rise until the dough has doubled in volume, about 1 hour.)

9 Preheat the oven to 375°F.

10 **Bake the loaves:** Make the egg wash by mixing the egg, water, and salt together in a small bowl. Gently brush the entire surface of the loaves (or rolls) with egg wash. You want a nice thin coating. Place the pans (or sheet pan) in the oven and immediately reduce the oven temperature to 325°F. Bake until the bread is golden brown, 25 minutes for loaves and 12 to 14 minutes for rolls. Remove from the oven and set aside to cool.

An Everyday Loaf

(Using Baguette Dough)

Makes 3 loaves (1,050 grams / 2⅓ pounds of dough)

This is a standard bread, a French baguette–type dough, baked in a bâtarde (short baguette) shape. The shorter, wider shape holds the bread's freshness better than a baguette, which dries out so quickly, making this, in my opinion, a great everyday loaf. I bake this in a couche, a folded and floured heavy-duty cloth, to help loosely guide the shape and create a more voluminous loaf. The dough is soft because of the high proportion of water, and if you don't let it rise in a loosely structured vessel, it will flatten during the process. If you don't want to use a couche, you can certainly bake this bread in a loaf pan for a nice Pullman-style sandwich bread, or try it free-form knowing that the bread will be flatter. This dough relies on a pre-ferment for a fuller flavor; it also allows for less yeast in the total recipe, meaning the dough will stay supple longer before going stale. Be sure to build in an extra day for the pre-ferment mixture to develop flavor; let it sit for 2 hours at room temperature and then 24 hours in the refrigerator.

PRE-FERMENT

Cool room-temperature water	150 grams (⅔ cup)
Fresh yeast	3 grams (1 teaspoon)
or active dry yeast	⅓ teaspoon
All-purpose flour (sifted, 11.7%)	150 grams (1¼ cups)

BREAD DOUGH

Cool room-temperature water	280 grams (1¼ cups)
Fresh yeast	10 grams (1 tablespoon)
or active dry yeast	5 grams (1 teaspoon)
All-purpose flour (sifted, 11.7%)	500 grams (4 cups), plus extra for kneading and shaping
Fine salt	15 grams (1 tablespoon)

1 **Prepare the pre-ferment:** Pour the water into a large bowl or airtight container. Add the yeast and whisk to combine. Whisk in the flour; the mixture should look like pancake batter. Cover the bowl with plastic wrap and set it aside at room temperature for 2 hours; then refrigerate it for 24 hours.

2 **The next day, make the bread dough:** Pour the water into the bowl of a stand

mixer. Crumble the yeast into the water and use your fingers to rub and dissolve it; if using active dry yeast, whisk the yeast into the water. Add the flour and salt, and then add the chilled pre-ferment. Attach the dough hook and mix the dough on low speed, scraping the sides and bottom of the bowl often, until combined, about 1 minute. Increase the speed to medium-low and continue to mix, scraping the bowl as needed, until the dough is well mixed, about 2 minutes longer. Increase the speed to medium and continue to mix until the dough reaches the windowpane stage (see photo on page 15), 7 to 8 minutes longer.

NOTE: EVERY MINUTE OF KNEADING increases the temperature of the dough. You want the temperature of the finished dough to be 70° to 73°F for optimal rising and flavor development. If the dough becomes too warm, it will "burn" the gluten, weakening the dough's elasticity. It's better to stop mixing once the dough reaches 73°F rather than overmix it, even if the dough hasn't reached the windowpane stage. At this point, set the dough in a cool place for 20 minutes. Then continue from step 3. This will help create a strong dough without compromising the gluten by overheating or overmixing the dough.

3 Stretch and fold the dough, then let it rise: Once the dough reaches windowpane stage, use a plastic dough scraper to turn it out onto a lightly floured work surface. Starting at one corner, stretch the dough until it tears, and then fold the corner up onto the center. Give the dough a quarter turn, and repeat until the dough resists stretching, about 20 times (1 to 2 minutes). The dough should be nice and soft, and should be tacky but shouldn't stick to your hands. Lightly flour a bowl, set the dough into the bowl, and lightly flour the top. Cover the bowl with plastic wrap and set

it aside in a warm, draft-free spot until the dough has risen by 50%, about 25 minutes.

4 Stretch and fold and rise again: Lightly flour the work surface and set the dough on top. Stretch and fold the 4 corners of the dough again, doing so very gently (don't tear the dough this time) by stretching a corner and lightly placing it on top of the dough ball so you don't press all the gas out of the dough. Lightly flour the bowl and place the dough, smooth-side up, in the bowl. Cover the bowl with plastic wrap and set it aside in a warm, draft-free spot until the dough has roughly doubled in volume, about 30 minutes (depending on how warm your kitchen is).

5 Divide and pre-shape the dough: Lightly flour the work surface and use a bench scraper to divide the dough into 3 equal pieces. Gently stretch a piece into a rectangular shape with a short side facing you, and then fold the top down to just above the middle. Lightly press the top edge into the dough, trying not to press the gas out of the dough. Fold 2 more times to make a cylinder. Place the dough on a lightly floured baking sheet (or leave it on the work surface). Repeat with the remaining pieces of dough, and set them aside at room temperature for 15 minutes.

6 Shape the dough again and proof it: On a lightly floured work surface, firmly press down on one of the cylinders of dough to press the gas out, and then pull it to make a 9-by-5-inch rectangle with a long side facing you. Fold the left side over to meet the middle, and then fold the right side to meet the middle (like an open book). Then use your fingers to fold the top edge a quarter

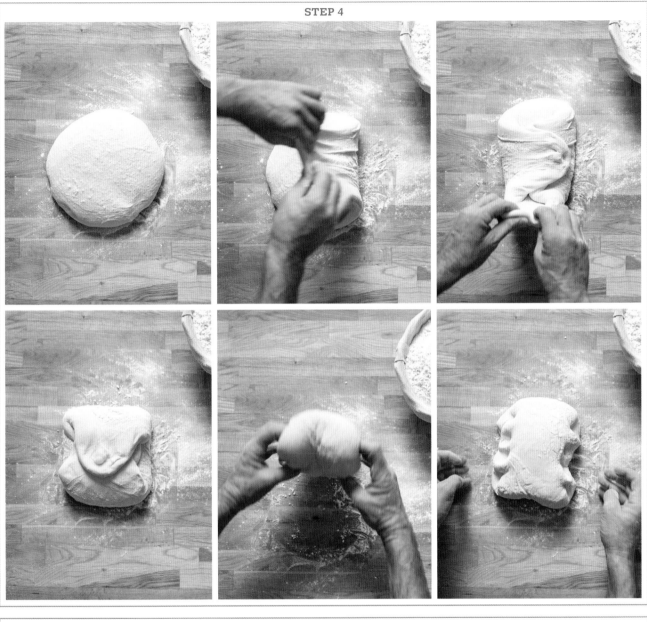

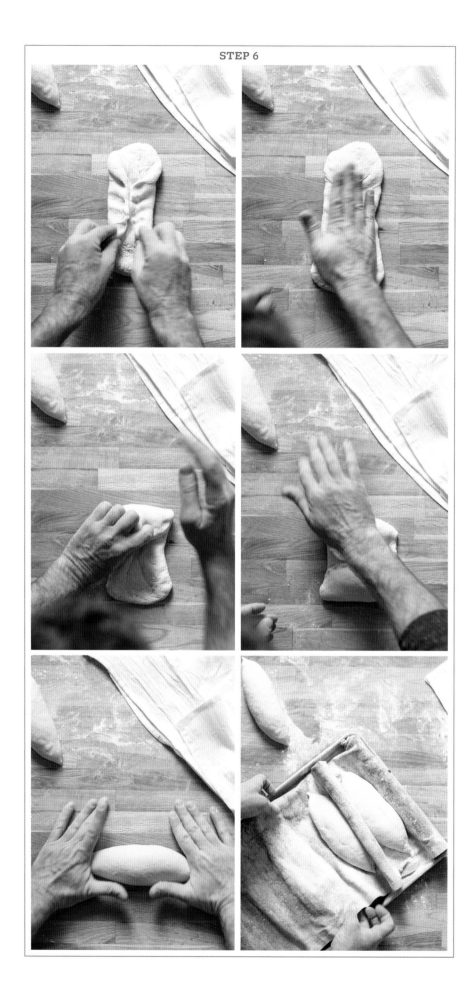

of the way down, and use the heel of your hand to seal the edge to the bottom part of the dough (see photos, opposite). Repeat 3 more times to make a cylinder. Set the dough horizontally, and use your hands to roll it back and forth as you would to make a rope, pressing down lightly on the edges to make a torpedo shape. Repeat with the other 2 pieces of dough. Place the dough on a lightly floured cloth (if using) and place in a lightly floured rimmed sheet pan, cover with a kitchen towel, and set aside at room temperature until it has doubled in volume and jiggles when the pan is tapped, 2 to 3 hours.

7 Set a rimmed sheet pan on the floor of the oven (or if not possible, on the lowest oven rack) and preheat the oven to 400°F. Use a razor or sharp paring knife to make 3 diagonal slashes in the top of each bâtarde. Set the sheet with the bâtardes in the oven and immediately add ¼ cup of water to the hot baking sheet on the oven floor. Close the door quickly and reduce the oven temperature to 350°F. Bake until the bread is nicely browned and cracked on top, about 20 minutes. Remove from the oven and set aside to cool before serving.

BAKERY-STYLE CRUSTS AT HOME

How do you get a nice crust at home? Well, you will never get a crust exactly like the one produced in a bakery oven because a home oven doesn't have the built-in steam and the vents used to control airflow, dryness, heat, and moisture. At home, the best solution I have found is to place a rimmed sheet pan on the oven floor (or, if not possible, on the lowest rack of the oven) and let it get very hot while the oven preheats. Once you place the bread in the oven, splash about ¼ cup of water onto the sheet pan and close the oven door immediately. The water will hiss and create steam so you get a nice blister effect on the bread's surface. You can splash more water onto the sheet pan about 2 minutes before the baking is finished, too, to help crackle the crust.

(continued)

Yeast is what gives bread its tang, its unique flavor. Like plants and animals, yeast is a living thing. It is not a powder that comes from a box; it is a living organism. Give yeast the right environment, and it will thrive and multiply. Like any living thing, yeast needs to eat and drink to live. That is where sugar and water come into play; sugar is yeast's daily bread, while water activates and encourages the yeast. The yeast divides and multiplies, creating carbon dioxide and alcohol, both of which are trapped by the gluten net (created when kneading the dough), giving the bread its desirable lift and holes.

There are many types of yeast. A true 100% sourdough loaf relies on a natural yeast starter (wild yeast) that, when more flour and water are added, multiplies within the dough (the dough is like a petri dish for the yeast). This starter is called a "mother," a webby, gooey, flour-and-water mass that is mixed with the flour and water in a bread recipe in place of commercial yeast. Ripe with natural yeast, the acidic sourness in a mother is what gives a sourdough its name. To host a mother at home, you need to take special care of her (just like a real mother, no?); you need to feed her often, nurture her, and not let her be ignored—otherwise, the mother will not create delicious bread. When the mother is mixed with more flour and water, magical things happen.

Bakers have discovered a somewhat less needy way to begin breads, one which requires less hand-holding than a mother and more flavor than commercial yeast: it's called a pre-ferment. Also called a poolish (in France) or a biga (in Italy), a pre-ferment is similar to a mother, but is made from commercial rather than wild yeast. A good example is a "quick poolish" method, whereby you mix a loose paste of flour, water, and yeast, cover it with more flour, and let it sit until the top layer of flour cracks. You get more layers of flavor in the bread by starting with this quick poolish than not. It also creates a more tender crumb and a moist open-holed interior texture. It's an extra step that requires extra time, but it really is worth it.

Another method is the "old dough" method. If you are making 1 pound of baguette dough, you save 10% of the dough (1½ ounces) and leave it in the refrigerator overnight to let it ferment and acquire a sour flavor. The next day, you add that fermented dough to your baguette dough. Then, before you make the baguettes, you reserve 10% (again) in the refrigerator for the next day's bread.

Jerusalem Baguette

Here is the marriage of the French baguette with the Jerusalem bagel. I created it for Union Square Café, the landmark Danny Meyer restaurant that used to be located across from Breads Bakery in New York City. They asked me to come up with a small and simple bread for their baskets. I created a mini baguette heavily coated in sesame seeds; thus, the Jerusalem Baguette was born. In the bakeries, I use this mini loaf for sandwiches, too.

After the dough has risen in step 4 (see page 170), set it on a lightly floured work surface and pull it (without pressing on the dough) into a rectangle. Divide the dough in half lengthwise and then cut it crosswise into 5 strips to make 10 pieces. Pre-shape the dough by gently rolling the top edge of a piece of dough onto the middle, lightly pressing the seam onto the bottom of the dough. Roll 3 more times. Repeat with each piece of dough. Cover the dough with a kitchen towel and let it rest at room temperature for 10 minutes. Create the final shape by using your hands to roll each piece back and forth to form a cylinder, pressing on the ends to taper the piece into a small, thin baguette shape.

Line 2 rimmed sheet pans with parchment paper. Soak a kitchen towel in water and place it on another sheet pan. Place 160 grams (1 cup) of sesame seeds on a large plate. Place a baguette facedown on the towel to dampen the top, set it in the sesame seeds and roll it a bit to coat it, and then place it on a prepared sheet pan, sesame seed–side up. Repeat with the remaining pieces of dough (about 5 baguettes will fit on each sheet pan). Cover with a dry kitchen towel and set aside in a draft-free spot at room temperature until the dough has doubled in volume, about 40 minutes.

Preheat the oven to 475°F.

Bake the baguettes for 10 minutes; then reduce the oven temperature to 375°F and bake for 13 minutes longer. Open the oven door a crack (for the crispiest crust) and bake until the loaves are golden brown and crisp, about 2 minutes more. Remove from the oven and let cool on the sheet pans.

Jerusalem Bagel

Makes 6 bagels

To be clear, the Jerusalem bagel has nothing to do with the American bagel. The only connection between the American bagel and the Jerusalem bagel is the hole they have in the middle. A Jerusalem bagel is a very airy, light, large oval-shaped ring; it's also sometimes called ka'ak (in Turkey, it's known as simit). There is also a Polish version that has a larger hole and a twisted ring. The dough is quite sweet, which is nice against the warm and toasty flavor of the sesame seeds and salt that coat the outside of the ring.

In Jerusalem, these bagels are sold with a little bit of za'atar and wrapped in a small square of newspaper. If you can wait until you get home, you rip off a piece of the bagel and dip it into a small dish of olive oil and then dunk it into the za'atar—wow, it is so good! I don't think there is one vendor in all of East Jerusalem who sells the bread ring without za'atar. This is a bread that *must* be eaten fresh—it dries out quickly and once it does, it isn't nearly as delicious. Many of the best vendors sell the fresh-from-the-oven rings throughout the day. The good news is that Jerusalem bagels freeze beautifully and defrost quickly— a brief warm-up in a hot oven brings them right back to life.

DOUGH

Cool room-temperature water	280 grams (1 cup plus 3 tablespoons)
Fresh yeast	25 grams (3 tablespoons)
or active dry yeast	8 grams (2¼ teaspoons)
All-purpose flour (sifted, 11.7% protein)	500 grams (4 cups), plus extra for kneading and shaping
Dry milk powder	60 grams (2½ teaspoons)
Granulated sugar	50 grams (¼ cup)
Fine salt	15 grams (1 tablespoon)
Extra-virgin olive oil	20 grams (1 tablespoon plus 1 teaspoon)

EGG WASH AND TOPPING

Large egg	1
Water	1 tablespoon
Fine salt	Pinch
Sesame seeds	60 grams (6 tablespoons)
Coarse salt	for sprinkling

1 Make the dough: Pour the water into the bowl of a stand mixer, add the yeast, and whisk briefly to combine. Add the flour, milk powder, sugar, and salt. Attach the dough hook and mix on low speed until the flour is about halfway incorporated, about 30 seconds. With the mixer running, slowly drizzle in the olive oil, and once the dough comes together, increase the speed to medium and knead the dough until it looks smooth, 3 minutes.

2 Stretch and fold the dough, then let it rise: Use a plastic dough scraper to transfer the dough to a lightly floured work surface. Take one corner of the dough and stretch the dough until it tears, then fold it on top of the center. Give the dough a quarter turn and repeat until it has been stretched and folded about 12 times and is shaped into a nice round ball. Lightly flour a large bowl, set the dough in the bowl, and lightly flour the top. Cover the bowl with plastic wrap and set it aside in a draft-free spot at room temperature until the dough has nearly doubled in volume, about 30 minutes.

3 Divide and round the dough, then let it proof: Remove the dough from the bowl and set it on a lightly floured surface. Divide it into 6 equal pieces. Fold the corners of one piece up onto the center, then flip the piece over and using a cupped hand, push and pull the dough in a circular motion on the work surface to create a round ball. Repeat with each piece. Cover with a clean kitchen towel or plastic wrap, and leave at room temperature for 30 minutes.

4 Shape the dough: Pick up a piece of dough and stick a finger into the center to create a hole (like a doughnut). Gently use 2 fingers to make the hole larger until the dough is the size of a large doughnut. Set the shaped dough on a parchment paper–lined sheet pan and repeat with the other pieces. Cover the shaped pieces of dough with a kitchen towel or plastic wrap and let them rest at room temperature for a few minutes. Then repeat, stretching the hole to be a little bit bigger (being careful not to deflate the dough), cover, and set the dough aside to rest for another 10 minutes.

5 Adjust one oven rack to the upper-middle position and one to the lower-middle position. Preheat the oven to 350°F. Line 2 sheet pans with parchment paper.

6 Bake the dough: Stretch each shaped piece of dough to make a 12-inch-long oval ring. Set 3 rings on each prepared sheet pan. Make the egg wash by whisking the egg, water, and salt together in a small bowl. Brush the top of each ring with egg wash (see Note), and then sprinkle heavily with sesame seeds and coarse salt. Place a sheet pan on each of the oven racks and bake for 8 minutes; then rotate the bottom sheet to the top and the top to the bottom, turning the sheets as well. Continue baking until the bagels are golden brown, 4 to 6 minutes longer. Remove from the oven and cool on the sheet pans. Jerusalem bagels are best eaten within a few hours of baking.

NOTE: ALWAYS BRUSH EGG WASH OVER DOUGH from two different directions so you don't get any drips. I like to brush all of the loaf or rolls in one direction, then turn the sheet pan around to brush from the opposite direction.

Ciabatta

Makes 3 loaves or 10 rolls (1.1 kilos / 2½ pounds of dough)

Israelis are always on the hunt for the newest thing. I'll have customers walk into Lehamim Bakery in Tel Aviv asking me, "Uri, what's new today?" They are perhaps as interested—or even more interested—in the new creations than in the classics. Food trends take on like wildfire in Israel, and ciabatta is a perfect example of a popular food that was probably experienced by a few savvy Israeli restaurateurs in Italy in the 1990s who brought it back to Tel Aviv.

This Italian bread has a very high percentage of water to flour, and the mixing method is a bit unusual and interesting. The dough needs to be very slack and bubbly. I use malt syrup (or corn syrup) for flavor, which also allows the yeast to produce more carbon dioxide in the dough. Because the mixing process is so lengthy, use ice water to keep the dough from getting too warm so the mixture doesn't "burn," or overheat and lose its elasticity. Since the dough is so loose, you can't really tear and fold it as I do with other bread doughs. Instead I use a folding technique that allows you to turn the sides of the dough onto itself to create a rectangular shape, achieving structure without overheating the flour and gluten.

Ice water	380 grams (1¾ cups)
Fresh yeast	18 grams (heaping 1 tablespoon)
or active dry yeast	6 grams (heaping 1 teaspoon)
Bread flour (sifted, 12.7%)	600 grams (4¼ cups), plus extra for kneading and shaping
Malt syrup, corn syrup, or granulated sugar	1 teaspoon
Fine salt	10 grams (2 teaspoons)
Cool room-temperature water	100 grams (scant ½ cup)

1 **Make the dough:** Fill a bowl with ice and water and stir for a few seconds to allow the water to get icy cold. Measure out 1¾ cups of the ice water and pour it into the bowl of a stand mixer fitted with the dough hook. Crumble the yeast into the water and use your fingers to rub and dissolve it; if using active dry yeast, whisk the yeast into the water. Add the bread flour, malt syrup, and salt, and knead on low speed until the dough comes together, 1 to 2 minutes. Increase the speed to medium and knead until the dough is very, very smooth, about 8 minutes (see page 182). With the mixer running, gradually add the cool water, about 1 tablespoon at a time, until all the water has been added. This will take 5 to 6 minutes (the total mixing time on medium speed is 13 to 14 minutes).

NOTE: EVEN THOUGH CIABATTA IS A WET dough, it is a strong one—it has to be in order to stretch enough to trap all the tunnels and holes created by the gas bubbles in the dough. Using higher-protein bread flour instead of all-purpose flour helps right off the bat, as does a long mixing time at the beginning of the dough-making process. If you added all the water at once in the beginning, the dough would be too slack and you wouldn't be able to activate the gluten enough to get a strong dough. So you add the ice water first and let the dough mix awhile (the ice water prevents the dough from overheating) until the dough is smooth and stretchy and *then* add the remaining water in small additions after you have developed the gluten in the dough. This way you can develop a strong dough *and* a very wet one to create the holes and tunnels and texture for which ciabatta is known.

2 Let the dough rise: Sprinkle a little flour on top of the dough and use a plastic dough scraper to help you transfer the dough to a large floured bowl. Cover the bowl with plastic wrap, and set it aside at room temperature until the dough has almost doubled in volume, about 40 minutes.

3 Stretch and fold the dough, then let it rise again: Flour the top of the dough and fold one side over the middle. Give the dough a quarter turn and repeat on each of the 4 sides. Turn the dough over and cover it with a kitchen towel. Let it rest at room temperature for another 30 minutes.

4 Divide and shape the dough, then let it proof: Generously flour the top of the dough and transfer it to a floured work surface. Use a bench knife to divide it into 3 equal pieces for loaves or 10 pieces for rolls. Loosely stretch each piece into a

narrow rectangle. Then, starting at one narrow end, fold the end of the dough over and onto the center. Press the edge down to tack it onto the center, and repeat 2 times, taking care not to press all the air bubbles out of the dough. Set the loaves (or rolls) on a floured sheet pan and flour the top. Cover the dough with a kitchen towel (see page 17 for other homemade proof box ideas) and set it aside until when pressed lightly with a finger, the depression in the dough fills in halfway, about 1 hour.

5 Set a rimmed sheet pan on the oven floor (or if not possible, on the lowest oven rack), set a baking stone (or upside-down sheet pan) on a middle rack, and preheat the oven to 475°F.

6 Bake the ciabatta: Invert the loaves (or rolls) onto a floured pizza peel or piece of cardboard so the seam is up, flour the top, and slide them off the cardboard and onto the hot stone (or upside-down sheet pan) in the oven. (You may need to bake them in 2 batches; if your kitchen is very warm, you can cover the other pieces of dough and refrigerate them.) Pour about ¼ cup of water onto the baking sheet on the oven floor (or bottom rack) to create steam, and quickly close the oven door. Bake just until the ciabatta sounds hollow when tapped and is a pale gold color (it will still be streaked with white from all of the flour), 10 to 12 minutes (8 to 10 minutes for rolls). Use a spatula to remove the loaves from the oven and transfer them to a wire rack to cool. Serve warm or at room temperature.

(continued)

STEP 1

STEP 2

KNEADING SOFT DOUGHS

You can make many general statements about bread for which there are often just as many exceptions to the rule. I always (well, most of the time—see, an exception!) try to incorporate as much water as I can into a bread dough. That way, the bread stays fresh and tender for longer because the dough is more hydroscopic (meaning it has more moisture). During fermenting and proofing, the dough will acquire bigger holes in the interior and get nice air pockets inside during baking (like ciabatta). But dough this wet can be challenging to work with, even for professional bakers; it is sticky on the hands and the table and hard to knead (and you don't want to overflour the dough or the work surface because then what is the point of the wet dough?), making it difficult to form an elastic dough that is strong enough to capture air pockets within the crumb.

So how do you knead such a soft dough? There is an alternative to over-kneading the dough in the mixer, where you risk "burning" it and compromising the gluten. Instead, you stretch and fold the dough in stages. So if the recipe calls for 40 minutes of resting after kneading the dough in the stand mixer, you can actually rest it for 20 minutes (in the mixer bowl), and stretch and fold from each side, rotating the dough after each stretch and fold (so 4 times total). Lightly dust the top of the dough with flour, then cover it with a kitchen towel and let it rest for another 20 minutes. Much like the No-Knead Focaccia on page 125, the dough will become stronger just through the resting and the small amount of folding done to punctuate the resting time.

Pain de Mie

Makes 16 rolls (800 grams / 1¾ pounds of dough)

Tender, sweet, and pillowy, pain de mie is very French but has been whole-heartedly adopted by Israelis. Also called "milk buns," this dough makes a soft-textured bun with just enough crust. It's closely related to challah, but pain de mie differs in that it calls for milk powder and butter rather than eggs and oil to enrich the dough. You could substitute 75 grams (⅓ cup) of milk for the milk powder—just remember to reduce the amount of water in the recipe by 75 grams (⅓ cup). For a slightly tangy flavor, substitute plain yogurt or buttermilk for the milk.

At the bakeries, we use pain de mie buns to make a lot of our sandwiches, including tuna salad, avocado, and egg salad.

DOUGH

Cool room-temperature water	180 grams (¾ cup)
Fresh yeast	15 grams (1 tablespoon)
or active dry yeast	5 grams (1 teaspoon)
All-purpose flour (sifted, 11.7%)	450 grams (3¼ cups), plus extra for kneading and shaping
Granulated sugar	75 grams (⅓ cup)
Dry milk powder	15 grams (1 tablespoon)
Fine salt	7 grams (1½ teaspoons)
Unsalted butter (at room temperature)	45 grams (3 tablespoons)
Nigella seeds, poppy seeds, or sesame seeds (optional)	75 grams (about ½ cup)

EGG WASH

Large egg	1
Water	1 tablespoon
Fine salt	Pinch

1 **Make the dough:** Pour the water into the bowl of a stand mixer fitted with the dough hook. Add the yeast and use a whisk or your fingers to dissolve it into the water. Add the flour, sugar, milk powder, and salt, and then add the butter in small pinches. Mix the dough on low speed, scraping the sides and bottom of the bowl, until combined, about 1 minute. Increase the speed to medium-low and continue to mix, scraping the bowl as needed, until the dough is well mixed, about 2 minutes longer. Then increase the speed to medium and mix until the dough is elastic and shiny, about 3 minutes.

2 **Stretch and fold the dough, then let it rise:** Use a plastic dough scraper to transfer the dough to a lightly floured work surface. Take one corner of the dough and stretch the dough until it tears, then fold it on top of the center. Give the dough a quarter turn and repeat the stretching and folding for 1 minute. Lightly flour a bowl and set the dough in it, lightly flour the top of the dough, and cover the bowl with plastic wrap. Set it aside at room temperature for about 1 hour.

3 **Divide and round the dough, then let it proof:** Uncover the dough and transfer it to a lightly floured work surface. Divide the dough into 16 equal pieces. Fold the corners of each piece up and over to create a roundish shape. Turn the dough over, seam-side down, and using a cupped hand, push and pull the dough, rolling it against the work surface, to create a nice ball (be very light-handed with the flour; otherwise, it will be difficult to get the dough to form a tight ball). Place the dough balls on a parchment paper–lined rimmed sheet pan,

cover with a kitchen towel (see page 17 for other homemade proof box ideas), and set aside at room temperature to proof for 1½ to 2 hours.

4 Preheat the oven to 350°F.

NOTE: RICH DOUGHS, SUCH AS PAIN DE MIE, challah (page 27), and babka (page 68) dough, freeze very well. (I don't freeze lean dough like focaccia—it doesn't bounce back from being frozen as nicely as richer doughs because the dough is too soft.) After shaping, proof the dough for 15 minutes, then freeze it on the sheet pan. Once the rolls are hard, transfer them to an airtight freezer-weight plastic bag and freeze for up to 1 month. To defrost, separate the rolls and refrigerate for a few hours; then continue to proof them at room temperature (and covered with a plastic bag or towel) until a finger lightly pressed into the dough leaves a depression that remains without deflating the dough or filling back in.

5 **Bake the bread:** Make the egg wash by whisking the egg, water, and salt together in a small bowl. Brush egg wash over the rolls, and then sprinkle with the seeds to coat the rolls evenly. Bake the rolls until they are golden brown and nicely risen, 8 to 10 minutes. Remove from the oven and let cool slightly on the baking sheet before serving.

NOTE: PAIN DE MIE RESPONDS REALLY WELL to mix-ins. Feel free to stir raisins, walnuts, chocolate chips, or your favorite bread ingredients into the dough. Add a total of about 170 grams (20% of the dough weight; about 6 ounces) of mix-ins for a nicely enhanced dough. That would be about 1 cup of chocolate chips or a heaping 1¾ cups of walnuts, just as an example.
  IF SOME OF YOUR PROOFED ROLLS ARE larger than others, place the larger rolls around the edges of the baking sheet and the smaller ones in the middle. The rolls at the perimeter get more heat than the rolls in the middle, so taking that into account, the larger rolls will be done at about the same time as the slightly smaller ones.

Dill Bread

Makes 3 loaves (1.6 kilos / 3½ pounds of dough)

I first saw the shape of this bread on the island of Djerba, off the coast of Tunisia, where there is a very small (about a thousand people) yet vibrant Jewish community that has lived there for 2,500 years. Unlike other Arab countries in North Africa and the Middle East whose Jewish communities have all but vanished after many people moved to Israel, the bulk of Djerba's Jewish community has remained on this beautiful island.

Dill, an herb favored in Scandinavia and Eastern Europe and even in Iran, is popular in Tunisia, too. This bread, a twist on Pain de Mie (page 186), is formed into a coil and then snipped with scissors to create the shape of a flower (kishlaya), which is how challah is traditionally shaped in Djerba, Tunisia. You'll need a generous amount of work surface to form the coils.

DOUGH

Cool room-temperature water	180 grams (¾ cup)
Fresh yeast	35 grams (¼ cup)
or active dry yeast	12 grams (2½ teaspoons)
All-purpose flour (sifted, 11.7%)	840 grams (6¾ cups), plus extra for kneading and shaping
Granulated sugar	50 grams (¼ cup)
Fine salt	15 grams (1 tablespoon)
Plain whole-milk yogurt	180 grams (¾ cup)
Unsalted butter (at room temperature)	75 grams (5 tablespoons), cut into small pieces
Yellow onion	50 grams (1 small onion), finely chopped
Fresh dill fronds	35 grams (2 cups), finely chopped

EGG WASH

Large egg	1
Water	1 tablespoon
Fine salt	Pinch

1 Make the dough: Combine the water and yeast in the bowl of a stand mixer and whisk until the yeast has dissolved. Add the flour, sugar, salt, yogurt, and butter pieces. Attach the dough hook and knead on low speed until the dough comes together, 1 to 2 minutes (if, after 2 minutes, the dough has dry spots at the bottom of the bowl or the dough looks very wet, add more water or flour—a little at a time—as needed). Once the dough comes together nicely, continue to mix on low speed for 3 minutes. Then increase the mixer speed to medium and knead until the dough looks shiny and cleans the bowl, about 5 minutes.

2 Stretch and fold the dough, then let it rise: Lightly flour a work surface and set the dough on it. Lightly flour the top of the dough. Take one corner of the dough and stretch the dough until it tears, then fold it on top of the center. Give the dough a quarter turn and continue the stretching/folding/turning for 2 minutes. Use a bench scraper or chef's knife to cut the dough into 12 pieces, and return the pieces to the mixer bowl (this helps incorporate the onion and dill easily). Add the onion and dill, and knead on low speed just until they are well incorporated, about 1 minute. Transfer the dough to a lightly floured work surface and fold again, giving it about 4 turns. Place the dough in a lightly floured large bowl, dust the top with flour, and cover the bowl with plastic wrap. Set it aside at room temperature until the dough has doubled in volume, about 1 hour.

3 Divide and shape the dough: Transfer the dough to a lightly floured surface and divide it into 3 equal pieces. Firmly press down on each piece of dough, and then pull it to make a 9-by-5-inch rectangle with a short side facing you. Fold the top edge a quarter of the way down and use the heel of your hand to seal the edge to the bottom part of the dough (see photos on page 172). Repeat 3 more times to make a cylinder. Repeat with the remaining pieces of dough. Use your hands to roll each piece to form a 20-inch-long cylinder. Then cover them with a clean kitchen towel and let them rest for 15 minutes.

4 Roll and shape the dough again, then let the dough proof: Flatten each cylinder to a rectangle again and repeat the process, folding the top down by a fourth, using the heel of your hand to seal the edge, then repeating 3 times to make a cylinder. Now use your hands to roll each cylinder to make a 40-inch-long rope. Use scissors to snip diagonal slits three-quarters of the way through the dough at 1-inch intervals. Coil the snipped rope into a spiral shape overlapping to create a tall pyramid-like shape and set it on a parchment paper–lined sheet pan. Repeat with the other 2 ropes, fitting 2 coils onto one of the sheets (you might have to refrigerate 1 coil of dough while the first 2 bake if your sheet pans aren't large enough to accommodate 2 loaves on one pan). Pull on each of the segments to separate them from one another, cover the sheet pans with a kitchen towel (see page 17 for other homemade proof box ideas), and set them aside in a warm, draft-free spot until the dough jiggles slightly when tapped, 1½ to 2 hours (depending on how warm the room is).

5 Set a rimmed sheet pan on the oven floor (or, if not possible, on the lowest oven rack). Adjust the oven racks to the upper-middle and lower-middle positions, and preheat the oven to 350°F.

6 Bake the dough: Make the egg wash by whisking the egg, water, and salt together in a small bowl. Use a pastry brush to lightly coat each loaf with egg wash. Place one sheet pan on the upper rack and the other on the lower rack, pour ¼ cup of water into the pan on the bottom of the oven, and quickly close the oven door. Bake for 12 minutes. Then rotate the bottom sheet pan to the top and the top to the bottom, and continue to bake until the loaves are browned, 5 to 8 minutes longer. Remove from the oven and let cool on the sheet pans before serving.

Spelt and Muesli Buns

Makes 24 buns (920 grams / 2 pounds of dough)

Muesli is a common ingredient in Danish and German breads. These breads often take on a more rustic, free-form shape since they are hearty and studded with dried fruits, nuts, seeds, and grains. But if you're expecting this to be a heavy fruit-laden bun, look somewhere else, because while they are made with spelt flour and loaded with apples, dried fruits, and seeds, they're still unbelievably fluffy. Of course you should feel free to change the goodies as you like—if you don't care for hazelnuts, try pecans or walnuts; if you don't have dried cranberries on hand, substitute raisins or figs or chopped dried apricots; if you aren't a fan of poppy seeds, leave them out and use extra sesame. The one ingredient I encourage you *not* to switch out is the fresh apple. It's very important because of the texture and moisture it adds to the dough.

SPELT DOUGH

Cool room-temperature water	230 grams (1 cup)
Flaxseeds	50 grams (⅓ cup)
Fresh yeast	20 grams (heaping 1 tablespoon)
or active dry yeast	5 grams (1 teaspoon)
All-purpose flour (sifted, 11.7%)	250 grams (2 cups), plus extra for shaping
Whole-grain spelt flour	250 grams (2½ cups)
Large egg	1
Dark brown sugar	50 grams (¼ cup, lightly packed)
Fine salt	10 grams (1½ teaspoons)
Extra-virgin olive oil	45 grams (3 tablespoons), plus extra for greasing the muffin tin

MUESLI BUN FILLING

Dried cranberries	50 grams (⅓ cup)
Dried pitted dates	50 grams (heaping ¼ cup), coarsely chopped
Toasted and skinned hazelnuts	50 grams (½ cup), finely chopped
Toasted sesame seeds	40 grams (¼ cup)
Roasted, unsalted sunflower seeds	35 grams (¼ cup)
Poppy seeds	30 grams (¼ cup)
Honey	30 grams (scant 2 tablespoons)
Green apple	1, peeled, cored, and finely chopped
Large eggs	2
Rolled oats	50 grams (½ cup)

EGG WASH

Large egg	1
Water	1 tablespoon
Fine salt	Pinch

1 Make the dough: Pour the water into the bowl of a stand mixer. Add the flaxseeds and let them sit in the water for 30 minutes.

2 Crumble the yeast into the water and use your fingers to rub and dissolve it; if using active dry yeast, whisk the yeast into the water. Add the all-purpose flour, spelt flour, egg, brown sugar, salt, and olive oil. Attach the dough hook and mix on low speed to combine the ingredients, stopping the mixer if the dough climbs up the hook or if you need to work in dry ingredients that have settled on the bottom of the bowl. Scrape the bottom and sides of the bowl as needed. It should take about 2 minutes for the dough to come together.

3 Increase the speed to medium and knead until a smooth dough forms, about 4 minutes. You may need to add a little water if the dough is too stiff, or a little flour if it is too sticky.

> NOTE: EVENTUALLY YOU'LL BE ABLE TO feel the dough and know if you need to add water or flour; it's always better to adjust the ratios when the dough is first coming together rather than during the kneading process, since it takes longer for ingredient additions to get worked into the dough mass at this later point.

4 Stretch and fold the dough: Lightly dust your work surface with a spare amount of flour, and use a plastic dough scraper to transfer the dough from the mixing bowl to the floured surface. Use your palms to knead/push the dough away from you in one stroke; then pinch the front portion and stretch it toward you to rip the dough slightly, and fold it on top of itself. Give the dough a quarter turn and repeat the push/pinch/tear/fold process. After 1 minute, the dough should be in a nice ball shape.

5 Let the dough rise: Lightly dust a bowl with flour, place the dough in the bowl, sprinkle just a little flour on top of the dough, and cover the bowl with a kitchen towel or plastic wrap. Set the bowl aside at room temperature until the dough has risen by about 70%, 30 to 40 minutes (depending on how warm your room is).

6 Cut in the dried fruits, nuts, and seeds: Gently use a plastic dough scraper to help lift the dough out of the bowl and onto a lightly floured work surface. Use a bench knife to make a checkerboard pattern on the dough (don't cut all the way through the dough—just make deep incisions). Pile the cranberries, dates, hazelnuts, sesame seeds, sunflower seeds, poppy seeds, honey, and chopped apple on top. Crack the eggs on top and use the bench knife to chop through the dough and fold the dough over onto itself, continuing to chop and fold to mix the ingredients in (see photo, opposite). You don't want it too well mixed—you want a very chunky dough.

7 Divide the dough and let it proof: Lightly grease the wells of two 12-cup muffin tins with olive oil and place about 50 grams (2 ounces) of the dough in each well. Sprinkle each with some oats, and set the muffin tins aside in a draft-free spot at room temperature until the dough has risen above the lip of the wells, 45 minutes to 1 hour.

8 Preheat the oven to 350°F.

9 Bake the buns: Make the egg wash by whisking the egg, water, and salt together in a small bowl. Brush the egg wash evenly over the buns, and bake until they are golden brown on top and sound hollow when lightly tapped, 15 to 18 minutes. Remove the tins from the oven and let the buns cool in the tins for 5 minutes. Remove them from the muffin tins and let them cool completely on a wire rack.

STUFFED BREADS

ISRAELIS LIKE TO EAT ON the run. We like convenient foods—falafel, shawarma, sandwiches, toasts—small meals that suit the fast pace of Tel Aviv and beyond. Burekas are the ultimate food on the go. You buy them from stands or vendors (and from supermarkets), warm them up, and have a cheap and filling snack or small meal. These stuffed pastries have long been the morning meal for workers and a snack for children after school because they can be eaten as is or split open and stuffed with sliced hard-boiled eggs and maybe a slice of tomato in addition to the potato or cheese or spinach filling baked into the bureka. Add a pickle and some tahina and you have a complete meal that is uniquely Israeli (though other Middle Eastern countries have their versions of burekas too; see page 204).

In Israel, burekas had become the mass-produced spaghetti and meatballs of the States, and like spaghetti and meatballs, they were given no respect. The dough was commercially made, shortcuts were taken, fillings were almost invisible—and if they were noticeable, they were surely unremarkable and often not tasty. In fact, low-budget movies in Israel are even called "bureka films." Of course, if you seek them out, you can always find great, flaky, homemade fresh-from-the-oven burekas in the shuks of Tel Aviv and Jerusalem, but most people will opt for the convenience of grocery store burekas made with less-than-high-quality pastry and fillings. It's kind of like comparing spongy, soft, and tasteless commercial croissants to the beautifully layered, buttery, and extra-crispy artisanal croissants of Paris. You can't compare them. It's as simple as that.

Burekas very much reflect what is happening with the food movement in Israel right now. We are looking at our traditions and asking ourselves, How do we make this better? How do we bring this food back to its original intent, its original glory? I decided to make fresh burekas at my bakery throughout the day, as they do in the shuks; they are overstuffed with high-quality filling.

The burekas have been such a success that I have extended the same concept to other recipes, like savory hamantaschen made from a buttery pie dough and filled with a mixture of potatoes or roasted beets and hazelnuts (see pages 234 and 238). I make savory and sweet stuffed boats and buns using the Light Brioche (page 165). Of course there are the Cheese Straws (page 241) too, which are so incredibly simple yet immensely satisfying. I add *a lot* of Gouda to the pastry dough and twist it in; as the cheese melts in the oven, some caramelizes and crisps and the result is truly decadent—they're so good stuffed with goat cheese, cherry tomatoes, jalapeños, and cilantro for a sandwich that hits all the flavor notes.

For the cheese twists as well as the burekas, the kind of puff pastry you buy is of the utmost importance. Look at the ingredients and make sure the pastry is made with 100% butter first and foremost. Then try a few brands and see what you like best. I haven't given a puff pastry recipe in this book because, truly, I think store-bought all-butter high-end puff pastry is good, and making homemade puff pastry is a very labor-intensive and discouraging process. Buy a good commercial brand and save yourself the time and headache. For more tips on buying puff pastry, see page 208.

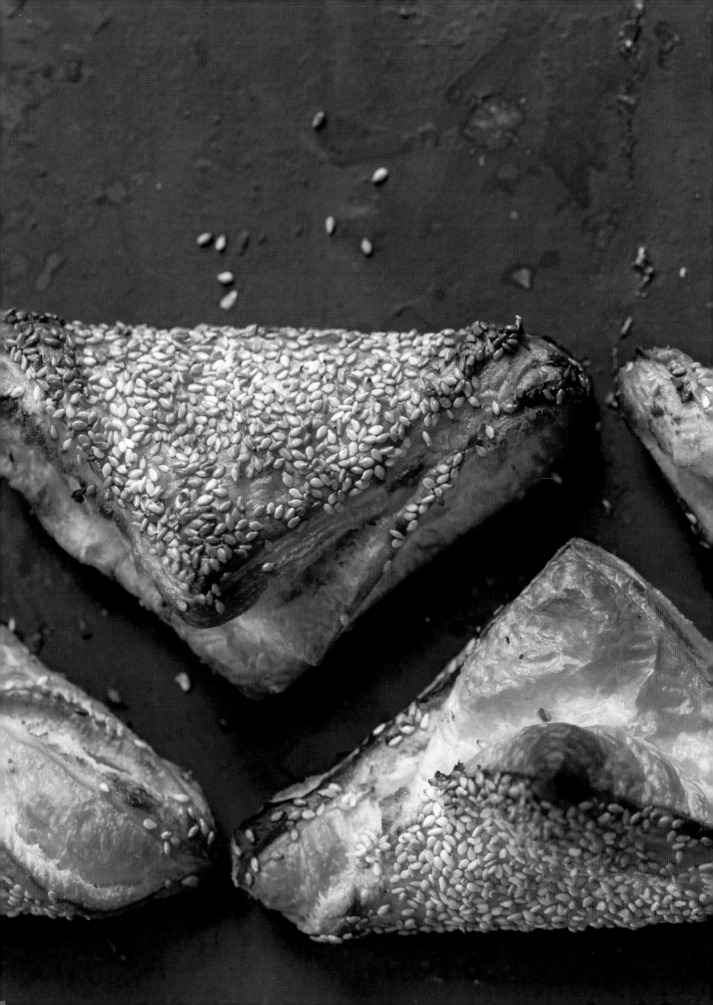

Cheese Burekas

Makes 8 burekas

While I was living in a moshav (a farming cooperative) near Netanya in Israel, everyone talked about one little bureka stand. People said the owner made the best burekas. His shop always had a line of people waiting, and in Israel this is a big deal because no one likes to wait in line for anything. Later I found out that he was not making his own dough—really! He was buying the dough premade just like everyone else. So why were his burekas better? The difference is that he was baking burekas fresh throughout the day, multiple times a day, so when people ordered a bureka, they would get one that was recently pulled out of the oven. His burekas weren't preheated or microwaved until hot. It's the freshness that made his burekas so great.

To Israelis, the bureka is like the American bagel—it's available almost everywhere and is eaten at all times of the day, from morning through late night. But what exactly is a bureka? In Israel and elsewhere, a bureka is a flaky turnover made with a very thin dough and filled with a savory stuffing. In Israel the classic fillings are cheese, potatoes, or spinach and the burekas are usually served with grated tomatoes or a hard-boiled egg and sometimes with tahini on the side. Burekas (börek) were brought to Israel by Jews from the Balkans, Turkey, and Greece, and were originally made with phyllo or yufka dough. Also referred to as sambousak or boyos, they can be stuffed with ground lamb and other combinations of cheeses, herbs, and vegetables.

A great bureka is the same no matter what it's called; if it's fresh, tender, and filled with quality ingredients, you're in for a treat. The key to a great bureka is to achieve a balance between the flakiness of the dough and a filling that has an assertive flavor but is also ample in amount. But really, more than anything else, a bureka is best when it is absolutely *fresh* and served hot from the oven. This recipe includes the classic ingredients for filling, but feel free to experiment—add peas, fried onions, olives or tapenade or sautéed mushrooms, or make a pizza bureka with matbucha (page 330), fresh mozzarella, and basil.

Cream cheese (at room temperature)	135 grams (²/₃ cup)
Feta cheese	80 grams (¾ cup), crumbled
Sour cream	70 grams (¹/₃ cup)
Large eggs	2
All-purpose flour	25 grams (3 tablespoons), plus extra for rolling and shaping
Store-bought puff pastry (see page 208)	455 grams (1 pound), thawed if frozen
Water	1 teaspoon
Fine salt	Pinch
Sesame seeds	50 grams (¹/₃ cup)
Nigella seeds	50 grams (¹/₃ cup)

1 Place the cream cheese and feta cheese in the bowl of a stand mixer fitted with the paddle attachment and beat on medium-low speed until smooth. Add the sour cream and mix until well combined. Add 1 egg and beat to combine, scraping down the sides and bottom of the bowl as necessary. Add the flour and mix until combined.

2 Set the puff pastry on a lightly floured work surface and roll it into a rectangle approximately 8½ by 16½ inches and about ⅛ inch thick. Trim the edges so you have a nice, clean rectangle, then divide the dough into eight 4-inch squares. In a small bowl, whisk the remaining egg with the water and salt; brush some of this egg wash over 2 adjacent edges of each square (see photo on page 206). Reserve the remaining egg wash.

3 Place about 3 tablespoons of the cheese filling in the center of each square and fold the non-egg-washed side of the dough over to meet the egg-washed edge—but do not press the edges to seal (see photo on page 206). Instead, lightly tap the sides together about ⅛ inch in from the edge; then use your finger to press down and seal the triangle along this line (this is so the edges puff when baked, letting you see the layers of the pastry at the edge of the bureka; see photo on page 206).

4 Set the burkeas on a parchment paper–lined sheet pan and refrigerate for at least 20 minutes and up to 24 hours (if refrigerating them longer than 1 hour, cover the sheet pan with plastic wrap).

5 Preheat the oven to 400°F.

6 Remove the burekas from the refrigerator and brush the top of each one with the remaining egg wash. Stir the sesame seeds and nigella seeds together in a small bowl, and sprinkle each bureka generously with the seed mixture (see photo on page 206). Bake the burekas until they are puffed and golden brown, about 25 minutes. Try to cool the burekas slightly before eating—if you have the willpower!

(continued)

Variation

Egg Burekas

Instead of making the cheese filling, place a heaping teaspoon of cream cheese on the center of each pastry square (40 grams / 3 tablespoons of cream cheese total) and top it with half of a hard-boiled egg (4 hard-boiled eggs total). Proceed with the egg-washing, sealing, chilling, and baking as described.

Spinach Burekas

Makes 8 burekas

In Israel, you know the filling of the bureka according to its shape. Triangular burekas are almost always filled with cheese, and rectangles with potato. Spinach is usually in a rectangle but is also sometimes shaped into a coil or snail (see page 224). I prefer rectangles; the pastry gets crisper and flakier around all the edges.

Extra-virgin olive oil	15 grams (1 tablespoon)
Yellow onion	½, diced
Garlic clove	1 large, minced
Fresh spinach	300 grams (10½ ounces; about 10 cups), tough stems removed, leaves coarsely chopped
Large egg	1
Feta cheese	120 grams (heaping 1 cup), crumbled
Cream cheese (at room temperature)	70 grams (⅓ cup)
All-purpose flour	40 grams (¼ cup plus 1 tablespoon), plus extra for rolling and shaping)
Fine salt	Few pinches
Freshly ground black pepper	for sprinkling
Water	1 teaspoon
Store-bought puff pastry (see page 208)	455 grams (1 pound), thawed if frozen
Sesame seeds, poppy seeds, or nigella seeds (or a combination)	110 grams (⅔ cup)

1 Heat the olive oil in a large skillet over medium heat. Add the onion, reduce the heat to medium-low, and cook, stirring occasionally, until it starts to brown, 7 to 8 minutes. Add the garlic and cook, stirring often, until it is fragrant, about 30 seconds; then stir in about half the spinach and cook until it starts to wilt, 2 minutes. Add the remaining spinach and cook, stirring and turning the mixture, until it is mostly wilted, 2 to 3 minutes longer. Transfer the spinach mixture to a large bowl and let it cool.

2 Whisk the egg in a medium bowl and transfer about 1 tablespoon of the beaten egg to a small bowl (this will be for your egg wash); set that aside. Mix the feta cheese and cream cheese into the remaining egg in the medium bowl, and then mix in the flour until smooth. Add the cooled spinach mixture along with a few pinches of salt (be careful when adding salt since feta cheese is salty) and a couple grinds of black pepper.

3 Add the water and a pinch of salt to the reserved beaten egg, and whisk to combine. Set the puff pastry on a lightly floured work surface and roll it into a rectangle approximately 10 by 15 inches and about ⅛ inch thick, with a long side facing you.

(continued)

Divide the dough into 8 rectangles. Brush the bottom third of each rectangle with some of the egg wash (reserve the remainder of the egg wash). Spoon (or pipe) about 2 tablespoons of the spinach mixture in a line across the bottom third of the dough and then fold the top over to meet the bottom (egg-washed) edge. Do not press the edges to seal. Instead, lightly tap them together about ⅛ inch in from the edge, and then use your finger to press down and seal the rectangle along this line (this is so the edges puff when baked, letting you see the layers of the pastry at the edge of the bureka).

4 Set the burekas on a parchment paper–lined sheet pan and refrigerate for at least 20 minutes and up to 24 hours (if refrigerating them longer than 1 hour, cover the sheet pan with plastic wrap).

5 Preheat the oven to 400°F.

6 Remove the burekas from the refrigerator and brush the top of each one with the remaining egg wash. Sprinkle each bureka generously with the seeds, then use a paring knife to score the top of each one 2 or 3 times. Bake the burekas until they are puffed and golden brown, about 25 minutes. Let them cool slightly before serving.

BUYING PUFF PASTRY

At my bakeries in New York City and Tel Aviv, we make our own puff pastry dough. This is no minor task—it takes many hours and a lot of patience, and we even have the help of a mechanical sheeter to help "laminate" the dough (that's what it's called when layer upon layer of butter is folded into the dough—it's the butter layers that create the flaky quality of the best puff pastries and, in this case, burekas).

At home, though, not many of us have the time and energy to make homemade puff pastry. There are many good-quality frozen brands of puff pastry for sale in higher-end grocery stores (or ask your local baker to sell some to you). I advise you to look for one made with all butter, as it will have the very best flavor. Additionally, some sheets are sold as rectangles and some rolled out as rounds. Buy the puff pastry in rectangular sheets if possible; it will be easier to divide into squares or rectangles for burekas or other pastries. Try to find the kind that comes as one pound to a box, but if the pastry weighs a few ounces less, it's really no big deal and shouldn't prevent you from making the burekas.

To defrost the pastry, let it sit in your refrigerator for a few hours. Unwrap it and work quickly, always refrigerating the dough if it starts to become very sticky. You want to keep puff pastry very cold so that when it goes into the oven to bake, the butter layers create lots and lots of flaky layers in your burekas (or whatever it is that you are making). If, when you unroll the dough, it looks speckled with little black-gray dots, this means the dough is not fresh. You should bring the dough back to the store where you bought it and get a new package (old dough isn't harmful, but puff pastry dough is not inexpensive to buy, so why settle for something that is not 100% perfect?).

Swiss Chard and Kashkaval Burekas

Makes 5 burekas

Kashkaval is a semi-hard sheep's-milk cheese that has an assertive, sharp flavor. It is common to Romania, Greece, Turkey, and other Balkan countries; if you can't find it, substitute a young pecorino-style cheese instead. These burekas are formed into large oval-shaped snails; however, you can make them into rectangles or triangles if you prefer smaller burekas.

Swiss chard (preferably rainbow chard)	1 bunch (about 10 stems)
Fresh spinach leaves	100 grams (3½ ounces)
Extra-virgin olive oil	15 grams (1 tablespoon)
Yellow onion	½, finely chopped
Celery ribs with leaves	1½, thinly sliced
Tomato	½, chopped
Garlic cloves	2 small, minced
Lemon zest	grated from ½ lemon
Dried red pepper flakes	⅛ teaspoon
Freshly ground black pepper	Several pinches
Lemon juice	from ½ lemon
Fine salt	¾ teaspoon, plus a pinch for the egg wash
Large egg	1
Water	1 tablespoon
All-purpose flour	for rolling the puff pastry
Store-bought puff pastry (see opposite)	455 grams (1 pound), thawed if frozen
Kashkaval cheese	150 grams (1⅓ cups), crumbled

1 Separate the chard stems from the leaves. Trim off and discard the tough ends of the stems. Cut the remaining stems in half crosswise, and then thinly slice them lengthwise to make thin matchsticks. Stack the Swiss chard leaves and slice them into 1-inch-wide ribbons. Repeat with the spinach leaves.

2 Heat the olive oil in a large skillet over medium heat. Add the onion, celery ribs and leaves, and the chard stems and cook,

stirring often, until the onion and celery are very soft, 5 to 8 minutes (if the onion starts to brown, reduce the heat to medium-low).

3 Stir in the tomato, garlic, lemon zest, red pepper flakes, and black pepper and cook, stirring often, until the tomatoes become juicy and are starting to break down, 2 to 3 minutes. Add half the chard leaves and cook, stirring, until they begin to wilt, then add the remaining chard leaves. Repeat with the spinach leaves, and once they wilt, stir in the lemon juice and the salt (see Note). Transfer the mixture to a medium bowl and let it cool completely (you can refrigerate the mixture for a few hours to get it extra-cold).

> NOTE: TASTE YOUR CHEESE FOR SALTINESS before salting the filling. Some types of Kashkaval (like feta) are saltier than others, so keep this in mind when seasoning the sautéed vegetables. You can always add more salt, but it's difficult to take it away.

4 Place the cooled filling in a sieve and drain off any extra liquid, lightly pressing down on the vegetables to extract even more moisture (but don't mash them). In a small bowl, beat the egg with the water and a pinch of salt to make an egg wash. Lightly flour your work surface and set the puff pastry on top. Lightly flour the top of the pastry, and then roll it into a rectangle approximately 20 by 12 inches and $\frac{1}{16}$ inch thick, with a long side facing you. Working quickly so the dough doesn't warm up, divide it lengthwise into 5 equal strips (each about 4 inches wide). Brush the strips of pastry with some of the

egg wash. Spoon about $\frac{1}{2}$ cup of the filling down the center of each strip, and top the vegetables with a generous $\frac{1}{4}$ cup of the crumbled Kashkaval. Reserve the remaining egg wash.

5 Fold the right edge of each strip over the filling to meet the left edge, and press the edges together to seal. If the dough starts to become sticky or difficult to work with, place it on a sheet of parchment paper and chill it until it firms up. Turn each filled strip over, seam-side down. Shape each strip into a U-shaped spiral, and place them on a parchment paper–lined rimmed sheet pan (leave space between the spirals so the sides can brown). Refrigerate the burekas until they are chilled.

6 Preheat the oven to 400°F.

7 Brush the burekas with the remaining egg wash and bake until they are golden brown, 30 to 35 minutes. Remove from the oven and serve warm or at room temperature.

Potato Burekas

Makes 8 burekas

Burekas are a great use for leftover mashed potatoes, to which you can add any herbs or spices you like. This recipe uses the traditional mashed potato filling, but as with all burekas, feel free to experiment. For smaller burekas that are good for cocktail parties, slice a rectangle crosswise into thirds before baking.

Russet potatoes	3 medium, peeled and chopped into 1-inch pieces
Unsalted butter	15 grams (1 tablespoon)
Fine salt	½ teaspoon, plus a pinch for the egg wash
Freshly grated nutmeg	⅛ teaspoon
Freshly ground white pepper	⅛ teaspoon
Fresh flat-leaf parsley leaves	15 grams (about ¼ cup), finely chopped
Large egg	1, lightly beaten
Water	1 teaspoon
Store-bought puff pastry (see page 208)	455 grams (1 pound), thawed if frozen
All-purpose flour	for rolling
Nigella, poppy, and sesame seeds, in any combination	100 grams (⅔ cup)

1 Bring a large pot of water to a boil. Add the chopped potatoes and cook until they are soft and tender but not falling apart, about 15 minutes. Drain the potatoes and return them to the pot. Add the butter, salt, nutmeg, and white pepper and mash the potatoes to a semismooth consistency. Stir in the parsley, taste, and add more salt if needed. Set aside until cool.

2 Set aside 1 tablespoon of the beaten egg. Whisk the remaining egg into the cooked potato mixture and refrigerate until it is cold.

3 In a small bowl, whisk the reserved beaten egg with the water and a pinch of salt to make an egg wash. Set the puff pastry on a lightly floured work surface and roll it to form a rectangle approximately 10 by 15 inches and about ⅛ inch thick, with a long side facing you. Divide the dough into 8 rectangles. Brush the bottom third of each rectangle with some of the egg wash (reserve the remainder of the egg wash). Spoon about 4 tablespoons of the potato mixture in a line across the top third of the dough, and then fold the top over to meet the bottom (egg-washed) edge. Do not press the edges to seal. Instead, lightly tap them together about ⅛ inch in from the edge, and then use your finger to press down and seal the rectangle along this line (this is so the edges puff when baked, letting you see the layers of the pastry at the edge of the bureka).

4 Set the burekas on a parchment paper–lined sheet pan and refrigerate for at least 20 minutes and up to 24 hours (if refrigerating them longer than 1 hour, cover the baking sheet with plastic wrap).

5 Preheat the oven to 400°F.

6 Remove the burekas from the refrigerator and brush the top of each one with the remaining egg wash. Sprinkle each bureka generously with the seeds. Bake the burekas until they are puffed and golden brown, about 25 minutes. Let them cool on the sheet pan slightly before serving.

FREEZING BUREKAS

Freeze some or all of the unbaked burekas (before brushing with the egg wash) on the sheet pan. Once they are frozen, transfer them to a gallon-size resealable freezer bag and freeze them for up to 1 month. When you want to serve them, they can go directly from the freezer to the hot oven to bake (they may need a few extra minutes to brown).

Poached Pear and Goat Cheese Brioche Buns

Makes 10 buns

I thought the idea of making stuffed open-faced buns was my invention alone, but when I went to Poland, I saw many versions. It just goes to show that there are very few original ideas, but that doesn't mean that great ones can't be repeated and emulated, right? You can make stuffed buns with an enriched dough—I use the Light Brioche here because it is so airy and tender, though you could absolutely use challah dough (page 27) too. Take the filling in any direction you like—for a quicker version, figs would be excellent instead of the poached pears, or try onions sautéed with some herbs.

Note that the poached pears must be prepared at least 2 days ahead.

POACHED PEARS

Fruity red wine	1 bottle
Granulated sugar	100 grams (½ cup)
Whole black peppercorns	5
Whole allspice berries	3
Bay leaves (fresh or dried)	2 if fresh, 3 if dried
Forelle pears	5, peeled; stems left on
or Bosc pears	5, peeled and cored

BUNS

½ recipe Light Brioche dough (page 165), prepared through step 5	
Large egg	1
Water	1 tablespoon
Fine salt	Pinch
Fresh goat's-milk cheese	85 grams (3 ounces)
Fresh thyme sprigs	4, leaves removed and reserved
Walnut halves	30

1 Poach the pears: Pour the wine into a medium saucepan. Add the sugar, peppercorns, allspice berries, and bay leaves and bring to a simmer over medium-high heat. Reduce the heat to medium-low and simmer gently until the mixture is slightly reduced, about 15 minutes. Then carefully drop the peeled whole pears into the wine, return it to a simmer, and cook until a paring knife just slips into the center of a pear without resistance, 10 to 12 minutes (you don't want the pear to be too soft; underripe pears may take a few minutes longer, while ripe pears may take a few minutes less).

Remove the pan from the heat and let the pears cool in the liquid; then transfer them to an airtight container and refrigerate for at least 2 days (or up to 1 week) before using.

2 **Make the buns:** Place the brioche dough on a lightly floured surface and divide it into 10 equal pieces. Gently fold the corners over the middle of a piece of dough (avoid pressing the gas out of the dough), and then flip the piece over. It won't be a perfect ball—this is called pre-shaping (it also ensures that the heat from your hand doesn't melt all the butter tucked into the dough). Repeat with the remaining pieces of dough. Then go back to the first piece and use both hands to lightly roll the dough into a cylinder, pressing down on the ends to create a torpedo shape; and set it on a parchment paper–lined sheet pan. Repeat with the remaining pieces of dough.

> NOTE: WHEN MAKING ROLLS OR SMALLER dough shapes from a large piece of dough, I like to pre-shape the dough by giving it a few folds or turns to get it into roughly the shape it will end up being. I continue with all the dough, and by the time I return to the first piece, it has had 5 to 10 minutes to rest, making the final shaping easier so I don't have to work the dough as hard to get it into its final shape as a ball, a boat, or a flat disk. The more you work dough, the more you strengthen the gluten and the stronger and less pillowy the interior of your dough will be. So for the most tender rolls, I like to work the dough as little as possible.

3 In a small bowl, whisk the egg, water, and salt together to make an egg wash. Brush a piece of the dough with some of the egg wash. Press your fingers down in the middle of the dough to create a deep oval depression that stretches along the body of the torpedo. Repeat with the other pieces of dough. Return to the first piece and repeat the pressing process. You should nearly be able to see the sheet pan through the bottom of the dough—it should be very thin.

4 Use a slotted spoon to remove the pears from the poaching liquid and set them on a paper towel–lined plate. Slice each whole pear in half (you can core the halves or leave them intact). Place a portion of the goat cheese in the center of each bun, followed by a pinch of thyme leaves. Add a pear half on top (if using Bosc pears and the halves are large, you can slice each one in half), and place 3 walnut halves just under the pear to prop it up a bit.

5 Cover the filled buns with a clean kitchen towel and set them aside in a draft-free spot at room temperature to rise until a finger pressed into the side of a bun leaves only a slight depression, about 1 hour.

6 Preheat the oven to 325°F.

7 Bake the buns until they are golden brown, about 8 minutes. Remove from the oven and set aside on the sheet pan to cool. Serve warm or at room temperature.

> NOTE: LAST NIGHT'S WINE CAN BECOME tomorrow's poaching liquid. Save your leftover wine and make the poaching liquid in advance, then store it in the refrigerator until you're ready to poach pears (or apples). The spiced wine also makes a great warm drink in the winter, or even a nice deglazing liquid to make a red wine sauce for a steak, pan-seared duck, or sautéed chicken.

Berry and Ricotta Brioche Buns

Makes 10 buns

It's very simple to take some dough and stuff it with what you have in your refrigerator—perhaps ricotta and jam, nuts, or other kinds of cheeses or fruits.

Ricotta cheese	200 grams (7 ounces)
Confectioners' sugar	8 grams (1 heaping tablespoon)
Cornstarch	8 grams (1 tablespoon)
Vanilla bean	½, split, seeds scraped out and reserved
½ recipe Light Brioche dough (page 165), prepared through step 5	
Large egg	1
Water	1 tablespoon
Fine salt	Pinch
1 recipe Streusel Topping (page 94)	
Fresh berries (blackberries, blueberries, or raspberries, or a combination)	30

1 Mix the ricotta, confectioners' sugar, cornstarch, and vanilla seeds together in a medium bowl. Set the mixture aside.

2 Place the brioche dough on a lightly floured work surface and divide it into 10 pieces. Gently fold the corners over the middle of a piece of dough (avoid pressing the gas out of the dough), and then flip the piece of dough over. It won't be a perfect ball—this is called pre-shaping. Repeat with the remaining pieces. Return to the first piece and use a cupped hand to push and pull the dough on the work surface to form a nice ball. Repeat with the remaining pieces, then place them on a parchment paper–lined sheet pan.

3 In a small bowl, whisk the egg, water, and salt together to make an egg wash. Brush each dough ball with some of the egg wash. Use your fingers to press down in the middle of a ball to make a deep depression, and slowly spread it out to within ½ inch of the edges of the dough. Repeat with the other pieces of dough, then return to the first piece and repeat the shaping process. You should nearly be able to see the sheet pan through the bottom of the dough—it should be very thin. Divide the streusel among the depressions in the buns, and then spoon the ricotta mixture over the streusel (or use a piping bag). Top each bun with 3 berries, cutting any large ones in half.

4 Cover the filled buns with a clean kitchen towel and set them aside to rise in a draft-free spot at room temperature until a finger pressed into the side of a bun leaves only a slight depression, about 1 hour.

5 Preheat the oven to 325°F.

6 Bake the buns until they are golden brown, about 8 minutes. Remove from the oven and set aside to cool on the sheet pan before serving. Serve warm or at room temperature.

Kalamata Tapenade Brioche Snails

Makes about 18 rolls

Instead of making boats or buns, here you take bread dough, roll it flat, add the filling, roll it up into a cylinder, and slice it crosswise. As with the other buns and boats, you could use challah dough (page 27) instead of the Light Brioche dough. I like to make one or two loaves of bread, then save some dough to stuff with pesto, roasted vegetables, or cheese—there is almost no limit to what works. In this version I fill the dough with a Kalamata olive tapenade, feta, Gouda, and oregano. Always taste your feta before adding salt because the tapenade and the halved olives will be salty already—you may not need to add any salt at all.

½ recipe Light Brioche dough (page 165), prepared through step 5	
All-purpose flour	for rolling and shaping
Kalamata Tapenade (page 328)	50 grams (¼ cup)
Feta cheese	55 grams (½ cup), crumbled
Pitted Kalamata olives	50 grams (¼ cup), halved
Young Gouda cheese	40 grams (⅓ cup), grated on the large-hole side of a box grater
Fresh oregano sprigs	4, leaves removed and reserved
Large egg	1
Water	1 tablespoon
Fine salt	Pinch

1 Set the brioche dough on a lightly floured work surface. Lightly flour the top of the dough, and then roll it into an 18-by-24-inch rectangle, about ⅛ inch thick, with a long side facing you. Spread the tapenade evenly over the dough, right to each edge. Sprinkle the feta, olives, Gouda, and oregano over the tapenade.

2 Roll the dough into a tight cylinder, pushing back on the dough after every roll to tighten the cylinder even more. Holding the cylinder by each end, lift and stretch it to tighten the cylinder even more. Then slice the cylinder crosswise into 1½-inch pieces (you should get about 18 pieces). Take the loose "tail" of each piece and tuck it over one of the exposed sides; then place the piece, with that side facing down, on a parchment paper–lined rimmed sheet pan. Repeat with the other pieces, then press down firmly on the center of each roll to make a depression (otherwise the roll will dome too much as it bakes and become cone-shaped). Cover them with a kitchen towel (see page 17 for other homemade proof box ideas), and set aside in a warm, draft-free spot until they have doubled in size, 30 to 40 minutes (this will depend on the warmth of your room).

3 Preheat the oven to 375°F.

(continued)

4 In a medium bowl, whisk the egg, water, and salt together to make an egg wash. Brush the tops and sides of the rolls with the egg wash. Bake until golden brown all over, 8 to 10 minutes. Remove the rolls from the oven and let them cool slightly before serving, or serve completely cooled.

Variations

Deconstructed "Pesto" Brioche Snails

Instead of using the olive tapenade and other filling ingredients, sprinkle the rolled-out brioche dough with grated Parmigiano-Reggiano cheese, untoasted pine nuts, minced garlic, extra-virgin olive oil, chopped fresh basil leaves, salt, and freshly ground black pepper. Roll up, slice, and bake as instructed.

Roasted Pepper and Goat Cheese Snails

Instead of using the olive tapenade and other filling ingredients, sprinkle the rolled-out brioche dough with sliced roasted red peppers, crumbled goat cheese, grated Parmigiano-Reggiano cheese, fresh thyme leaves, extra-virgin olive oil, salt, and freshly ground black pepper. Roll up, slice, and bake as instructed.

Mutabak

Makes 5 cheese mutabaks

There is a small shop in East Jerusalem's Christian quarter, tucked into a long corridor (it actually shares a wall—which was discovered to be the original main entrance—with the Church of the Holy Sepulchre, which contains the last four stations of the Via Dolorosa and is the site where many believe Jesus was crucified as well as the tomb where it is said he was buried and resurrected). This is where the Zalatimo family has been making a thin, crisp stuffed pastry called a mutabak (which means "folded" in Arabic) for more than a hundred years. The savory pastries are made one at a time, rolled to order, and filled by hand each and every time. The Zalatimos sell only two versions of the stuffed pastry: one with cheese and the other with walnuts. It comes out from the oven browned and crispy, folded like a square envelope—and it's so good that instead of calling it a mutabak, people just call it a Zalatimo.

After coming out of the oven, the stuffed pastry is brushed with a simple syrup that offers a lightly sweet counterpoint to the dough. Bite into the Zalatimo and you get layer upon layer of shattering dough that is wafer-thin and cushioned by crumbles of cheese. When I was traveling in Italy learning about focaccia, I tasted a very similar cheese-stuffed flatbread called focaccia formaggio—paper-thin, crisp, and filled with stracchino cheese instead of the drier cheese that the Zalatimo family uses. I never got the recipe for the Zalatimo (it's a closely guarded family secret), but I'm so enchanted by this ultra-crisp stuffed pocket (the dough is so thin that it rivals strudel dough) that I had to come up with my version; maybe one day it will just be known as a "Scheft"!

Note that the dough is refrigerated overnight before it is shaped and baked.

Cool room-temperature water	240 grams (1 cup)
Extra-virgin olive oil	15 grams (1 tablespoon), plus extra for the baking sheet and dough
Fine salt	10 grams (2 teaspoons)
All-purpose flour (sifted, 11.7%)	450 grams (3²/₃ cups), plus extra for kneading and shaping
Crumbly lean sheep's-milk cheese (such as a dry ricotta) or goat's-milk farmer's cheese	250 grams (8 ounces / 2¼ cups)

SIMPLE SYRUP

Granulated sugar	160 grams (¾ cup plus 1 tablespoon)
Water	120 grams (½ cup)

1 **Make the dough:** Place the water, olive oil, salt, and flour in the bowl of a stand mixer fitted with the dough hook. Set the mixer on low speed and mix, scraping the bottom and sides of the bowl as needed, until the dough forms a mass, 1 to 2 minutes. Increase the speed to medium and knead until the dough is smooth and not sticky, about 4 minutes longer.

2 **Divide the dough and shape it into rounds:** Place the dough on a lightly floured work surface and divide it into 5 equal pieces. Using your cupped hand, push and pull each piece on the work surface to shape it into a ball. Lightly grease the surface of each dough ball with oil, then wrap each ball of dough in plastic wrap and refrigerate them overnight or for up to 2 days (it is very important to chill the dough at least overnight; otherwise, it will not stretch paper-thin and will tear).

3 **Let the dough rest at room temperature:** Unwrap the dough balls and set them on a floured work surface. Cover them with a kitchen towel, and leave them until they are at room temperature, 1 to 2 hours (depending on how warm your kitchen is). It is very important for the dough to be at room temperature so it stretches easily.

4 **Meanwhile, make the simple syrup:** Combine the sugar and water in a small saucepan and bring to a boil over high heat. Reduce the heat to medium-low and simmer, stirring occasionally to dissolve the sugar. Turn off the heat and set aside the syrup to cool.

5 Set a pizza stone on the middle oven rack and preheat the oven to 450°F.

6 **Roll and stretch the dough:** Grease your work surface with a little olive oil. Dip your fingers into some oil and lightly grease 1 piece of dough, coating the top and bottom; then start to roll the dough with a rolling pin to form a flat round. Continue to roll the dough, adding oil when needed, until it is very, very thin. When the dough cannot be rolled any thinner, start to stretch it, pushing and pulling it by hand, stretching it in all directions and trying not to rip the dough until it gets to a large squarish shape, about 22 inches around (don't worry if you get a few small holes or rips). Cut away the thick edges.

7 **Fill the dough:** Add one-fifth of the cheese to the center of the dough. Fold the bottom of the dough up and over the middle, then fold the top and sides in to create a square. Take each corner of the square and fold it in toward the center (see photos on pages 228 and 229). Use a spatula to help you transfer the mutabak to the sheet pan (at this point you can bake the mutabak immediately or you can wait and bake them all together). Repeat with the remaining pieces of dough and the remaining cheese.

8 **Bake the dough:** Set the sheet pan on the hot pizza stone and bake until the mutabak is crisp and browned, 10 to 12 minutes. Remove from the oven, brush with the simple syrup, and serve immediately.

(continued)

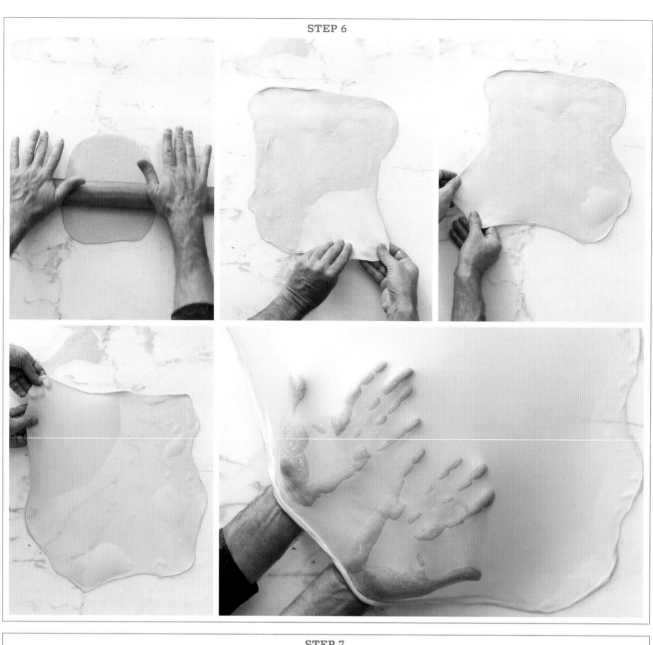

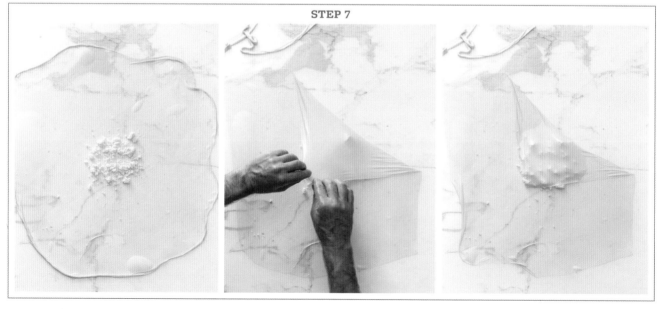

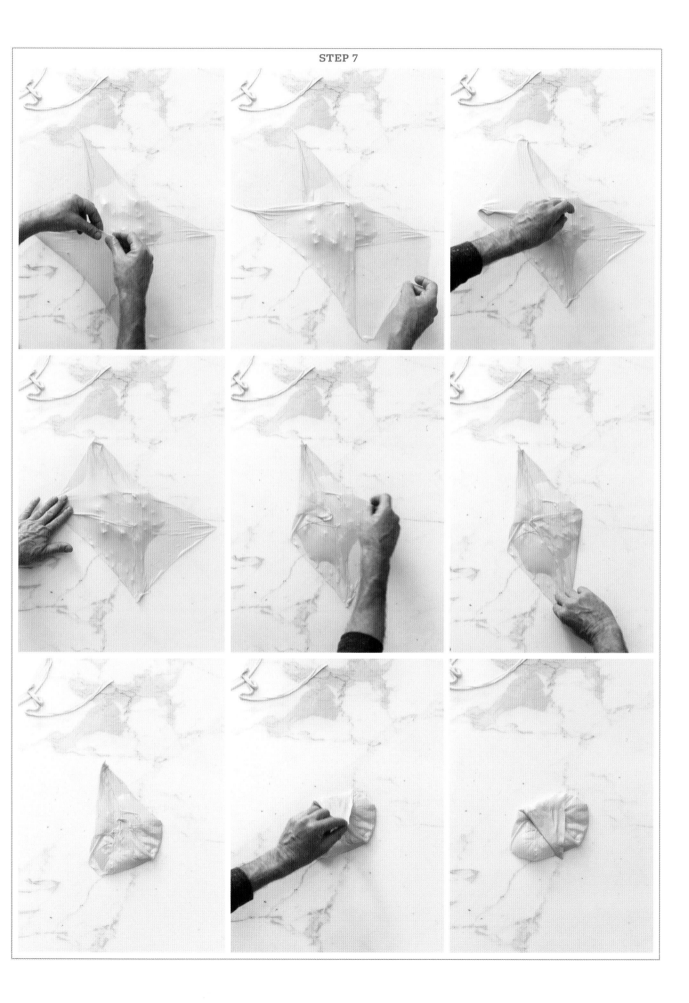

Cheese and Herb Mutabak

Fill each rolled-out round of dough with 55 grams (½ cup) of the cheese and about 15 grams (¼ cup) of mixed fresh herbs (such as chopped cilantro, parsley, and dill).

Cinnamon-Sugar Mutabak

Granulated sugar	100 grams (½ cup)
Ground cinnamon	3 grams (1 teaspoon)
Unsalted butter	75 grams (5 tablespoons)

Fill each rolled-out round of dough with 2 tablespoons of the cinnamon-sugar and 1 tablespoon of the butter (break the tablespoon into small bits). This version is also great fried in a pan.

Skillet Gozlome

This Turkish stuffed flatbread is almost like a quesadilla. I use the same dough as the mutabak and stretch one piece into a thin round, sprinkle the filling over the dough, and then fold the dough in half. The stuffed gozlome is cooked in a pan until browned on both sides, then sliced into small pieces.

Follow the instructions for making and chilling the mutabak dough.

Mix together 150 grams (about 2¼ cups) of finely chopped herbs (I like to use a combination of cilantro, dill, and parsley), 6 minced fresh mint leaves, 3 minced garlic cloves, 2 finely chopped large scallions, 1 seeded and minced jalapeño, the juice of 1 lemon, and 1 teaspoon of fine salt. In a separate bowl, mix together 115 grams (4 ounces) crumbled feta cheese (preferably a sheep's-milk feta), and 115 grams (4 ounces) grated Gouda cheese.

Divide the chilled dough into 6 pieces instead of 5 (as is done in the mutabak recipe). Use a rolling pin to roll each piece of dough into a 16- to 18-inch oval, and add some of the herb mixture and some of the cheese mixture to the bottom half of the oval, leaving a 1-inch border around the bottom. Fold the top over the bottom, use a knife to trim the edges, and then use your fist to pound and seal the edges together.

Heat a 12- or 14-inch skillet over medium heat. Add the gozlome to the skillet and cook until the first side is browned, 2 to 3 minutes. Carefully flip it over and cook on the other side until browned, 1 to 2 minutes. While the first gozlome is cooking, stretch the next piece of dough. Repeat with the remaining dough and filling. Slice the gozlome into pieces and serve hot. Makes six 6-inch gozlome.

Savory Potato Hamantaschen

Makes 24 to 30 hamantaschen

In Israel, of all the holiday-related pastries, cookies, breads, and cakes, my holiday hamantaschen are the best known (though my sufganiyot doughnuts, page 292, are not far behind!). Hamantaschen are triangle-shaped shortbread cookies filled with poppy seeds or apricot or other sweets; they are made for Purim (a Jewish holiday with elements of Halloween). I'm always looking for new ways to make hamantaschen, and this savory version is one result: pie dough is stuffed with savory fillings to make something that is close to a turnover like a bureka. Savory hamantaschen are excellent as little appetizers to serve at a cocktail party.

Be sure to roll the dough very thin and cut it into pieces that are just large enough to hold a generous amount of the goodies that go into the middle. The dough does need to rest for some time—ideally overnight—so plan ahead.

PIE DOUGH

All-purpose flour (sifted, 11.7%)	350 grams (1¾ cups), plus extra for dusting and shaping
Unsalted butter, (freezer chilled, not frozen)	250 grams (2 sticks)
Ice water	70 grams (¼ cup plus 2 teaspoons), plus another 2 teaspoons if needed
Granulated sugar	5 grams (¾ teaspoon)
Fine salt	5 grams (1 teaspoon)

POTATO FILLING

Yukon Gold potatoes	2, peeled and cut into ½-inch cubes
Fine salt	20 grams (4 teaspoons), plus a pinch
Fresh flat-leaf parsley leaves	15 grams (about 3 tablespoons), roughly chopped
Extra-virgin olive oil	5 grams (1 teaspoon)
Mayonnaise	20 grams (scant 1½ tablespoons)

EGG WASH AND TOPPING

Large egg	1
Water	1 tablespoon
Kosher salt	Pinch
Black sesame seeds	75 grams (½ cup)

1 **Make the pie dough:** Place the flour in the bowl of a stand mixer and chill it in the freezer for 20 minutes. Remove the bowl from the freezer and set it on your work surface. Sprinkle a little of the flour over the butter, and working quickly so the butter

doesn't warm up, cut the butter crosswise into very thin pieces. Sprinkle the pieces of butter with a little more of the cold flour and chop them very fine, until the butter looks like grated cheese. If the butter starts to warm up and soften, put it in a bowl and freeze it for 10 minutes before continuing.

2 Fill a small bowl with ice and water and stir for a few seconds to allow the water to get icy cold. Measure out ¼ cup plus 2 teaspoons of the ice water and pour it into a large bowl. Add the sugar and salt, and whisk until dissolved.

3 Use a bench scraper to transfer the butter and any bits of flour from the work surface to the mixer bowl containing the remaining flour. Set the bowl onto the stand mixer, attach the paddle, and cut the butter into the flour on medium-low speed until there aren't many pieces left that are larger than a small lentil, about 2 minutes.

4 With the mixer running, pour 3 tablespoons of the water mixture over the flour mixture, adding it around the edges of the bowl. Let the mixer run for 10 seconds, then stop the mixer and grab and squeeze the dough several times with your hands. Return to medium-low speed, add the remaining water around the edges of the bowl, and let the mixer run for a few seconds. The dough should start to come together but still be crumbly around the edges of the bowl (if it doesn't come together, add up to another 2 teaspoons of ice water). Stop the mixer and squeeze a small knob of dough in your hand. It should hold together. If it crumbles or feels dry, add a little more water, a small spoonful at a time, until the dough holds together without crumbling apart.

5 Transfer the dough (it will be crumbly) to a lightly floured work surface. Press and squeeze the dough into a mound, and then knead it 3 times. Press it into a ¾-inch-thick square and wrap it in plastic wrap. Refrigerate the dough for at least 30 minutes or up to 2 days (an overnight rest in the refrigerator is best for well-chilled and well-relaxed dough).

6 Make the filling: Bring a large pot of water to a boil over high heat. Add the potatoes and 10 grams (2 teaspoons) of the salt, and cook until the potatoes are just tender, 12 to 15 minutes. Drain the potatoes in a colander or fine-mesh sieve and set aside to cool completely. Place them in a large bowl and stir in the remaining 10 grams (2 teaspoons) salt, the parsley, olive oil, and mayonnaise.

7 Flour the work surface and set the dough on top; lightly dust the top of the dough with flour. Roll the dough to form a very thin square about ¹⁄₁₆ inch thick, dusting the top of the dough with flour and dusting beneath the dough as necessary to keep it from sticking to the work surface.

8 Use a 4-inch round cookie cutter to stamp out as many rounds as possible from the sheet of dough (you should get about 24). Gather the scraps, gently press them together (don't knead the dough—just press it so it holds together), and refrigerate for 20 minutes.

9 While the dough scraps are chilling, fill the rounds: In a small bowl, whisk the egg, water, and kosher salt together to make an egg wash. Pour the sesame seeds into a shallow dish. Brush the entire surface of each dough round with egg wash and then press the egg-washed side into the sesame seeds. Set the rounds, sesame-side down, on a parchment paper–lined rimmed sheet pan, and then brush them with more egg wash. Chill the rounds in the refrigerator for 20 minutes if they have become too soft to work with easily.

10 Set a small bowl of water on your work surface and use a pastry brush to lightly dab the outer edges of each hamantaschen round. Add 1 heaping tablespoon of the potato filling to the center of each round. Use your thumb and forefinger to pinch 2 edges of the dough together, and then pinch the other edges together to create the classic triangle-shaped hamantaschen (see photo, opposite). Place the filled hamantaschen in the refrigerator for at least 20 minutes (or up to overnight) to chill before baking.

11 Flour the work surface, place the dough scrap ball on top, flour the top, and roll it into a very thin square as before. Cut out as many rounds as possible, and repeat steps 9 and 10. Discard any remaining dough scraps.

12 Preheat the oven to 375°F.

13 Bake the hamantaschen until browned, 10 to 15 minutes. Remove from the oven and let them cool completely on the sheet pan before serving.

NOTE: IF YOU PLAN ON FREEZING PIE DOUGH to use in a month or two, add 2 or 3 drops of distilled white vinegar to the water-sugar-salt mixture before adding it to the flour-butter mixture. The vinegar in the dough preserves it and prevents it from getting speckled dark spots.

THE FLAKIEST PIE DOUGH

My method for making pie dough is unique. Instead of cutting butter into small cubes and adding them to the dry ingredients using a food processor, a stand mixer, a pie cutter, or even my fingers, I take sticks of freezer-chilled (but not frozen) butter, sprinkle the butter with flour, and slice it into thin leaves. I sprinkle the butter with more flour, slice it crosswise into thin pieces, and then chop it all quite fine, until it looks almost like shredded cheese. Cutting the butter into such fine pieces enables you to combine the butter with the flour mixture without risking overhandling the dough. You want to see thin butter streaks throughout the dough after it is rolled—in the oven, these streaks will melt and create a flaky pie dough that is nearly as delicate as puff pastry. In addition to cutting the butter small and thin and sprinkling it with flour so the pieces stay separate, the key to retaining the small butter specks is to work with the dough as quickly as possible so it doesn't get too warm. In the summertime when the house runs hot, I'll even put the bowl of sifted flour in the freezer along with the butter to chill it too. Use this pie dough for quiche, hamantaschen, and pie—it's very versatile.

Beet Hamantaschen

Makes about 24 to 30 hamantaschen

This savory hamantaschen with its beet and hazelnut filling makes a great salad (salatim) on its own—add a plate of hummus, some olives, maybe some pita or a bureka, and you have a great meal. At the bakeries, we buy peeled hazelnuts in bulk, but in most grocery stores it is more common to find unskinned hazelnuts. To easily remove the skin, roast the nuts at 350°F until they are fragrant and toasted, usually 6 to 8 minutes (use your timer—when nuts roast too long, they turn bitter and burnt very quickly and you'll have to start over), then rub them in a cloth while they are still warm. The skins will, for the most part, just flake away.

If you want a variety, use half the pie dough to make beet hammantaschen and the other half to make potato (page 234).

All-purpose flour	for rolling and shaping
1 recipe hamantaschen pie dough (page 234), prepared through step 5	
Large egg	1
Water	1 tablespoon
Kosher salt	Pinch
Black sesame seeds	75 grams (½ cup)
Roasted beets	255 grams (9 ounces; about 2 beets), chopped into ½-inch pieces
Toasted and skinned hazelnuts	30 grams (1 ounce), finely chopped
Garlic cloves	3, minced
Fresh cilantro leaves	1 bunch, finely chopped (about ½ cup)
Extra-virgin olive oil	10 grams (2 teaspoons)
Fine salt	¾ teaspoon
Freshly ground black pepper	½ teaspoon
Goat's- or sheep's-milk feta cheese	135 grams (heaping 1 cup), crumbled

1 Flour a work surface, set the dough on top, and lightly dust the top of the dough with flour. Roll the dough to form a very thin square about ¹⁄₁₆ inch thick, dusting the top of the dough with flour and dusting beneath the dough as necessary to keep it from sticking to the work surface.

2 Use a 4-inch round cookie cutter to stamp out as many rounds as possible from the sheet of dough (you should get about 24). Gather the scraps, gently press them together (don't knead the dough—just press it so it holds together), and refrigerate for 20 minutes.

3 **While the dough scraps are chilling, fill the rounds:** In a small bowl, whisk the egg, water, and kosher salt together to make an egg wash. Pour the sesame seeds into a shallow dish. Brush the entire surface of each dough round with egg wash and then

press the egg-washed side into the sesame seeds. Set the rounds, sesame-side down, on a parchment paper–lined rimmed sheet pan, and then brush them with more egg wash. Chill the rounds in the refrigerator for 20 minutes if they have become too soft to work with easily.

4 **Make the filling:** Place the beets, hazelnuts, garlic, cilantro, olive oil, salt, and pepper in a large bowl and toss to lightly combine. Add the feta and stir once or twice (you don't want the feta to color too much from the beets).

5 Set a small bowl of water on your work surface and use a pastry brush to lightly dab the outer edges of each hamantaschen round. Add 1 heaping tablespoon of the beet filling to the center of each round. Use your thumb and forefinger to pinch 2 edges of the dough together, and then pinch the other edges together to create the classic triangle-shaped hamantaschen (see photo on page 237). Place the filled hamantaschen in the refrigerator for at least 20 minutes (or up to overnight) to chill before baking.

6 Flour the work surface, place the dough scrap ball on top, flour the top, and roll it into a very thin square as before. Cut out as many rounds as possible, and repeat steps 3 and 5.

7 Preheat the oven to 375°F.

8 Bake the hamantaschen until browned, 12 to 15 minutes. Remove from the oven and let them cool completely on the sheet pan before serving.

Cheese Straws

Makes 20 cheese straws

These cheese straws are the ultimate snack. I am by no means the first baker to ever press grated cheese into puff pastry and twist it, but I do like to think that my cheese straws are the best. That's because I use a lot of cheese. *A lot.*

I am a huge cheese lover—that must be the Danish in me. When I moved back to Israel from Denmark as a young man—which was at a time before you could get good cheese in Israel—whenever someone was coming from Denmark to visit, I would say, "Bring coffee, bring licorice, bring cheese, and definitely don't forget the smoked fish!"

For baking you don't want to use strong, bold, well-aged cheeses. Because they are more mature, they have less moisture, which means they won't melt nicely in the oven. A young Gouda works well for this recipe. It has the right balance of sharp to sweet and it melts beautifully.

To load these sticks with cheese, press both sides of the puff pastry dough into the grated cheese so there isn't just cheese on the outside of the twist but trapped on the inside too. As the puff pastry bakes, the cheesy bits on the outside of the stick become golden and crisp, while the interior stays rich and mellow. In the bakeries we sell hundreds a day, baking some every hour or two so they're warm and fresh when people eat them. That's when cheese sticks are at their best—within a few hours of baking (not that they'll last any longer than that). For mini appetizer or hors d'oeuvre cheese straws, slice the unbaked straws crosswise into thirds after twisting them.

Large egg	1
Water	1 tablespoon
Kosher salt	Pinch
All-purpose flour	for rolling
Store-bought puff pastry (see page 208)	450 grams (1 pound), thawed if frozen
Young Gouda cheese	340 grams (12 ounces), grated on the large-hole side of a box grater

1 Line a rimmed sheet pan with parchment paper. In a small bowl, whisk the egg, water, and salt together to make an egg wash, and set it aside.

2 Lightly flour a work surface and set the puff pastry on top. Roll it to form a 15-by-10-inch rectangle with a long edge facing you, flouring the bottom and top of the dough as needed so it doesn't stick (don't overflour the pastry or it will toughen—you just want a light coating so it doesn't stick to the work surface).

3 Use a pastry brush to lightly coat the entire surface of the rectangle with the egg wash, and then sprinkle half the cheese evenly over the entire surface. Press lightly on the cheese with a rolling pin to smash the cheese into the dough (try to do this without further rolling or flattening the dough—you just want to get the cheese to stick).

4 Use the rolling pin to lift and flip the dough over. Egg-wash the second side, cover it with the remaining cheese, and press it in. Use a pizza wheel, chef's knife, or bench knife to divide the dough in half lengthwise so you have two 5-by-15-inch strips. Then slice each strip crosswise into 1½-inch-wide strips (you'll end up with 20 strips).

5 Hold the ends of a strip and twist it like the threads on a screw. Place the twisted strip on the prepared sheet pan, and repeat with the remaining dough. Cover with plastic wrap and refrigerate for at least 20 minutes or up to overnight.

6 Preheat the oven to 375°F.

7 Bake the cheese twists, rotating the sheet pan midway through, until they are golden brown and the cheese is nicely melted, 12 to 15 minutes total. Remove from the oven and let them cool on the sheet pan before serving.

NOTE: FREEZE SOME OR ALL OF THE UNBAKED cheese twists on the sheet pan. Once they are frozen, transfer them to a resealable freezer bag and freeze for up to 1 month. When you want to serve them, they can go directly from the freezer to the hot oven to bake (they may need a few extra minutes to brown). You can also cut them into thirds crosswise to make mini hors d'oeuvres-size twists.

SWEETS & COOKIES

WE ISRAELIS ARE VERY PARTICULAR about our coffee and tea, and enjoying a hot cup in the morning or midafternoon (or after dinner or anytime, really) is like pausing for a sacred ritual, whether it's for an espresso or macchiato, a Turkish coffee, or a nana tea made with bunches of mint and several spoonfuls of sugar. There is so much tension and stress in the region and in the everyday Israeli's life that allowing ourselves to take a moment for a coffee or tea is like giving ourselves a needed break, a moment to sit and catch up with a friend or discuss politics (which for us is relaxing and invigorating!). While dessert after dinner isn't always a guarantee, a cookie with your morning coffee or a krembo (page 299) in the afternoon is an inexpensive and easy burst of happiness. Israelis have a major sweet tooth and have no problem indulging it throughout the day.

The tradition of eating something sweet in the afternoon extends beyond Israel to many cultures—throughout the Middle East there is mint tea and nut-filled mamoul or dry cookies like barouj; in England tea cookies and scones are a favorite, as are a piece of strudel in Austria and a biscotti in Italy. In Israel, especially in the summer, when it can become unbearably hot, it was once quite customary for people to rest between two and four o'clock in the afternoon. Kids are expected to be quiet and respectful during this time. When you wake up, it's common to make coffee and have something sweet on the side, maybe a tahini cookie, maybe some rugelach.

This ritual of small sweet bites throughout the day was such a part of my experience as a child that even now when we serve a coffee or tea at the bakeries, it comes with a bite-size piece of cake on the saucer. I like to think of it as a sweet and unexpected treat to help lift your day. Aside from the strudel (page 283), the sweets in this chapter aren't necessarily "desserts" but are more what you might find Israelis snacking on in the early morning or afternoon (or evening for that matter—we don't discriminate). The assortment is wide and diverse, pulling from many influences, from Morocco to Lebanon, Denmark to Austria. Perhaps if there is one thing we can agree on in the Middle East, it is that sweet things lift the spirit and sweeten the day.

Chocolate Rugelach

Makes 48 rugelach

American rugelach are made with a flaky pastry dough that usually contains cream cheese, either instead of or in addition to butter. The dough is sprinkled with chopped chocolate and nuts or raisins and cinnamon, rolled into a log, and sliced crosswise into small pieces. My rugelach are more of a pastry than a cookie. I use babka dough rolled very thin, spread the dough with Nutella and bittersweet chocolate ganache, and then shape the rugelach into mini croissants. The key to the success of the rugelach is for the dough to be rolled extra-thin, and since the dough is yeasted (remember, you're using babka dough), it's important to refrigerate it whenever it starts to resist your rolling pin, which I guarantee will happen. A marble surface is excellent for rolling this pastry. You can get the effect of cool marble by placing a couple of bags of ice on the counter to chill it before rolling.

Heavy cream	140 grams (½ cup plus 1 tablespoon)
Bittersweet chocolate (at least 55% cacao)	120 grams (4 ounces), finely chopped
Dark brown sugar	60 grams (¼ cup plus 1 tablespoon, lightly packed)
Cocoa powder (sifted)	30 grams (2 tablespoons)
Unsalted butter (at room temperature)	30 grams (2 tablespoons)
Nutella	120 grams (½ cup)
1 recipe Basic Babka Dough (page 68), refrigerated for 24 hours	
All-purpose flour	for rolling

EGG WASH

Large egg	1
Water	1 tablespoon
Fine salt	Pinch

SIMPLE SYRUP

Granulated sugar	160 grams (¾ plus 1 tablespoon)
Water	120 grams (½ cup)

1 Bring the heavy cream to a simmer in a small saucepan. Place the chocolate and the dark brown sugar in a heat-safe bowl and pour the hot cream over it. Set aside for 5 minutes, then stir until smooth. Sift in the cocoa powder (yes, it is sifted twice), then stir in the butter until it's completely melted. Stir in the Nutella until the mixture is smooth, and set aside until it is cooled to room temperature (this is very important).

2 Set the dough on a lightly floured work surface and roll it, flouring the top as needed, into a rectangle that is about 8 by 22 inches with the short side facing you. Smear half the chocolate mixture over the bottom two-thirds of the dough. Fold the top third of the dough over the middle, then fold the bottom third of the dough over the middle (this is called a simple fold). Wrap the dough in plastic wrap and refrigerate it for 20 minutes.

3 Lightly flour the work surface and set the dough on top with the seam of the dough facing to the right. Repeat step 2, rolling the dough out to an 8-by-22-inch rectangle and spreading the remaining chocolate mixture over the bottom two-thirds. Fold the dough again into a simple fold. Wrap the dough and refrigerate it for 30 minutes.

> NOTE: IT IS VERY IMPORTANT TO CHILL THE filled dough for exactly the amount of time as directed. If the filled dough is chilled too long, when you go to roll the dough the filling will break and the rugelach will look tiger-striped.

4 Set the dough on a lightly floured work surface with the opening facing left. Lightly dust the top with flour, and roll the dough into a 15-by-28-inch rectangle with a long side facing you. When the dough resists rolling and bounces back (and it will), cover it with a kitchen towel and let it rest for 10 minutes (if resting longer than 10 minutes, place it in the refrigerator), then try again.

5 Divide the dough lengthwise into three 5-by-28-inch strips. Following the photo on page 251, make a small cut in the right edge of one of the strips of dough, about 1 inch from the bottom right corner of the strip. Then, starting at that notch, make another notch every 2½ inches. Repeat on the top left edge of the strip, making the first notch at 2½ inches and repeating in 2½-inch lengths all the way down. Place a dough cutter or a chef's knife in the first notch at the bottom right edge and angle the knife up to the next notch on the left

edge to make the first diagonal cut. Repeat in the other direction and continue, connecting the notches to create triangles.

6 Following the photo on page 251, make a small notch in the center of the wide base of each triangle. Hold a triangle in your hand and gently stretch to elongate it. Repeat with the remaining triangles, then roll the triangles up, starting at the wide base and ending at the narrow tip. Place the rugelach, with the pointy end tucked under the dough, on parchment paper–lined sheet pans. (You'll have enough rugelach to fill 2 to 3 sheets; you may need to bake the cookies in batches if you run out of sheet pans.)

7 Cover the sheet pans with kitchen towels (see page 17 for other homemade proof box ideas) and set them aside in a warm, draft-free spot to proof until they jiggle when the sheet pan is tapped, about 1½ hours.

8 Preheat the oven to 325°F.

9 Make the egg wash and brush each rugelach so the top is lightly coated. Bake the rugelach until they are nicely browned and cooked through, about 15 minutes (do this in batches if necessary), rotating the pan midway through baking.

10 **Meanwhile, make the simple syrup:** Combine the sugar and water in a saucepan and bring to a boil over high heat. Reduce the heat to medium-low and simmer, stirring occasionally to dissolve the sugar. Turn off the heat and set aside the syrup to cool. Transfer the rugelach to a wire rack set over a sheet of parchment paper, and brush the still-warm rugelach with the simple syrup. Serve warm or at room temperature. Store the rugelach in an airtight container for up to 5 days.

(continued)

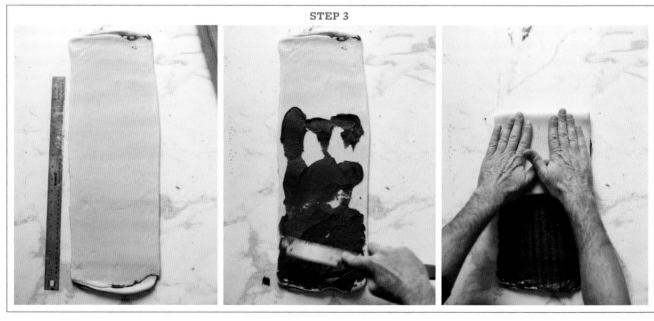

STEP 4

STEP 5

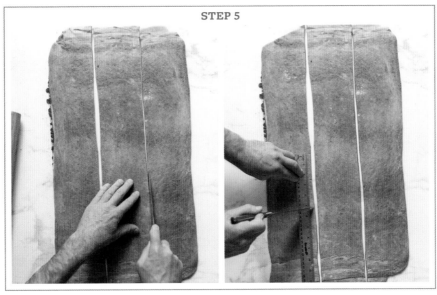

STEP 6

Pistachio and Marzipan Pull-Apart Rugelach

Makes 48 rugelach

Rugelach dough can be a canvas for any kind of filling, from chocolate (page 248) to the creamy, nutty sweetness of marzipan with little bits of chopped pistachio throughout. You can use other combinations, too, like finely chopped walnuts with currants, or raisins and cinnamon-sugar, or even a very simple filling of raspberry jam. This recipe shows another way to shape the rugelach, more similar to the American version, in which the dough is rolled into a log and sliced crosswise. Slice all the way through for separate cookies, or keep the slices attached at the bottom for a pull-apart rugelach.

RUGELACH

Best-quality marzipan (see page 338)	90 grams (3 ounces)
Granulated sugar	45 grams (scant ¼ cup)
Pistachio paste (optional)	30 grams (2 tablespoons)
Unsalted butter (at room temperature)	45 grams (3 tablespoons), cut into small pieces
½ recipe babka dough (either Basic, page 68, or Advanced, page 70), refrigerated overnight	
All-purpose flour	for rolling
Unsalted pistachios	100 grams (scant ¾ cup), finely ground
Chopped pistachios	for finishing

EGG WASH

Large egg	1
Water	1 tablespoon
Fine salt	Pinch

1 Place the marzipan and the sugar in a medium bowl and knead with your fingers until combined. Add the pistachio paste (if using) and the butter, 1 piece at a time, mixing by hand until the marzipan is creamy and smooth. Set it aside.

2 Set the dough on a lightly floured work surface and roll it, flouring the dough as needed to keep the rolling pin from sticking, to form a rectangle about 8 by 22 inches, with a long side facing you. Smear the marzipan all over the dough, leaving a ½-inch border at the bottom of the dough, and then sprinkle it with the ground pistachios. Use your hand or a rolling pin to lightly press the pistachios into the marzipan. Using your hands, roll the dough from the top down, pushing back on the roll after every turn to tighten the cylinder.

(continued)

BREAKING BREADS

254

Once it is completely rolled, hold one end in each hand and lift and stretch the cylinder to tighten it even more. Cut the cylinder in half crosswise and set each half on a parchment paper–lined sheet pan.

3 Make the egg wash: Whisk the egg, water, and salt together in a small bowl. Brush the top of each cylinder with egg wash, then slice the cylinders crosswise into 1-inch-thick pieces (you can slice completely through the cylinder for individual pieces, or three-quarters of the way through for an accordion effect; see photo on page 255). Sprinkle with the chopped pistachios. Cover with a kitchen towel (see page 17 for other homemade proof box ideas) and set aside in a warm, draft-free spot to proof until they jiggle when the baking sheet is tapped, about 1 hour.

4 Preheat the oven to 325°F.

5 Bake the rugelach until they are nicely browned and cooked through, 15 to 20 minutes, turning the sheet pan midway through baking. Transfer the cookies to a wire rack to cool. Serve them warm or at room temperature. Store the rugelach in an airtight container for up to 3 days.

Poppy Seed Hamantaschen

Makes 40 hamantaschen

In late winter around Purim time, hamantaschen floods every bakery and grocery store in Israel. But like with most things, homemade is always best. This recipe will let you make this old-fashioned cookie the right way, with a buttery and delicious shortbread-type dough and lots of goodies on the inside. It has become one of the most popular items we sell at Lehamim Bakery. When I bite into one, I want to taste the poppy seeds. This is why it's important to take your time and roll the dough very thin. After baking, the dough turns into a crisp, buttery shell to hold the filling. And this is what makes these cookies so special. Poppy seeds, though they seem dry, actually contain quite a bit of natural oil that comes out when we pulverize them into a paste. Then we cook the poppy seeds in milk, which makes the filling even more special. Because the seeds are rich, make sure to taste your poppy seeds before using them. They shouldn't taste off, sour, or bitter—if yours have been on a cupboard shelf for a long time, invest in a new batch before making the filling.

ALMOND SHORTBREAD

Unsalted butter (cold)	230 grams (2 sticks)
Confectioners' sugar	100 grams (scant 1 cup)
Granulated sugar	50 grams (¼ cup)
Large eggs	1½, beaten
All-purpose flour (sifted, 11.7%) or cake flour	400 grams (3 cups plus 2 tablespoons), plus extra for dusting and rolling
Almond flour	50 grams (½ cup)
Fine salt	5 grams (1 teaspoon)

POPPY SEED FILLING

Poppy seeds	220 grams (1⅔ cups)
Whole milk	315 grams (1⅓ cups)
Granulated sugar	110 grams (heaping ½ cup)
Lemon zest	grated from 1 lemon
Unsalted butter	45 grams (3 tablespoons)
Apricot jam	15 grams (1 tablespoon)
Cake or muffin crumbs (see page 106)	20 grams (¼ cup)

EGG WASH

Large egg	1
Water	1 tablespoon
Fine salt	Pinch

1 **Make the shortbread dough:** Set the butter on a piece of parchment paper and use a rolling pin to whack it—you want to soften the butter but keep it cold. Place the smashed butter, confectioners' sugar, and granulated sugar in the bowl of a stand mixer fitted with the paddle attachment, and mix on low speed until combined, about 30 seconds. Increase the speed to medium-low and beat for 30 seconds (you want the mixture to be well mixed but not airy—you don't want volume).

2 Add the beaten eggs and mix on low speed until just combined, stopping the mixer to scrape down the sides and bottom of the bowl as needed. Add the all-purpose flour, almond flour, and salt and mix just until almost combined. Turn off the mixer, remove the bowl from the mixer base, and use a plastic dough scraper to continue to fold and work the dough until it is of one consistency (finishing the dough by hand prevents overmixing and ensures that the shortbread will be very tender).

3 Transfer the dough to a large sheet of parchment paper and use plastic wrap or another sheet of parchment to press it into a 5-by-10-inch, ½-inch-thick rectangle. Leaving the plastic wrap (or parchment) on top, refrigerate the dough for 1 hour (the dough can be refrigerated for up to 5 days before using or frozen for up to 1 month).

4 **Make the poppy seed filling:** Pour the poppy seeds into a food processor and grind them until they are almost finely ground, stopping before they start to turn into a paste (or grind them in batches in a spice grinder or coffee mill). Pour the milk and sugar into a medium saucepan, set it over medium heat, and stir often until the sugar

dissolves, about 2 minutes; then stir in the ground poppy seeds, grated lemon zest, and butter. Reduce the heat to low and cook, stirring continuously (otherwise the poppy seeds could stick to the bottom of the pan and burn), until the mixture thickens and the poppy seeds have absorbed all of the milk and sugar mixture and it starts to bubble, about 5 minutes. Immediately remove the pan from the heat. Stir in the apricot jam and the cake crumbs, transfer the filling to a shallow bowl or baking dish, cover the surface directly with plastic wrap, and set it aside (or refrigerate) to cool completely.

5 Set the dough on a lightly floured work surface. Lightly flour the top, and roll the dough into an 18-inch square that is ⅛ inch thick. As you roll it, move the dough often, flouring the top and underside lightly so it doesn't stick to the work surface or rolling pin. If the dough becomes warm and starts to stick or become difficult to work with, slide it onto a sheet pan and refrigerate it until it becomes firm again—about 20 minutes should do it (if the dough is too thin to move easily, then cut out the circles in step 6, transfer them to the prepared baking sheet, and chill them before filling).

6 **Make the egg wash:** In a small bowl, whisk the egg, water, and salt together. Brush off the dough to remove any excess flour and then use a 3-inch round cookie cutter (or an upside-down glass) to stamp out as many rounds as possible, leaving as little space between them as possible so you don't end up with lots of scraps. Divide the rounds between 2 parchment paper–lined sheet pans, setting them about 1½ inches apart. Gather the scraps and lightly press them together into a ball (don't knead the dough—just firmly press it), flatten the ball,

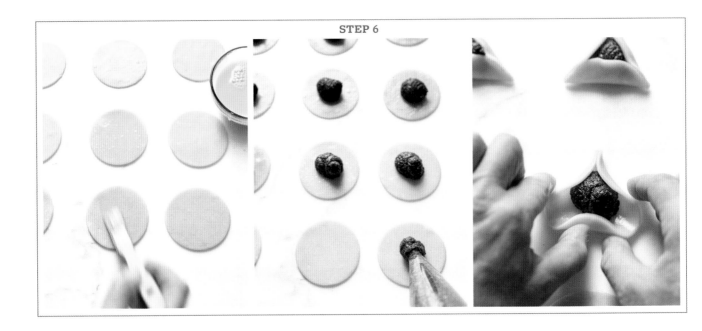

wrap it in plastic wrap, and set it aside in the refrigerator for 10 minutes. Use a pastry brush to brush the entire surface of each shortbread round with egg wash. Using a spoon or a piping bag, place 1 tablespoon of the poppy seed filling (about 15 grams) on the center of each round (don't put too much filling on the shortbread round or you won't be able to shape the hamantaschen). Be sparing with the filling for the first few as you get the hang of shaping the hamantaschen—if too much filling is used, the cookie can be difficult to shape. Follow the photo above to pinch the dough into the classic triangular hamantaschen shape around the filling.

7 Flour the work surface and roll out the ball of scraps. Repeat the stamping, filling, and shaping process, refrigerating the dough for

15 to 20 minutes if it becomes too sticky to work with. Discard any remaining dough scraps, add the shaped cookies to the others on the sheet pans, and refrigerate the hamantaschen for at least 30 minutes or overnight.

8 Adjust the oven racks to the upper-middle and lower-middle positions. Preheat the oven to 350°F.

9 Bake a sheet of hamantaschen on each oven rack for 6 minutes; then rotate the top sheet to the bottom rack and the bottom to the top rack and bake until the pastry is evenly browned, 5 to 6 minutes. Remove the sheet pans from the oven and set the cookies aside to cool. Store the hamantaschen in an airtight container for up to 3 days.

Apple Hamantaschen

Makes about 30 hamantaschen

When I was a beginner baker in Denmark, I begged my teacher at cooking school to find me a place to work in Paris, a place where I could learn to make croissants and brioche and chaussons aux pommes. He found me an opening at a patisserie that specialized in tarts and quiche, so I left Denmark to live in Paris for a few months—where, little did I know, I'd be shaping and crimping tart dough all day, every day, for hours and hours. I was not even making the dough—just shaping it! But my reward for this hard and repetitive work was that if I finished quickly enough, I'd get to roll croissants for an hour—not make the dough, just roll and shape the croissants. Even so, this opportunity was pure pleasure. I went on to work in other patisseries and shops in Paris, but this first experience has stayed with me, and when I was thinking of different filling ideas for hamantashen, I thought, why not apples? These cookies are like a handheld French apple tart. They bring me back to my youth and to the happiness and simplicity of doing one thing at a time and doing it really, really well.

Granny Smith apples	3, peeled, cored, and cut into ¼-inch cubes
Granulated sugar	90 grams (heaping ⅓ cup)
Lemon zest	grated from ½ lemon
Fresh lemon juice	45 grams (3 tablespoons)
Unsalted butter	45 grams (3 tablespoons)
Vanilla bean	½, split, seeds scraped out and reserved
Honey or apricot jam	30 grams (heaping tablespoon)
1 recipe Almond Shortbread dough (see page 258)	
All-purpose flour	for rolling the dough
Fine cake crumbs	40 grams (heaping ⅓ cup)

EGG WASH

Large egg	1
Water	1 tablespoon
Fine salt	Pinch

1 **Make the apple filling:** In a medium bowl, toss the apples with the sugar, lemon zest, and lemon juice. Melt the butter in a medium saucepan set over medium-high heat. Once it is light brown and nutty smelling, add the vanilla seeds (save the pod for another use) and the apple mixture. Increase the heat to high and cook, stirring often, until the apples just start to color, 2 to 3 minutes. Then stir in the honey and continue to cook until the juices are a deep mahogany color and the apples are tender (but not too soft), 6 to

7 minutes. Transfer the apples to a fine-mesh sieve set over a medium bowl and drain the apples, reserving the juices in the bowl. Transfer the drained apples to another bowl.

2 Pour the drained-off juices into a small saucepan and simmer until they have reduced by half and are thick. Stir this reduced syrup into the apples and refrigerate until completely cooled.

3 Set the shortbread dough on a lightly floured work surface. Lightly flour the top and roll the dough into an 18-inch square that is ⅛ inch thick. As you roll it, move the dough often, flouring the top and underside lightly so it doesn't stick to the work surface or rolling pin. If the dough becomes warm and starts to stick or become difficult to work with, slide it onto a sheet pan and refrigerate it until it becomes firm again—about 20 minutes should do it.

4 Make the egg wash: In a small bowl, whisk the egg, water, and salt together. Use a 3-inch round cookie cutter (or an upside-down glass) to stamp out as many rounds as possible, leaving as little space between the circles as possible so you don't end up with lots of scraps. Place the rounds on a parchment paper–lined sheet pan about 1½ inches apart and refrigerate for 10 minutes to chill them. Gather the scraps and lightly press them together into a ball (don't knead the dough—just firmly press it), flatten the ball, wrap in plastic wrap, and set it aside in the refrigerator for

10 minutes. Brush the surface of each chilled pastry round with egg wash and place a pinch of cake crumbs in the center. Spoon a scant tablespoon (don't overfill the pastry or you won't be able to shape the hamantaschen) of the apple filling onto the center of each round. Follow the photo on page 260 to pinch the dough into the classic triangular hamantaschen shape around the filling.

5 Flour the work surface and roll out the ball of scraps. Repeat the stamping, filling, and shaping process, refrigerating the dough for 15 to 20 minutes if it becomes too sticky to work with. Discard any remaining dough scraps, add the shaped cookies to the others on the sheet pan, and refrigerate the hamantaschen for at least 30 minutes or overnight.

6 Adjust the oven racks to the upper-middle and lower-middle positions. Preheat the oven to 350°F.

7 Use a pastry brush to lightly brush the sides of each hamantaschen with egg wash. Bake a sheet of hamantaschen on each oven rack for 8 minutes; then rotate the top sheet to the bottom rack and the bottom to the top rack and continue to bake until the pastry is evenly browned, 5 to 7 minutes. Remove the sheet pans from the oven and set the cookies aside to cool. Store the hamantaschen in an airtight container for up to 3 days.

Chocolate Chip and Vanilla Cream Hamantaschen

Makes about 40 hamantaschen

Pastry cream is the master cream of all pastry chefs and is used as a filling for tarts, cookies, doughnuts, and so many other baked goods. Be sure to let the cream cool completely before using it. The pastry cream can also be refrigerated for up to two days before you make the cookies; just give it a good whisking before mixing it with the chocolate chips. This hamantaschen and the apple-filled one (on page 261) are the most delicate of the hamantaschens and are best enjoyed within a day or two of baking.

Large egg yolks	120 grams (6 yolks)
Granulated sugar	125 grams ($2/3$ cup)
Cornstarch	45 grams ($1/3$ cup)
Whole milk	480 grams (2 cups)
Vanilla bean	1, split, seeds scraped out and reserved
1 recipe Almond Shortbread dough (page 258)	
All-purpose flour	for rolling the dough
Bittersweet chocolate chips	150 grams (1 cup)

EGG WASH

Large egg	1
Water	1 tablespoon
Fine salt	Pinch

1 Place the egg yolks in a heat-safe medium bowl, add the sugar, and whisk until well combined. Whisk in the cornstarch and set the bowl aside.

2 Whisk the milk and vanilla seeds together in a heavy-bottomed medium saucepan, and set it over medium heat. Cook, stirring occasionally, until the milk comes to a simmer. Whisk a drizzle of the hot milk mixture into the egg mixture—you want to warm the yolks gently so they don't curdle. Whisk in more milk, a little at a time, until

the bottom of the bowl is warm to the touch. Then pour all the egg yolk mixture into the saucepan and whisk well to combine. Set the saucepan over medium heat and cook, stirring, making sure that the pastry cream doesn't burn on the bottom of the pan, until the pastry cream is smooth, steam rises off the top, and one or two bubbles burst at the surface, 4 to 6 minutes. Pour the pastry cream into a medium bowl. Cover the cream with plastic wrap pressed directly against its surface and refrigerate until well chilled, at least 2 hours (it will keep for up to 2 days).

3 Set the shortbread dough on a lightly floured work surface. Lightly flour the top, and roll the dough into an 18-inch square that is ⅛ inch thick. As you roll it, move the dough often, flouring the top and underside lightly so it doesn't stick to the work surface or rolling pin. If the dough becomes warm and starts to stick or become difficult to work with (before it gets too large—otherwise it is tricky to move), slide it onto a sheet pan and refrigerate it until it becomes firm again—about 20 minutes should do it.

4 **Make the egg wash:** In a small bowl, whisk the egg, water, and salt together. Use a 3-inch round cookie cutter (or an upside-down glass) to stamp out as many rounds as possible, leaving as little space between the rounds as possible so you don't end up with lots of scraps. Place the rounds on a parchment paper–lined sheet pan about 1½ inches apart and refrigerate for 10 minutes to chill them. Gather the scraps and lightly press them together into a ball (don't knead the dough—just firmly press it), flatten the ball, wrap in plastic wrap, and set it aside in the refrigerator for 10 minutes. Lightly brush the surface of each chilled pastry round with egg wash. Using a spoon or a pastry bag,

place a mound of pastry cream (1½ to 2 tablespoons) on the center of each round. Press 5 chocolate chips into the mound of filling. Follow the photo on page 260 to pinch the dough into the classic triangular hamantaschen shape around the filling.

5 Flour the work surface and roll out the ball of scraps. Repeat the stamping, filling, and shaping process, refrigerating the dough if it becomes too sticky to work with. Add these hamantaschen to the others on the sheet pan. Discard any remaining dough scraps, and refrigerate the hamantaschen for at least 30 minutes to chill thoroughly.

6 Adjust the oven racks to the upper-middle and lower-middle positions. Preheat the oven to 350°F.

7 Use a pastry brush to lightly brush the sides of each hamantaschen with egg wash. Bake a sheet of hamantaschen on each oven rack for 8 minutes; then rotate the top sheet to the bottom rack and the bottom to the top rack and continue to bake until the pastry is evenly browned, 5 to 7 minutes. Remove the sheet pans from the oven and set the cookies aside to cool. Store the hamantaschen in an airtight container for up to 3 days.

MORE IDEAS FOR HAMANTASCHEN

While I agree that the classic fillings are delicious, it's fun to come up with new combinations and finishing techniques for the cookies. Here are a few ideas—see what others can you come up with.

- Combine apple filling (page 261) with poppy seed filling (page 258).
- Dip the baked and cooled hamantaschen in melted chocolate on one side or on just the bottom.
- Zigzag melted chocolate over the cookies.

Charoset Hamantaschen

Makes about 40 hamantaschen

Charoset is the chopped fruit and nut spread that is a part of the Passover Seder plate. It seemed natural to me to try the nut-filled charoset inside a hamantaschen. Ashkenazi charoset is made with apples and walnuts and honey, but the Sephardic version includes almonds, sesame seeds, dates, and spices. It makes such a good filling that this might become your new favorite hamantaschen.

Whole almonds (preferably with skin)	25 grams (¼ cup)
Sesame seeds	15 grams (2 tablespoons)
Water	3 tablespoons
Granulated sugar	15 grams (1 tablespoon)
Granny Smith apple	1, peeled, cored, and grated on the large-hole side of a box grater
Honey	20 grams (1 tablespoon)
Chopped walnuts	50 grams (½ cup)
Pitted Medjool dates	250 grams (8 ounces)
Ground cinnamon	½ teaspoon
Ground cardamom	¼ teaspoon
Ground cloves	¼ teaspoon
1 recipe Almond Shortbread dough (page 258)	
All-purpose flour	for rolling the dough

EGG WASH

Large egg	1
Water	1 tablespoon
Fine salt	Pinch

1 Place the almonds in a small or medium skillet set over medium heat and toast them, shaking the skillet often, until they are golden, 5 to 7 minutes. Transfer the almonds to a cutting board. Add the sesame seeds to the same skillet and toast them, shaking the skillet often, until they are golden brown, 3 to 4 minutes. Pour the sesame seeds into a bowl. Coarsely chop the almonds, add them to the sesame seeds, and set aside.

2 Pour the water into a large saucepan, stir in the sugar, and bring the mixture to a simmer over medium-high heat. Add the apple and honey and simmer, stirring occasionally, for 2 minutes. Add the walnuts, almonds, and sesame seeds and stir until well combined. Remove from the heat.

3 Place the dates in a medium bowl and add the apple mixture, cinnamon, cardamom, and cloves. Once the mixture is cool enough to handle, use your hands to mash it together until it is well combined. Cover the bowl with plastic wrap and refrigerate until chilled.

4 Set the shortbread dough on a lightly floured work surface. Lightly flour the top, and roll the dough into an 18-inch square that is ⅛ inch thick. As you roll it, move the dough often, flouring the top and underside lightly so it doesn't stick to the work surface or rolling pin. If at any time the dough becomes warm and starts to stick or become difficult to work with, slide it onto a sheet pan and refrigerate it until it becomes firm again—about 20 minutes should do it.

5 Make the egg wash: In a small bowl, whisk the egg, water, and salt together. Use a 3-inch round cookie cutter (or an upside-down glass) to stamp out as many rounds as possible, leaving as little space between the rounds as possible so you don't end up with lots of scraps. Place the rounds on a parchment paper–lined sheet pan about 1½ inches apart and refrigerate for 10 minutes to chill them. Gather the scraps and lightly press them together into a ball (don't knead the dough—just firmly press it), flatten the ball, wrap in plastic wrap, and set it aside in the refrigerator for 10 minutes.

Lightly brush the surface of each chilled pastry round with egg wash. Using a spoon or a piping bag (cut a large opening since the filling is chunky), place about 2 tablespoons of the charoset filling on the center of each round. Follow the photo on page 260 to pinch the dough into the classic triangular hamantaschen shape around the filling.

6 Flour the work surface and roll out the ball of scraps. Repeat the stamping, filling, and shaping process, refrigerating the dough for 15 to 20 minutes if it becomes too sticky to work with. Add these hamantaschen to the others on the sheet pan. Discard any remaining dough scraps, and refrigerate the hamantaschen for at least 30 minutes or overnight.

7 Adjust the oven racks to the upper-middle and lower-middle positions. Preheat the oven to 350°F.

8 Use a pastry brush to lightly brush the sides of each hamantaschen with egg wash. Bake a sheet of hamantaschen on each oven rack for 8 minutes; then rotate the top sheet to the bottom rack and the bottom to the top rack and continue to bake until the pastry is evenly browned, 5 to 7 minutes. Remove the sheet pans from the oven and set the cookies aside to cool. Store the hamantaschen in an airtight container for up to 3 days.

Napoleon Hats

Makes about 40 cookies

You will find Napoleonshatte, or "Napoleon hats," in every pastry shop in Denmark. It is a shortbread cookie filled with marzipan, egg white, and sugar. Some like to dip the bottom or the corners in melted chocolate, but I like to keep the almond flavor at the forefront. Instead of folding the pastry to make the hat shape, you could make this in a hamantaschen shape instead (see page 260). The almond filling can also be piped into a series of small-to-large rings that are baked on their own, and then stacked to form a kransekake ("ring cake"). The stacked cake rings are often drizzled with a white icing and served for holidays, weddings, and special occasions.

Marzipan (see page 338)	120 grams (4¼ ounces)
Granulated sugar	50 grams (¼ cup)
Large egg white	½ (about 14 grams)
1 recipe Almond Shortbread dough (page 258)	
All-purpose flour	for rolling the dough

EGG WASH

Large egg	1
Water	1 tablespoon
Fine salt	Pinch

1 Place the marzipan in a medium bowl. Add the sugar and combine with a spoon or your hands until the mixture is smooth. While continuing to mix, use a spoon to mix in the egg white a little at a time. You don't want to beat air into the mixture—you just want it to be creamy. Scrape the mixture into an airtight container and refrigerate it for at least 2 hours or overnight.

2 Shape the chilled marzipan into 40 generous 2 tablespoon–size balls.

3 Set the shortbread dough on a lightly floured work surface. Lightly flour the top, and roll the dough into an 18-inch square

sheet that is ⅛ inch thick. As you roll it, move the dough often, flouring the top and underside lightly so it doesn't stick to the work surface or rolling pin. If the dough becomes warm and starts to stick or become difficult to work with, slide it onto a sheet pan and refrigerate it until it becomes firm again—about 20 minutes should do it.

4 Use a 3-inch round cookie cutter (or an upside-down glass) to stamp out as many rounds as possible, leaving as little space between the rounds as possible so you don't end up with lots of scraps. Place the rounds on a parchment paper–lined sheet pan about 1½ inches apart. Gather the scraps and lightly press them together into a ball (don't knead

the dough—just firmly press it), flatten the ball, wrap in plastic wrap, and set it aside in the refrigerator for 10 minutes. Place a marzipan ball on the center of each round. Follow the photo on page 260 to pinch 3 sides together to make a hat.

5 Flour the work surface and roll out the ball of scraps. Repeat the stamping, filling, and shaping process, refrigerating the dough for 15 to 20 minutes if it becomes too sticky to work with. Add these hats to the others on the sheet pan. Discard any remaining dough scraps, and refrigerate the cookies.

6 Adjust the oven racks to the upper-middle and lower-middle positions. Preheat the oven to 375°F.

7 **Make the egg wash:** In a small bowl, whisk the egg, water, and salt together. Use a pastry brush to lightly brush the sides of each cookie with egg wash. Bake until the pastry is just set and not yet browning or turning golden, 6 to 7 minutes. Then remove the sheet pans from the oven and set the cookies aside to cool. Store the cookies in an airtight container for up to 5 days.

Variation

Tunisian Marzipan Flowers

In Tunisia there is another interpretation of the Danish marzipan kransekake. There bakers roll the marzipan into a ball and then create the most beautiful decorations on the surface using pistachios, almonds, and pine nuts. The cookies are kept as small one- or two-bite-size petit four–type sweets and are baked just until the marzipan and nuts are browned. See some examples on the opposite page for inspiration.

Rahat Lokum Crescents

Makes about 48 cookies

This is the kind of cookie you find only in home kitchens. It happens to be one of my friend Hanoch Bar Shalom's favorite cookies, and I developed this recipe just for him. The shortbread dough has a bit of baking powder as well as egg yolks and sour cream in it to make it very rich and tender, and it gets wrapped around a chewy piece of rose-flavored Turkish delight (see page 339), which is a little floral and a little sweet. The cookies are so delicate-tasting and beautiful . . . they are truly special.

Unsalted butter (cold)	100 grams (7 tablespoons)
All-purpose flour (sifted, 11.7%)	250 grams (2 cups), plus extra for dusting and rolling
Baking powder	½ teaspoon
Fine salt	½ teaspoon
Granulated sugar	25 grams (2 tablespoons)
Grapeseed oil or vegetable oil	25 grams (1 tablespoon plus 2 teaspoons)
Large egg yolks	2
Sour cream	100 grams (7 tablespoons)
Rose-flavored Turkish delight (rahat lokum)	225 grams (8 ounces)
Confectioners' sugar	15 grams (1 tablespoon)

1 Set the butter on a piece of parchment paper and use a rolling pin to whack it—you want to soften the butter but keep it cold. Sift the flour, baking powder, and salt together into a bowl, and set it aside.

2 Put the smashed butter and the granulated sugar in the bowl of a stand mixer fitted with the paddle attachment, and mix on low speed until combined, about 30 seconds. Increase the speed to medium and beat for another 30 seconds.

3 Add the oil and cream the mixture on medium speed until combined, stopping the mixer to scrape down the sides and bottom

of the bowl as needed. Add the egg yolks one at a time, mixing on medium speed until well combined and scraping the bowl as needed. Add the sour cream and the sifted flour mixture. Mix on medium speed until combined. Increase the speed to medium-high and beat for 5 seconds. Turn the mixer off.

4 Transfer the dough to a sheet of parchment paper and use plastic wrap or another sheet of parchment to press it into a 5-by-10-inch, ½-inch-thick rectangle. Leaving the plastic wrap (or parchment) on top, refrigerate the dough for 1 hour (the dough can be refrigerated for up to 2 days before using).

(continued)

5 While the dough chills, slice the Turkish delight into 48 strips. Place them in a medium bowl and toss with the confectioners' sugar so they don't stick to one another.

6 Use a bench knife or a chef's knife to divide the chilled dough in half. On a lightly floured work surface, roll one of the dough pieces to form a 6-by-16-inch rectangle that is very thin, about ⅛ inch thick, with a long side facing you. Cut the dough in half horizontally so you have two 3-by-16-inch strips.

7 Make a small notch in the bottom edge of one of the strips of dough, about 1 inch from the bottom right corner of the strip. Then, starting at that notch, make another notch every 2½ inches. Repeat on the top edge of the dough, making the first notch at 2½ inches and repeating in 2½-inch lengths all the way across. Place a dough cutter or a chef's knife in the first notch at the bottom right edge and angle the knife up to the right corner to make the first diagonal cut. Repeat in the other direction and continue, connecting the notches to create about 12 dough triangles.

8 Place a piece of Turkish delight in the bottom center of each triangle, pressing two strips together if needed so the Turkish delight is slightly longer than the widest part of the triangle (you may need to slice more Turkish delight), and roll the triangle up to form a crescent shape. Repeat with the other triangles. Set the cookies, seam down, on a parchment paper–lined rimmed sheet pan, about 1½ inches apart, and refrigerate for at least 30 minutes or overnight. Repeat with the other 3-by-16-inch strip of dough and the remaining Turkish delight, and then with the remaining piece of dough.

9 Adjust one oven rack to the upper-middle position and another rack to the lower-middle position. Preheat the oven to 350°F.

10 Bake the cookies, one sheet on each rack, for 7 minutes. Then rotate the top sheet to the bottom rack and bottom to the top and continue baking until they are golden, about 2 to 3 minutes more. Remove the sheet pans from the oven and let the cookies cool completely on the pans. Store the crescents in an airtight container for up to 5 days.

Tahini Cookies

Makes about 40 cookies

Tahini is like the Middle Eastern peanut butter—in this recipe, the sesame "butter" gives the cookie a very tender, melt-in-your-mouth quality. The ingredients are combined until the dough just holds together when squeezed in your palm, and then it is shaped into balls and baked. Roll them in sesame seeds for a deeply nutty taste.

All-purpose flour (11.7%)	280 grams (2¼ cups)
Baking powder	½ teaspoon
Fine salt	¼ teaspoon
Almond flour (preferably with skin)	70 grams (¾ cup)
Granulated sugar	75 grams (⅓ cup)
Unsalted butter (at cool room temperature)	75 grams (5 tablespoons)
Tahini sesame paste	100 grams (⅓ cup)
Honey	150 grams (scant ½ cup)
Vanilla extract	¼ teaspoon
White rum (optional)	5 grams (1 teaspoon)
Sesame seeds	40 grams (¼ cup), plus more if needed

1 Sift the all-purpose flour, baking powder, and salt together into the bowl of a stand mixer. Add the almond flour and sugar. Using the paddle attachment, mix on low speed to combine, about 15 seconds. Then add the butter, tahini, honey, and vanilla, and mix on medium-low speed until the mixture is pebbly, with no butter pieces larger than a small pea, 2 to 3 minutes. Add the rum, if using. Continue to mix just until the dough is combined and looks like streusel.

2 Pour the sesame seeds into a small bowl and set it aside.

3 Line 2 rimmed sheet pans with parchment paper. Adjust one oven rack to the upper-middle position and another to the lower-middle position, and preheat the oven to 325°F.

4 Using your hands, roll the dough into small balls, each about the size of a large marble (you should get about 40). Dip one side of a ball in the sesame seeds, place it on a prepared sheet pan, and then lightly press it with your finger to flatten it slightly. Repeat with the remaining balls.

5 Bake the cookies, turning the sheets and rotating them between top and bottom racks midway through, until they are firm to the touch and just barely golden, about 8 minutes. The cookies will seem soft and look like they need more time to bake, but this is exactly when you want to pull them out from the oven. Remove from the oven and let them cool completely on the pans.

Barouj Tea Cookies

Makes about 54 cookies

This is a simple Moroccan tea cookie, much like a biscotti, that is purposefully dry and just sweet enough, which means it is excellent served alongside a cup of strong Moroccan mint tea (a blend of black tea and fresh mint) or an espresso. The cookies are made with fennel seeds, apricot kernels, and whole blanched almonds. Bitter almonds are a traditional ingredient, but since they're prohibited in the United States, apricot kernels add a similar bitter-toasty almond flavor (if you can find bitter almond extract, you can add a splash of that, too). If you can't find apricot kernels, use an equal amount of whole almonds instead.

Sesame seeds	60 grams (heaping ¼ cup)
Fennel seeds	5 grams (2 teaspoons)
All-purpose flour	500 grams (4 cups)
Confectioners' sugar	300 grams (2⅓ cups)
Baking powder	7 grams (1¾ teaspoons)
Fine salt	½ teaspoon
Medium eggs	4, lightly beaten
Sunflower seed oil or vegetable oil	125 grams (½ cup)
Vanilla extract	1 teaspoon
Whole blanched almonds	50 grams (heaping ¼ cup)
Apricot kernels	50 grams (heaping ¼ cup)

1 Scatter the sesame seeds and fennel seeds in a small skillet and toast them over medium heat, shaking the skillet often, until they are lightly golden and fragrant, 2 to 3 minutes. Transfer the toasted seeds to a small plate and set aside.

2 Sift the flour, confectioners' sugar, baking powder, and salt into a medium bowl. Pour the eggs, oil, and vanilla into the bowl of a stand mixer fitted with the paddle attachment. Add the sifted flour mixture and the toasted seeds, and mix on low speed to combine. Add the almonds and the apricot kernels, and mix on low speed until combined, stopping the mixer occasionally

to scrape down the sides and bottom of the bowl (the dough will be very sticky).

3 Place half the dough on a piece of plastic wrap and roughly shape it into a 3-inch-wide log. Wrap it in plastic wrap and repeat with the other half of the dough. Refrigerate for 20 minutes (or up to 2 days).

4 Adjust one oven rack to the upper-middle position and another rack to the lower-middle position. Preheat the oven to 325°F.

5 On a lightly floured surface, roll one log into a 12-inch-long rope. Transfer the rope to a parchment paper–lined sheet pan (place

the rope diagonally on the sheet if it doesn't fit straight across). Pat the dough down so you have a ¾-inch-thick strip of dough. Repeat with the other log and a second sheet pan.

6 Place one sheet pan on the top rack and the other on the bottom rack. Bake for 15 minutes; then rotate the top sheet pan to the bottom rack and the bottom to the top. Continue to bake until the strips are golden and the edges are firm, about 10 minutes more. Remove the sheet pans from the oven and set the logs aside to cool slightly. Reduce the oven temperature to 275°F.

7 Once the logs are cool enough to handle, transfer them to a cutting board and using a bread knife, slice them on the diagonal into ¼-inch-thick pieces with a sawing motion. (Don't press down to slice—they will crumble; you have to use a sawing motion.) Set a wire rack on top of a sheet pan. Arrange the pieces, cut-side down, so they run against the grain of the rack (so the cookies don't fall through). Fill the rack with as many cookies as possible, and bake until they are very dry, 30 to 40 minutes. Repeat with any remaining cookies that didn't fit on the rack the first time. Let the cookies cool before serving, and store them in an airtight container for 1 to 2 weeks (depending on how humid your home is).

NOTE: USING A WIRE RACK TO DRY OUT cookies like barouj (or biscotti) is helpful— it means you don't have to flip the cookies over midway through baking. If you don't have a wire rack, simply place a few sheets of aluminum foil on the bottom rack of the oven (to catch crumbs) and arrange the cookies directly on the oven rack.

Date Mamoul

Makes 40 cookies

Mamoul is like the falafel of cookies, at home in Jewish kitchens and Muslim ones, served at Rosh Hashanah or Ramadan and sometimes even as an Easter sweet. It is a semolina cookie that is sometimes stuffed with a date paste or walnuts or pistachios. The dough surrounding the filling is shaped and pinched, or sometimes the cookie is pressed into a mold to decorate the surface with ridges and grooves. They can be domed or flat, and they keep very well for more than a week in an airtight container.

MAMOUL DOUGH

Hot water	90 grams (6 tablespoons)
Neutral oil (such as vegetable oil)	60 grams (¼ cup plus ½ tablespoon)
All-purpose flour (11.7%)	260 grams (2 cups plus 1 tablespoon), plus extra for shaping
Semolina	125 grams (¾ cup)
Granulated sugar	25 grams (2 tablespoons)
Baking powder	5 grams (1¼ teaspoons)
Vanilla bean	1, split, seeds scraped out and reserved
Neroli oil, rose water, or orange blossom water	¼ teaspoon
Fine salt	¼ teaspoon
Unsalted butter (at room temperature)	105 grams (7 tablespoons)

DATE FILLING

Pitted soft Medjool dates	300 grams (1¾ lightly packed cups)
Neutral oil (such as vegetable oil)	20 grams (1½ tablespoons), plus extra for your hands
Hot water	20 grams (1 tablespoon plus 2 teaspoons)
Ground cinnamon	½ teaspoon
Ground cardamom	¼ teaspoon
Walnuts	80 grams (heaping ¾ cup), chopped
Confectioners' sugar	for finishing

1 **Make the mamoul dough:** Pour the water and oil into the bowl of a stand mixer fitted with the paddle attachment. Add the flour, semolina, sugar, baking powder, vanilla seeds, neroli oil, and salt and mix on low speed until combined, about 30 seconds.

With the mixer on medium-low speed, begin to add the butter, 1 tablespoon at a time, waiting a few seconds before adding the next bit of butter. Continue to mix the dough until it is smooth and of one consistency.

(continued)

2 Transfer the dough to a large sheet of plastic wrap and press it into a rectangle about 1 inch thick. Wrap the dough well in the plastic wrap and refrigerate for 2 hours.

3 While the dough chills, make the date filling: Place the dates, oil, hot water, cinnamon, and cardamom in a medium saucepan and stir over medium-low heat until the mixture is sticky and jammy. Add the walnuts and stir to combine, then transfer the mixture to a bowl and set it aside to cool.

4 Pour a few tablespoons of oil into a small bowl and use it to lightly grease your hands. Scoop up a large-marble-size portion of the date mixture and roll it between your palms into a ball. Repeat; you should end up with about 35 date balls.

5 Unwrap the dough and place it on a lightly floured work surface. Divide the dough lengthwise into 4 equal strips, and then cut each strip crosswise into 10 equal squares (you should end up with 40 pieces of dough). Roll each square of dough between your palms to form a ball, and then flatten the ball into a thin disk. Place a date ball in the middle, and fold the edges of the dough around the date ball. Pinch the seams together to seal the ball, and roll again to make sure the date ball is nicely enclosed. Place the mamoul on a parchment paper–lined sheet pan. Repeat with the remaining pieces of dough. Refrigerate the mamoul for 30 minutes.

6 Adjust one oven rack to the upper-middle position and another rack to the lower-middle position. Preheat the oven to 325°F.

7 Use a fork or a dough crimper to create a pattern on each mamoul (dip in flour each time to prevent the fork or crimper from sticking; if the dough becomes too sticky, refrigerate the balls until they are once again easy to work with), or pinch the dough to create fluted, crimped ruffles. Divide the mamoul among 2 parchment paper–lined sheet pans and bake, turning the sheets and rotating them between the bottom and top racks midway through, until the bottoms of the cookies are golden and the tops are baked but not browned at all, about 10 minutes. Remove from the oven and let the cookies cool completely on the pans before dusting them with confectioners' sugar.

Apple Strudel

Makes four 12-inch strudels (750 grams / 1⅔ pounds of dough)

Part of my responsibility as a baker is to preserve the past with the sweets and breads that I bake. I approach these recipes with care and respect for tradition, and my goal is to create versions that are as delicious as our grandparents remember. One example is apple strudel. Strudel is such a big part of Israeli culture that even the "@" sign in an e-mail address is called the "strudel," referring to how a strudel is rolled into a cylinder before baking.

Here is the traditional way to make strudel using a hand-stretched flaky, delicate dough, the kind Austrian grandmothers have been making on their kitchen tables for centuries. What makes strudel so challenging and time-consuming is the dough. It must be chilled for at least 12 hours before stretching it very, very thin over the length of an entire table until it is transparent. Making it right requires patience and skill. It's critical to involve many hands in stretching the dough; it has to be done slowly and from multiple angles. This one recipe makes 4 strudels, enough for yourself and your strudel helpers!

DOUGH

Ice water	205 grams (¾ cup plus 2 tablespoons)
Large egg	1
Vegetable oil	50 grams (3 tablespoons plus 1 teaspoon), plus extra for coating the dough
All-purpose flour (11.7%)	450 grams (3⅔ cups), plus extra for dusting and rolling
Fine salt	½ teaspoon

APPLE FILLING

Large firm apples (such as Granny Smith or Spartan)	1½ kilos (3¼ pounds; about 10 apples)
Lemon zest	grated from 2 lemons
Ground cinnamon	5 grams (1 teaspoon)
Unsalted butter (melted)	150 grams (1¼ sticks)
Granulated sugar	200 grams (1 cup)
Fine cake crumbs, such as crumbled layer cake, muffins, biscuits, or cornbread	200 grams (7 ounces)
Raisins	120 grams (¾ cup)

Confectioners' sugar	for dusting

(continued)

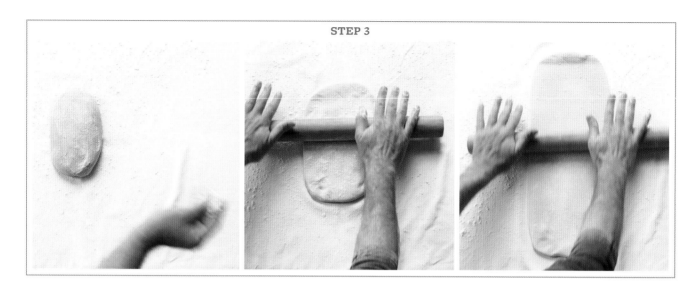

1 **Make the dough:** Fill a bowl with ice and water and stir for a few seconds to allow the water to get icy cold. Measure out 240 grams (¾ cup plus 2 tablespoons) of the ice water. Put the egg, oil, ice water, flour, and salt in the bowl of a stand mixer fitted with the dough hook. Mix on low speed, scraping down the sides and bottom of the bowl, until combined, 1 to 2 minutes. Increase the speed to medium-high and mix the dough until it is very soft and smooth, about 5 minutes. Use a dough scraper to transfer the dough to a lightly floured work surface. Form the dough into a ball and lightly coat it with oil. (Oiling the dough not only helps prevent it from sticking to the plastic wrap but also helps roll and stretch it.) Wrap the dough in plastic wrap and refrigerate for 12 to 48 hours.

2 Remove the dough from the refrigerator and let sit for 1 to 2 hours before rolling.

Meanwhile, prepare the apple filling: Peel, core, halve, and slice the apples very thin (preferably using a mandoline). Place the apples in a large bowl, and toss with the lemon zest and cinnamon. Set aside.

3 Flour a large tablecloth or sheet (one you don't mind getting dirty) and place it on a work surface (it should be as close as possible to 4 feet long by 2 feet wide) and set the dough on top. Flour the top of the dough and roll it with a rolling pin until it's about 18 inches long (don't worry about the width right now).

4 Line 2 rimmed sheet pans with parchment paper and preheat the oven to 425°F.

NOTE: GRAB A HELPER! FOUR HANDS ARE definitely easier than two when it comes to stretching strudel dough. Be sure to work with clipped and filed fingernails and take off any rings so nothing snags the dough and tears it.

FREEZING STRUDEL

Strudel can easily be frozen before baking. Freeze it on a parchment paper–lined sheet pan until firm, then wrap it in plastic wrap and aluminum foil. To defrost, remove the foil and plastic wrap and let the strudel sit out at room temperature.

(continued)

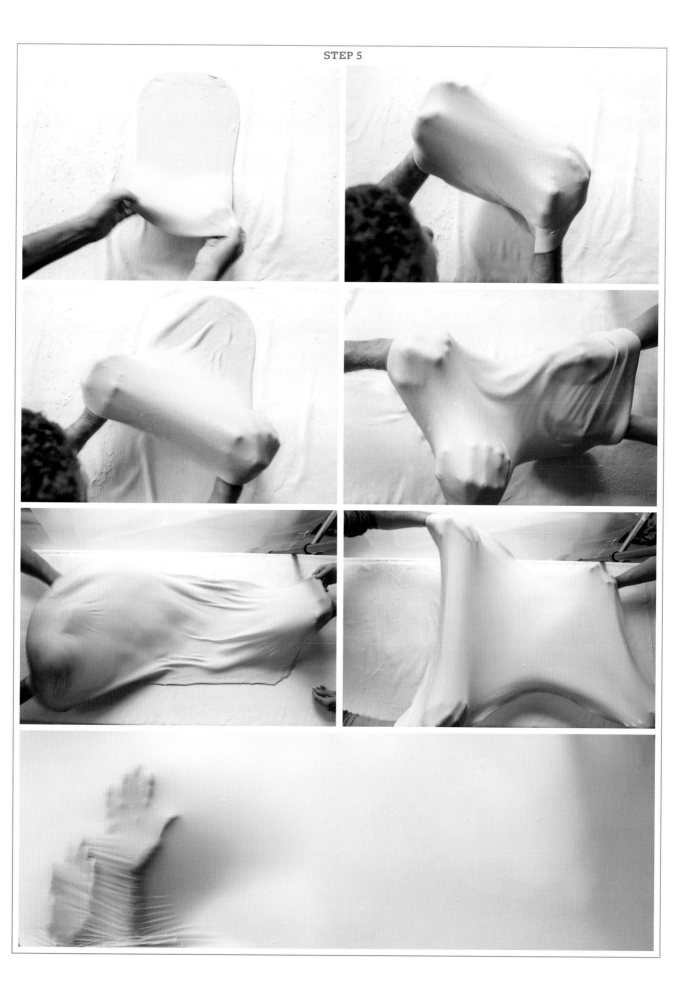

5 Stretch the dough: Use your fingers to start to stretch and pull the dough to one end of the table. Take care not to rip the dough. It helps to place your hands beneath the dough (see photos on page 285) and use your knuckles to stretch it out. The dough often thins at the center first, so make sure to pay attention to the edges and stretch the dough evenly from end to end. Once the stretched dough reaches one end of the table, hook it over the corners of the table to secure it and continue to pull and stretch the dough in the opposite direction until the dough is draped over all the edges and corners of the table.

6 Fill the strudel: Dip your fingers into the melted butter and spread/drizzle about ½ cup of the butter over the entire surface of the dough. Sprinkle the seasoned apples in a long strip along one long side of the dough; the apples should cover about a third of the width of the dough. Sprinkle the sugar over the dough and over the apples. Then sprinkle the cake crumbs and raisins over the apples. Use a paring knife to trim off any dough that is draped over the sides of the table.

7 Roll the strudel: Pick up the long side of the tablecloth that's under the apple strip, and use the cloth to lift and turn the dough over. Let the cloth fall back down, and use your hands to press and pull the apple-filled cylinder of dough toward you (see photos, opposite), pressing the apples into the dough so you have an even cylinder. Pick up the cloth and repeat, stopping to press the dough into an even cylinder and pull/press the apple portion toward you to create a tighter cylinder of dough with each turn. Once you are about halfway through the dough, just keep rolling until you get to the very end (use a paring knife to trim the excess dough). Use a sharp chef's knife to divide the strudel into 4 equal pieces. Carefully transfer the strudel sections to the prepared sheet pans (2 strudels on each sheet) and brush each one with melted butter to lightly coat the top and sides.

8 Bake the strudels until they are golden brown, about 10 minutes. Then reduce the oven temperature to 375°F and continue to bake until the strudels are evenly browned and the dough is crisp, 15 to 20 minutes longer. Cool completely before sprinkling each one with a generous amount of confectioners' sugar. Slice the strudels crosswise into 2-inch-wide pieces to serve. Rewarm leftovers in a warm oven for a few minutes to recrisp the dough before serving.

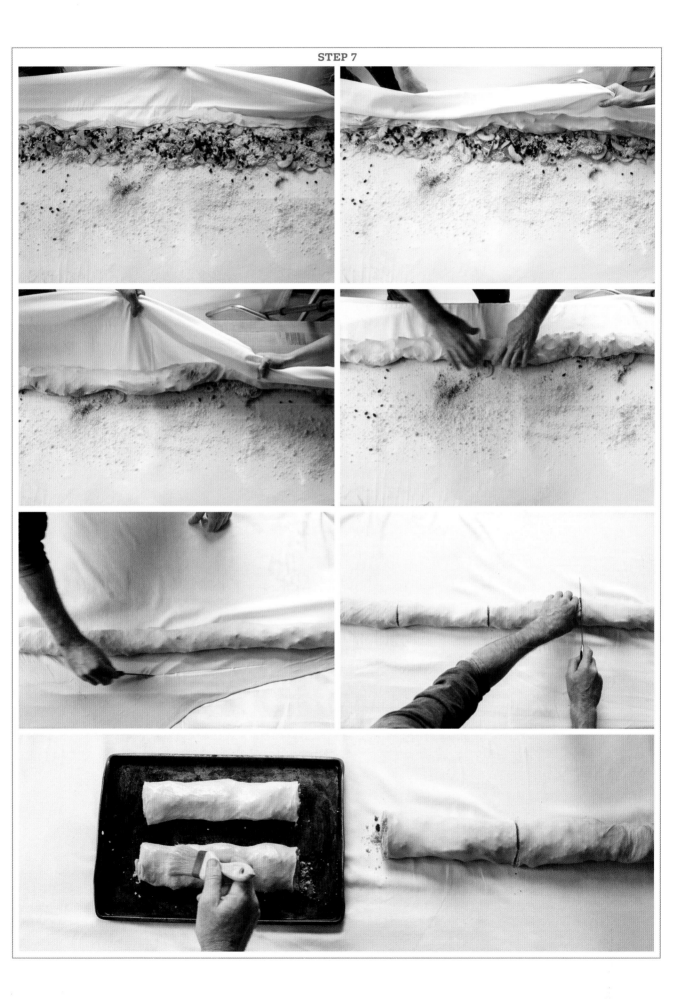

Moroccan Sfinge

Makes 18 to 20 doughnuts

Sfinge is an airy and very light doughnut made with a sticky, almost batter-like yeasted dough that fries up like an Italian zeppole. To make the doughnuts, use wet hands to simply pinch off a knob of the batter and gently stretch the bit of dough into a ring shape before dropping it into hot oil. In Morocco, vendors sell these in the street, suspended from a wire that hooks through the doughnut holes. They should be eaten warm, either coated in sugar or doused in honey syrup, soon after frying.

Cold water	450 grams (scant 2 cups)
Fresh yeast or active dry yeast	15 grams (2 tablespoons) 5 grams (1 teaspoon)
Cake flour (sifted)	650 grams (5¼ cups)
Granulated sugar	20 grams (1 tablespoon plus 1 teaspoon)
Fine salt	5 grams (1 teaspoon)
Vegetable oil	about 1 liter (4½ cups) or as needed for frying
Granulated sugar or Honey Simple Syrup (recipe follows)	for finishing the doughnuts

1 Pour the water into the bowl of a stand mixer fitted with the dough hook. Crumble the yeast into the water and use your fingers to rub and dissolve it; if using active dry yeast, whisk the yeast into the water. Add the flour, sugar, and salt, and mix on low speed until the ingredients come together, about 30 seconds (the mixture will be very loose, sticky, and runny and not like a traditional dough). Grease a large bowl with a drop of oil, and use a plastic dough scraper to transfer the very sticky and loose batter to the oiled bowl. Cover the bowl with plastic wrap and set it aside at room temperature for 30 minutes (the batter should just about double in volume).

2 Remove the plastic wrap, wet your hands, and flop one side of the batter over on top of itself. The batter is very loose and sticky,

so just do the best you can (wet hands help prevent sticking). Give the bowl a quarter turn and flop the next side over. Repeat until all 4 sides of the batter have been folded over; then repeat 3 more times so you have folded each quarter of the batter over 4 times. Cover the bowl with plastic wrap and set it aside at room temperature for 30 minutes.

3 Heat the oil in a medium or large saucepan over high heat until it reaches 350°F on an instant-read thermometer. Reduce the heat to medium. Set the bowl of batter to one side of the saucepan and place a paper towel–lined sheet pan on the other side. Place a bowl with cool water next to the batter.

4 Fill a medium bowl with water. Dip your hands in and then break off a fistful of the

batter, and force your thumb through the center of the mass. It may seem awkward because the dough is so soft and sticky but this is a key characteristic of the spongy sfinge. Gently use both hands to pull the dough into a rough doughnut shape (again, the dough is very sticky and loose, so this needs to be done quickly and without too much thought). Carefully place the doughnut in the hot oil—it should not look perfect! Repeat with 1 or 2 more doughnuts—don't overcrowd the pan, or the doughnuts will stick together. Use a soup spoon to baste the top of the doughnuts with hot oil—this helps them puff up as the first side fries.

5 Fry the doughnuts until they are golden brown on both sides, using a slotted spoon or frying spider to turn them often so both sides cook evenly. Once both sides are golden brown, after just 2 to 3 minutes, transfer the doughnuts to the prepared sheet pan and repeat with more batter.

6 While the next batch fries, roll the still-warm doughnuts in granulated sugar or brush them with honey simple syrup. Serve warm or within 1 hour of frying.

Honey Simple Syrup

Combine 200 grams (1 cup) sugar and 240 grams (1 cup) water in a medium saucepan, and bring to a simmer. Add a few spoonfuls of honey (2 to 3 tablespoons is a good amount—you can always add more) and stir until dissolved. Remove from the heat and let the syrup cool before using.

Sufganiyot

Makes 25 sufganiyot

Talk about anticipation! People in Israel and New York City go crazy for the bakeries' debut of sufganiyot; they'll wait in long, winding lines outside the stores to get a half dozen of these yeasty, airy fried doughnuts that are a special Chanukkah treat. While doughnuts are a common morning food year-round in the United States, in Israel they are typically sold only for Chanukkah, to celebrate the miracle of the eight days of light. Unlike traditional doughnuts, sufganiyot do not have a hole in the center. They are more like a Boston cream doughnut or a bomboloni, filled from the top with strawberry jam, chocolate, vanilla cream, or other variations like dulce de leche. I make sure to fill the doughnuts with lots of jam or cream—the goal is to have a little filling with every bite of dough (when there is just a dot of filling, you feel so cheated!). Try making these with your children. You can roll the dough and let them use an upside-down glass to stamp out the rounds; then watch their eyes light up in wonder as you fry them in a pot of oil.

Fresh yeast	30 grams (¼ cup)
or active dry yeast	12 grams (2¼ teaspoons)
Warm water	30 grams (2 tablespoons)
All-purpose flour (sifted, 11.7%)	500 grams (4 cups), plus extra for kneading and rolling
Granulated sugar	65 grams (¼ cup plus 1 tablespoon)
Large egg yolks	2
Large egg	1
Warm whole milk	120 grams (½ cup)
Grated orange zest	Pinch
Fresh orange juice	30 grams (2 tablespoons)
Brandy (optional)	15 grams (1 tablespoon)
Fine salt	½ teaspoon
Vanilla extract	½ teaspoon
Unsalted butter (at room temperature)	90 grams (6 tablespoons)
Vegetable oil	about 1.8 liters (8 cups) or as needed for frying
Strawberry jam	490 grams (1½ cups)
Confectioners' sugar	for finishing

1 **Make the dough:** In the bowl of a stand mixer, use your fingers to dissolve the yeast into the warm water. Stir in 10 grams (1 tablespoon) of the flour and 5 grams (1 tablespoon) of the sugar, and set aside until the mixture is bubbling, about 15 minutes.

2 Add the egg yolks, whole egg, warm milk, orange zest and juice, brandy (if using), salt,

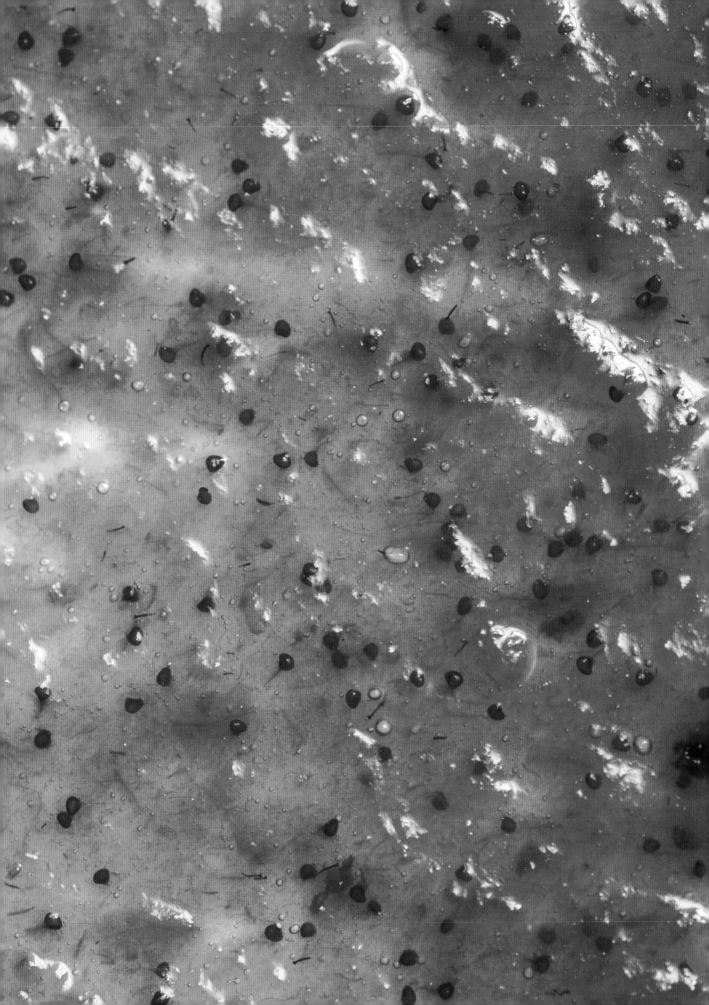

vanilla, the remaining sugar, and the flour to the yeast mixture. Attach the dough hook and mix on low speed until the dough comes together, 1 to 2 minutes.

3 With the mixer running on medium speed, gradually add the butter, a pinch at a time. Continue to mix until the dough pulls away from the sides of the bowl (add a few spoons of flour if needed), is smooth and shiny, and is beginning to climb up the dough hook. This will take about 4 minutes.

4 **Stretch and fold the dough, then let it rise:** Turn the dough out onto a lightly floured work surface and lightly dust the top of the dough with flour. Stretch the top piece of the dough until it tears, then fold it on top of the center. Give the dough a quarter turn and repeat, tearing and folding, adding more flour as needed, until the dough isn't sticky, 2 to 3 minutes. Transfer the dough to a lightly floured bowl, sprinkle the top with flour, and cover the bowl with plastic wrap. Set it aside in a warm and draft-free spot until the dough has doubled in volume, about 1 hour.

5 **Roll and stamp the dough:** Set the dough on a lightly floured work surface, and use a rolling pin to roll it into a ½-inch-thick sheet. Use a 2½-inch round cookie or biscuit cutter to stamp out rounds of dough. Stamp them out as close together as possible to minimize the amount of scraps; after pressing the cutter into the dough, twist it before pulling it out from the sheet of dough (to help strengthen the seal so the doughnut puffs nicely during frying). Gather the scraps;

press them together; rest for 5 minutes, covered; and then gently reroll them to stamp out a few more sufganiyot. Discard the remaining bits of scraps.

6 **Let the dough proof:** Place the dough rounds on a lightly greased (use a little oil) parchment paper–lined sheet pan and cover with a kitchen towel. Let the dough rise in a draft-free spot at room temperature until nearly doubled in volume, 40 to 50 minutes. (At this point, after rising, the dough can be refrigerated for up to 3 hours before frying.)

7 **Fry the dough:** Fill a large saucepan with enough oil to reach a depth of 4 inches. Heat the oil over medium-high heat until it reads 350°F on an instant-read thermometer. Start with one sufganiya and fry, turning it with a slotted spoon or frying spider, until both sides are golden, about 2 minutes. Use the spider or slotted spoon to transfer the doughnut to a paper towel–lined plate or sheet pan. Continue frying the remaining doughnuts in batches, taking care not to crowd the pan; otherwise, the oil will cool and the doughnuts will absorb more oil and become greasy. Let the doughnuts cool completely before filling them.

8 **Fill the sufganiyot:** Place the jam in a food processor and process until smooth. Scrape the jam into a piping bag fitted with a ¼-inch round tip and insert the tip into the top of a doughnut. Squeeze jam into the doughnut until the jam begins to ooze out of the hole at the top. Repeat with the remaining sufganiyot. Sprinkle with confectioners' sugar before serving.

Coconut Macaroons

Makes 48 macaroons

Flour-free and Passover-friendly, these macaroons are my favorite of all time. They are delicious on their own, or can be used as the base for the chocolate-dipped meringue-topped krembos, opposite.

Large egg whites	4 (120 grams / about ½ cup)
Granulated sugar	230 grams (1 cup plus 2 tablespoons)
Desiccated unsweetened coconut	210 grams (2½ packed cups)
Apricot jam	30 grams (2 tablespoons)

1 Pour enough water into a medium saucepan to reach a depth of 2 inches and bring it to a simmer over medium heat. In a heat-safe medium bowl, whisk the egg whites and the sugar together. Reduce the heat under the saucepan to low and set the bowl of egg whites on top. Heat the egg whites, whisking continuously, until the sugar is dissolved.

2 Remove the bowl from the saucepan and stir in the coconut and apricot jam. Cover the mixture directly with plastic wrap and refrigerate for 30 minutes.

3 Adjust one oven rack to the upper-middle position and another to the lower-middle position. Preheat the oven to 450°F.

4 Line 2 rimmed sheet pans with parchment paper. Take a scant 1 tablespoon of the coconut mixture (about 11 to 12 grams) and shape it into a small ball. Place the ball on the sheet pan and flatten it out as even as possible (wet your fingers to keep the mixture from sticking). Repeat until the sheet pan is full; then repeat the process with the remaining dough on the other prepared sheet pan. If there are a lot of cracks around the edges of the macaroons, use a wet finger to patch and smooth the edges.

5 Bake the macaroons, rotating the sheets between the top and bottom racks midway through baking, until they are golden brown, 4 to 6 minutes total. Remove the pans from the oven, and let the macaroons cool completely on the sheets. Then serve them or store them in an airtight container for up to 3 days. (The macaroons can also be frozen on the sheet pans and then transferred to a resealable plastic freezer bag and frozen for up to 1 month.)

Chocolate-Dipped Vanilla Krembos

Makes 48 krembos

How do you eat a krembo? From the top? All at once? Or the cookie at the bottom first? A variation of an English Whippet, a Mallomar, or a Danish flødeboller (which is the origin of the krembo—the Hebrew translation means "cream here"), the krembo is a mounded, chocolate-covered marshmallowy treat available in Israel throughout the winter (because in the summer they would just melt). Krembos are a bit of a national obsession; they're often sold alongside gum and candy bars in convenience stores. In my homemade version, I use a chewy coconut macaroon as the base, flavor the whipped Italian meringue topping with vanilla, and dip the whole thing in chocolate. Glucose keeps the meringue stable, so you can refrigerate the cookies for a few days (glucose is available online or in cake or specialty baking stores). Another way to enjoy the krembo is smashed over ice cream, which is how I used to eat it as a child in Denmark.

1 recipe Coconut Macaroons (opposite), baked and cooled

Large egg whites	5 (150 grams / about ½ cup plus 1 tablespoon)
Granulated sugar	260 grams (1⅓ cups)
Water	75 grams (¼ cup plus 1 tablespoon)
Glucose	120 grams (¼ cup plus 1 tablespoon)
Fine salt	Pinch
Vanilla beans	1½, split, seeds scraped out and reserved
Bittersweet chocolate (70% cacao)	750 grams (1⅔ pounds), finely chopped
Sunflower seed oil or grapeseed oil	45 grams (3 tablespoons)
Block of white chocolate	shaved with a chef's knife or vegetable peeler, for finishing the krembos

1 Place the macaroons in the freezer while you make the meringue topping.

2 Place the egg whites in the very clean bowl of a stand mixer fitted with the whisk attachment. Combine the sugar, water, glucose, and salt in a medium saucepan and set it over medium heat. Place an instant-read thermometer in the glucose mixture and once it reads 220°F, begin to whip the egg whites in the mixer until you get medium peaks. Once the syrup reaches 243°F, keep the egg whites whipping while you slowly pour the hot syrup down the side of the bowl and into the beating whites. Once all of the syrup is added, increase the mixer speed to high and beat the meringue until it is glossy and stiff and the outside of the bowl isn't warm to the touch. Add the vanilla seeds and whip until combined.

(continued)

3 Remove the macaroons from the freezer and arrange them on a large sheet of parchment paper. Add the meringue to a pastry bag fitted with a 1-inch tube tip. Pipe the meringue on top of the macaroons as shown on page 303, so it stands tall. The width at the bottom of the meringue should be nearly the same width as the macaroon. Place the sheet pan in the refrigerator for 30 minutes to chill the meringue.

4 Place the bittersweet chocolate in a microwave-safe bowl and microwave on high power, stirring every 20 seconds, until all the chocolate is melted. Stir in the oil and mix until combined. Transfer the mixture to a tall, narrow container.

5 Holding a macaroon by the base, dip it upside down (meringue going in first) into the melted chocolate. Remove it slowly, turn it right side up, and place it on the parchment. Dip a few more cookies and then sprinkle them quickly with shaved white chocolate before the shell hardens. Repeat with the remaining macaroons and meringue. Serve immediately or refrigerate in an airtight container for up to 3 days before serving.

Variations

Raspberry Krembos

Fold 135 grams (4½ ounces) of crumbled freeze-dried raspberries into the meringue along with the vanilla seeds. Substitute white chocolate for the bittersweet chocolate, and finish the krembos with more crumbled dehydrated raspberries and some optional chopped unsalted pistachios.

Mocha Krembos

Use a rolling pin, heavy skillet, or the blunt end of a wooden spoon to crush 10 coffee beans until they are very fine. Fold the coffee beans into the meringue along with 90 grams (3 ounces) of finely chopped bittersweet chocolate. Substitute milk chocolate for the bittersweet chocolate for dipping, and finish the krembos with more crushed coffee beans and shaved milk chocolate.

Parmesan Cookies

Makes 96 cookies

Parmesan cookies are essentially a cheese shortbread; they are a crisp, thin, savory cookie—delicious plain or when used like a crostini and topped with a little goat cheese or tapenade. Or you can sandwich two cookies together for a crisp one-bite sandwich. The trick to their melt-in-your-mouth deliciousness is that they have a higher ratio of butter, cheddar cheese, and Parmigiano-Reggiano cheese to flour than usual. After shaping the cookie dough into logs, you can slice and bake them all, or freeze a log for another time. Nigella seeds add a wonderful oniony flavor and nice color contrast to the edges of the cookies; if you don't have any, use poppy seeds instead.

Pastry or cake flour (8.5 to 9%)	180 grams (1¾ cups)
Baking powder	3 grams (¾ teaspoon)
Unsalted butter (at cool room temperature)	180 grams (1½ sticks)
Young Gouda cheese	80 grams (2¾ ounces), grated on the large-hole side of a box grater (⅔ cup)
Parmigiano-Reggiano cheese	80 grams (2¾ ounces), finely grated (¾ cup plus 1 tablespoon)
Large egg	1
Fine salt	½ teaspoon
Freshly ground black pepper	3 grams (1½ teaspoons)
Sesame seeds	75 grams (½ cup)
Nigella seeds	40 grams (¼ cup)

1 Sift the flour and the baking powder together into a bowl and set it aside. Place the butter in the bowl of a stand mixer fitted with the paddle attachment and beat it on low speed until it is soft and smooth, about 1 minute. Add the Gouda and Parmigiano-Reggiano cheeses and mix on medium speed, scraping down the sides and bottom of the bowl as needed, until combined.

2 Add the egg, flour mixture, salt, and black pepper, and combine the mixture on medium-low speed, scraping down the sides and bottom of the bowl as needed, until well mixed, about 1 minute.

3 Set half the dough on a large sheet of parchment paper and use the parchment to roll it into a 9-inch-long cylinder that is about 1 inch wide. Repeat with the remaining dough on another sheet of parchment. Wrap and refrigerate both dough logs until they are well chilled, at least 20 minutes or up to 3 days. (Or freeze the logs—or one of the logs—then wrap them in aluminum foil, place in a plastic freezer bag, and freeze for up to 3 months. Wait to slice the cookies until just before baking—they need to be sliced fairly thin, and if frozen as sliced disks, they could crack or break in the freezer. Freezing the log as a whole piece ensures that it won't dry out as much.)

4 Pour the sesame seeds and nigella seeds onto a long sheet of parchment paper and toss them around to combine them evenly. Unwrap 1 dough log and roll it in the seed mixture so all sides are well coated (if the seeds won't stick because the dough is too cold, leave the dough log at room temperature for 5 to 10 minutes to allow it to soften slightly). Repeat with the other log. Then rewrap each log and refrigerate them for 20 minutes.

5 Adjust the oven racks to the upper-middle and lower-middle positions, and preheat the oven to 375°F. Line 2 or 3 sheet pans (if you have that many) with parchment paper.

6 Slice the logs crosswise as thin as you can without them breaking, about ⅛ inch thick (this is what makes these cookies so special), and place the rounds ½ inch apart on the prepared sheet pans. Bake the cookies, turning the sheets and rotating the bottom sheet to the top and the top to the bottom midway through, until they are deep golden brown, 6 to 7 minutes. Remove the sheet pans from the oven, slide the sheets of parchment onto wire racks, and let the cookies cool completely.

7 Store the cooled cookies in an airtight container for up to 1 week.

Arak and Sesame Sticks

Makes 24 sticks

Arak is an aniseed liqueur similar to ouzo or pastis and the Tunisian liqueur called Boukha Bokobsa. In Morocco, it is commonly offered as an aperitif to guests when they enter a home before sitting down to dinner. It adds an extra anise-y taste to these very tender shortbread sticks. With the rest of the bottle of arak, do what they do in Lebanon and make a drink by mixing a little with some water and ice (like pastis), or beat the heat with a cocktail made of arak and grapefruit soda or arak and orange juice.

Sesame seeds	65 grams (¼ cup plus 2½ tablespoons)
Cake flour (sifted, 8 to 8.5%)	330 grams (3 cups)
Baking powder	4 grams (1 teaspoon)
Granulated sugar	15 grams (1 tablespoon)
Fine salt	15 grams (1 tablespoon)
Unsalted butter (at cool room temperature)	75 grams (5 tablespoons)
Extra-virgin olive oil	70 grams (5 tablespoons)
Arak, ouzo, pastis, or water	80 grams (⅓ cup), plus an extra 15 grams (1 tablespoon) if needed
Fennel seeds	30 grams (3 tablespoons)

EGG WASH AND TOPPING

Large egg	1
Water	1 tablespoon
Fine salt	Pinch
Coarse sea salt or kosher salt	as needed for finishing

1 Heat a medium skillet over medium heat. Add the sesame seeds and toast them, shaking the skillet often, until they are golden, 2 to 3 minutes. Transfer the seeds to a medium plate to cool.

2 Place the flour and baking powder in the bowl of a stand mixer fitted with the paddle attachment and combine on low speed. Add the sugar, salt, butter, olive oil, and liqueur or water, and mix on medium-low speed until the dough starts to come together (add the extra 15 grams / 1 tablespoon of liqueur or water if the dough seems dry). Add 3 tablespoons of the sesame seeds and the fennel seeds, and continue to mix until the dough is well combined, about 2 minutes.

3 Use a plastic dough scraper to transfer the dough to a piece of plastic wrap. Press the dough into a 1-inch-thick rectangle and refrigerate it for 1 hour or overnight.

(continued)

4 Preheat the oven to 300°F.

5 Place the dough on a work surface, and use a bench knife to divide it into 24 pieces. Roll each piece into a cylinder that is 7 to 8 inches long and ¼ inch thick. Transfer the sesame sticks to a parchment paper–lined sheet pan.

6 In a small bowl, beat the egg with the water and fine salt to make an egg wash. Use a pastry brush to lightly coat the top of the sticks with egg wash, and then sprinkle them with the remaining sesame seeds and some coarse salt. Bake the sticks until they are golden and very dry, 18 to 20 minutes. Remove the sheet pan from the oven and let the sesame sticks cool completely on the sheet. Store in a parchment paper–lined airtight container for up to 1 week.

Variation

Toasted Cumin Sticks

Substitute 10 grams (1 tablespoon plus 1 teaspoon) cumin seeds for the sesame seeds in step 1, toasting them as instructed. After brushing the sticks with egg wash, sprinkle them with coarse salt and bake as instructed.

WITH . . .

ONCE YOU LEARN TO MAKE the breads in this book, you'll need something to eat with them. It is almost impossible to sit down to a meal at an Israeli restaurant or in an Israeli household without starting off with an assortment of salatim: salads, dips, and spreads. We even have our own hand gesture to cover this genre: bring your fingers and thumb together to a point, then motion from right to left in a swooping half circle to signal "Do you have a little something to dip into?" We can't imagine pita or fresh bread without some kind of creamy dip or chunky salad to scoop up.

I call these recipes "Muddled" Eastern—they are a combination of a little of this and a little of that, from a multitude of cultures and countries that have become part of the standard definition of Israeli food. Hummus bi tahina is the obvious go-to, as is babaghanouj. Are these Israeli? Are they Palestinian? Are they Turkish or Egyptian, Yemenite, Albanian, Lebanese, or Moroccan? The answer is yes! They are the foods of all these places. These foods are fantastic served on small plates as part of an array of little dishes for snacking, but you can also use them as a spread for sandwiches, as a stuffing for burekas, a topping for focaccia, or even as an accompaniment to an omelet. They are healthy and fresh, composed of vegetables and beans, olives and olive oil, chiles and spices, which is why none of us can imagine a meal without at least a few of these to enjoy with our bread.

Hummus

Makes about 7 cups

Everyone in Israel has an opinion about hummus, and I do too. The most important thing about hummus is that it is served fresh, ideally warm, and within 4 to 5 minutes of being made. Hummus truly changes once refrigerated—it's still good, but try it warm and fresh and you will never want to eat it another way. It's like eating a bureka or bread straight from the oven: irresistible and at its best. Try to find small chickpeas—Bulgarian chickpeas—which make the smoothest hummus because they have a thin skin.

Dried chickpeas	500 grams (1 pound)
Baking soda	10 grams (1 tablespoon)
Tahini sesame paste	100 grams (heaping ⅓ cup)
Fresh lemon juice	30 grams (2 tablespoons)
Garlic cloves	3, finely minced or grated on a Microplane
Fine salt	5 grams (1 teaspoon)
Ground cumin	Large pinch
Extra-virgin olive oil	2 teaspoons, plus extra for serving
Bread or pita	for serving

1 Place the chickpeas in a large bowl and add enough water to cover them by 3 inches. Stir in 5 grams (1½ teaspoons) of the baking soda and let the chickpeas soak at room temperature for 24 hours.

2 Transfer the chickpeas and the soaking liquid to a large pot and add the remaining 5 grams (1½ teaspoons) baking soda. If the chickpeas are not covered, add more water. Bring the liquid to a boil over high heat; then reduce the heat to medium-low and simmer gently (you want just a few bubbles bursting on the surface), skimming off any impurities that rise to the surface, until the chickpeas are very soft and easy to mash against the side of the pot, 45 minutes to 1 hour.

3 Set a fine-mesh sieve over a large bowl and drain the chickpeas, reserving the cooking liquid. Set about ½ cup of the cooked chickpeas aside and pour the rest into a food processor. Add 70 grams (⅓ cup) of the reserved cooking liquid to the food processor along with the tahini, lemon juice, garlic, salt, cumin, and olive oil.

4 Process the hummus until it is very creamy, 3 to 4 minutes. Taste and adjust the thickness with more cooking liquid and the flavor with more salt or lemon juice as needed. Scoop some of the hummus onto a serving plate and use the back of a spoon to make a well in the center. Drizzle olive oil into the well, and then finish with the cooked chickpeas. Serve the hummus with bread or pita.

Tahina

Makes 2¼ cups

Tahina is a must with burekas and babaghanouj; it's also delicious as a dressing for salad, over raw or roasted vegetables, or on roasted chicken or cauliflower. Tahina is almost always present as part of the Israeli table. I like my tahina with lots of garlic; some prefer just lemon, water, and salt. Of course, great tahina starts with the best-quality tahini. Buy it from a store with high turnover so you can be sure to get the freshest product. You want to be able to taste the toasted sesame—a warm, deeply nutty flavor. Ice water makes the tahina extra thick and creamy. A little date syrup (silan) adds a touch of sweetness, which can be very nice drizzled over tahina instead of parsley and without the garlic.

Ice water	about 1 cup (or use less for a thicker tahina)
Tahini sesame paste	290 grams (1 cup)
Fresh lemon juice	1 tablespoon to ¼ cup, to taste
Garlic cloves (optional)	2, minced or grated
Fine salt	¼ teaspoon
Fresh flat-leaf parsley leaves (optional)	Pinch, finely chopped

Fill a small bowl with ice and water and stir for a few seconds to allow the water to get icy cold. Measure out 1 cup of the ice water. In a medium bowl, whisk together the tahini, ice water, 1 tablespoon of the lemon juice, the garlic (if using), and the salt. Stir in the parsley (if using). Taste and adjust the flavor and thickness with more water, lemon juice, or salt as needed. Refrigerate in an airtight container for up to 1 week.

Red Z'hug

Makes 2 cups

Z'hug is a Yemenite hot sauce that Israelis have adopted wholeheartedly (see page 164 for more information about Yemen's contribution to Israeli food). It comes in two varieties: red, based on dried red chiles, and green, based on fresh green chiles. Either is important to cut the heaviness and richness of many dishes like falafel and hummus, burekas, malawach, and jachnun. Z'hug is essentially the Middle Eastern equivalent of Sriracha, yet it is much simpler to make at home—and let's face it, homemade is always the best. If you can, buy fresh cayenne chiles when they are in season and dry them (by hanging—see photo on page 320). The flavor difference is enormous.

Whole fresh red chiles (such as cayenne chiles)	700 grams (1½ pounds), stemmed and halved lengthwise
Garlic cloves	15 (from about 1½ heads of garlic)
Fresh cilantro leaves	5½ ounces (about 3 packed cups, from about 3 bunches)
Fine salt	1½ teaspoons
Whole cumin seeds	1½ teaspoons
Ground cardamom	1 teaspoon
Ground coriander	1 teaspoon
Freshly ground black pepper	1 teaspoon
Extra-virgin olive oil	225 grams (1 cup)

1 Place the chiles, garlic, cilantro, and salt in a blender jar (or food processor) and pulverize as best as you can, stopping the blender as needed to stir or to scrape the solids and reincorporate them into the mixture.

2 Add the cumin, cardamom, coriander, and black pepper. With the blender running, slowly add the olive oil until well combined. Transfer the z'hug to a glass jar or other airtight container and refrigerate for up to 2 weeks.

Green Z'hug

Makes 2 cups

Green z'hug is made with lots of green chiles, garlic, and cilantro. For less heat, seed some of the chiles by using a melon baller to scrape out the seeds from a chile half. You can use less spicy jalapeños instead of Thai chiles (the closest in taste and heat to the Yemenite chile used) or serrano chiles, or a combination of the two to create a tamer z'hug. This is not salsa—it's supposed to make you sweat!

Whole fresh green chiles (such as Thai or serrano chiles)	700 grams (1½ pounds), stemmed and halved lengthwise
Garlic cloves	22 (from about 2 large heads of garlic)
Fresh cilantro leaves	5½ ounces (about 3 packed cups, from about 3 bunches)
Fine salt	20 grams (1 tablespoon plus 1 teaspoon)
Ground cumin	5 grams (1 tablespoon)
Freshly ground black pepper	1 teaspoon
Ground cardamom	½ teaspoon
Extra-virgin olive oil	225 grams (1 cup)

1 Place the chiles, garlic, cilantro, and salt in a blender jar (or food processor) and pulverize as best as you can, stopping the blender as needed to stir or to scrape the solids and reincorporate them into the mixture.

2 Add the cumin, black pepper, and cardamom. With the blender running, slowly add the olive oil until well combined. Transfer the z'hug to a glass jar or other airtight container and refrigerate for up to 2 weeks.

ABOUT SPICES

It is always best to buy whole spices and grind them fresh for the purest, freshest flavor. The difference in taste is huge—a freshly ground spice becomes a totally different product from the store-bought version. If buying bags of bulk spices, be sure to buy from a shop that specializes in spices and one that has a lot of turnover so you know the product is fresh; it makes an enormous difference in cooking and baking. In fact, some spice shops will even grind whole spices to a powder for you while you wait. This is ideal!

Babaghanouj

Makes about 2 cups

What makes a plate of babaghanouj really special is the smokiness that comes from charring the eggplant—preferably on a grill over coal or wood, or under a broiler, or directly over a gas flame.

Vegetable oil	for oiling the grill
Eggplants	3 large
Garlic clove	1, grated on a Microplane
Fine salt	1 teaspoon, plus more if needed
Extra-virgin olive oil	15 grams (1 tablespoon)
Tahina (page 316)	80 grams (⅓ cup)
Bread or pita	for serving

1 Prepare a charcoal or gas grill and heat to medium-high heat.

2 Use tongs to dip a folded paper towel into a small bowl of vegetable oil and use it to grease the grill grates. Prick each eggplant a few times with a fork, and then place them on the grill. Cook until they are charred on all sides, 8 to 12 minutes. Once an eggplant is charred, move it to a cooler side of the grill so it can continue to roast until cooked through, 20 to 25 minutes total. When the eggplants are completely deflated and tender to the center, remove them from the grill and set them aside to cool.

3 Once the eggplants are cool enough to handle, peel away the charred skin, remove the stem ends, and cut the eggplants in half. Use a spoon to scoop out the flesh and place it in a large bowl. You should end up with about 500 grams (1 pound) of cooked eggplant.

4 Stir the garlic and the salt into the cooked eggplant. Stir in the olive oil and tahina. Taste and adjust the seasoning with more salt if needed. Serve with bread or pita. Scrape any leftover babaghanouj into an airtight container and refrigerate for up to 5 days.

SMOKY EGGPLANT OFF THE GRILL

You can get your eggplant smoky indoors by charring it slowly over your stovetop's gas flame—use tongs to turn it every so often until the skin is blackened. You can also char the eggplant under the broiler, turning it every 5 to 8 minutes. For an extra smoky flavor, use a handheld torch (see page 340) to char the skin before opening the eggplant and scooping out the flesh.

Rinat's Salad

Serves 6 to 8

Smoke is key to this eggplant, tomato, and pepper salad, made with vegetables cooked over a live fire so they can become infused with the taste of the grill. To cheat, you can roast the vegetables in the oven and then use a handheld torch to char the skin and the outside of the vegetables. Rinat and I like to serve this salad with grilled steaks or kebabs—and freshly baked bread, of course.

Vegetable oil	for oiling the grill
Eggplant	1 large
Tomatoes	6
Red bell peppers	2
Jalapeños	2
Yellow onion	1, quartered (skin left on)
Extra-virgin olive oil	45 grams (3 tablespoons)
Garlic cloves	2, finely chopped
Fine salt	10 grams (2 teaspoons)
Bread or pita	for serving

1 Prepare a charcoal or gas grill and heat it to medium-high heat.

2 Use tongs to dip a folded paper towel into a small bowl of vegetable oil and use it to grease the grill grates. Prick the eggplant a few times with a fork and place it on the grill. Add the tomatoes, bell peppers, jalapeños, and onion to the grill and cook until the vegetables are charred on all sides, 5 to 8 minutes; then transfer them to a rimmed sheet pan or plate. Once the eggplant is charred, move it to a cooler side of the grill so it can continue to roast until cooked through, 20 to 25 minutes total. Remove the eggplant from the grill once it is completely deflated and tender to the center. Set all the vegetables aside until they are cool enough to handle.

3 Remove the stem from the eggplant, halve it lengthwise, and use a spoon to scoop out the flesh and place it in a large bowl. Peel away the skin from the bell peppers and jalapeños, stem them, cut them in half lengthwise, and scrape away the seeds (keep the seeds in the jalapeño if you want the salad to be spicy). Coarsely chop the peppers and add them to the eggplant in the bowl. Peel the tomatoes and the onion. Seed and chop the tomato, chop the onion, and add these to the bowl with the eggplant. Use your fingers to shred and stir everything together. You want the salad to be rustic and chunky.

4 Stir in the olive oil, garlic, and salt. Taste and adjust the seasoning with more salt if needed. The flavors in the salad will continue to come together the longer it sits. Eat at room temperature or cold, with bread or pita.

Algerian Salad

Makes 1½ cups, serves 4 to 6

I learned to make lahmis, or Algerian salad, from a few Breads Bakery employees who are Algerian. One day they were making it for themselves for lunch and gave me a taste. After one bite, I knew I had to offer this wonderfully savory-smoky salad in the bakery. It's perfect with pita or focaccia, with hummus, or on its own.

Green bell peppers	3 large
Ripe tomato	1 large
Jalapeño	1
Extra-virgin olive oil	15 grams (1 tablespoon)
Fine salt	½ teaspoon
Bread or pita	for serving

1 Adjust an oven rack to the upper-middle position and heat the broiler to high (or heat a charcoal or gas grill to high heat). Set the bell peppers, tomato, and jalapeño on a rimmed sheet pan and broil until charred all over (watch the vegetables closely, as broiler intensities vary), using tongs to turn them often. Remove the vegetables from the oven and place everything in a heat-safe bowl. Cover the bowl with plastic wrap and set it aside for 15 minutes.

2 Once the vegetables are cool enough to handle, peel away the charred skins. Open the bell peppers and remove the seeds; then slice them into long, very thin strips; place them in a medium bowl. Do the same with the jalapeño, keeping some of the seeds if you like things spicy.

3 Heat a small nonstick skillet over high heat. Squeeze the peeled tomato over the hot skillet, releasing the juice, and then use your fingers to shred the flesh to bits, adding it to the skillet. Cook the tomato, stirring often, until the liquid has completely evaporated, 1 to 2 minutes.

4 Add the tomato to the peppers in the bowl and stir in the olive oil and salt. Use the back of a fork to mash everything up a little bit. Serve immediately with bread or pita, or refrigerate in an airtight container for up to 5 days.

Kalamata Tapenade

Makes about 1¼ cups

Olives are a part of every meal in Israel. The cracked, briny, slightly bitter green olives are what I most love; they're often served in a small dish with maybe some spicy finger-length pickled cucumbers or pickled pink turnips. Those olives would be too bitter for tapenade, however, so I rely on the briny flavor of less intense Kalamata olives instead. This tapenade provides a nice counterpoint in a simple cheese sandwich, makes a savory topping for focaccia, and is also great spread onto dough for stuffed brioche snails (page 223).

Pitted Kalamata olives	250 grams (1⅓ cups)
Garlic cloves	5, coarsely chopped
Fresh thyme sprig	1, leaves removed and reserved
Extra-virgin olive oil	25 grams (1 tablespoon plus 2 teaspoons)
Fine salt	½ teaspoon

Combine the olives, garlic, thyme leaves, olive oil, and salt in a small food processor and process until semismooth. Taste and add more salt if needed (this will depend on how salty the olives are). Store in an airtight container for up to 1 week.

Moroccan Charoset

Makes about 2½ cups

Charoset is one component of the traditional Pesach Seder plate. This North African version counts on spices like cinnamon and cardamom for sweetness and warmth along with the sesame seeds, dates, and almonds. Traditional ingredients like apples and walnuts are included, too. Use it to fill hamantaschen (page 266) or spread it onto matzo or bread.

Raw whole almonds (preferably with skin)	25 grams (¼ cup)
Sesame seeds	15 grams (2 tablespoons)
Granulated sugar	15 grams (1 tablespoon)
Water	45 grams (3 tablespoons)
Granny Smith apple	1, peeled, cored, and grated on the large-hole side of a box grater
Honey	25 grams (1½ tablespoons)
Chopped raw walnuts	50 grams (½ cup)
Pitted Medjool dates	250 grams (½ pound)
Ground cinnamon	½ teaspoon
Ground cardamom	¼ teaspoon
Ground cloves	¼ teaspoon

1 Place the almonds in a medium skillet set over medium heat. Toast the almonds, shaking the pan often, until they are golden, 5 to 7 minutes. Transfer the almonds to a cutting board. Add the sesame seeds to the pan and toast them, shaking the pan often, until they are golden brown, 3 to 4 minutes. Pour the sesame seeds into a bowl, and then coarsely chop the almonds and add them to the sesame seeds. Set aside.

2 Combine the sugar and water in a large saucepan set over medium-high heat and bring the mixture to a simmer. Add the apple and honey and simmer, stirring occasionally, for 2 minutes. Add the walnuts, almonds, and sesame seeds and stir until well combined; remove from the heat.

3 Place the dates in a medium bowl and add the apple mixture, cinnamon, cardamom, and cloves. Once the mixture is cool enough to handle, use your hands to mash it together until it is well combined. Cover the bowl with plastic wrap and refrigerate to chill. The charoset tastes best after a few hours once the flavors have come together and is best eaten within 2 days, though it will keep in the refrigerator for up to 1 week.

Matbucha

Makes 2 cups

Matbucha is a simple tomato sauce made by slowly cooking tomatoes, chiles, and garlic down until the mixture reaches a jamlike consistency. It is excellent as a salad or a condiment or used as the base for shakshuka with eggs for breakfast. If you are using out-of-season tomatoes, consider adding a teaspoon of sugar to enhance their flavor.

Tomatoes	12
Extra-virgin olive oil	30 grams (2 tablespoons)
Garlic cloves	6, slivered
Jalapeños or serrano chiles	1 or 2, quartered lengthwise; seeded if desired for less heat
Fine salt	20 grams (1 tablespoon plus 1 teaspoon)
Granulated sugar (if needed)	1 teaspoon

1 Bring a large pot of water to a boil. Fill a large bowl with ice and water and set it aside.

2 Cut a small X in the bottom of each tomato. Blanch the tomatoes in the boiling water until the skin at the X starts to curl, about 2 minutes (if the tomatoes are very under-ripe, they may need a minute or two longer; if they are very ripe, check at 30 seconds to 1 minute). Use a slotted spoon to transfer the tomatoes to the bowl of ice water.

3 Heat the olive oil in a large saucepan over medium-low heat. Add the garlic and jalapeños and cook, stirring often, until the garlic is lightly golden, 5 to 7 minutes. Reduce the heat to low.

4 Drain the cooled tomatoes. Peel the skin off a tomato, and holding the tomato over the saucepan, shred it with your fingers so the pieces drop into the pan. Repeat with the remaining tomatoes; then stir in the salt and the sugar (if using). Cook the tomato mixture, stirring every 5 to 10 minutes, until the liquid has completely evaporated and the tomatoes have broken down to a jamlike consistency, about 1½ hours.

5 Let the matbucha cool a bit and serve it warm, at room temperature, or cold. Refrigerate the matbucha in an airtight container for up to 1 week.

Labne

Makes about 1 cup

Labne is a Lebanese strained yogurt into which salt and a little lemon juice are stirred to give the extra-thick yogurt a strong, tangy flavor. It's an essential part of a Middle Eastern platter with olives, pita, and hummus or babaghanouj and perhaps Algerian Salad (page 327) or Rinat's Salad (page 324) on the side. To make labne, you need a spot where you can let the yogurt drain over a bowl. Get creative and see what you come up with—a towel bar, shower rod, or even a broomstick or mop handle adjusted to shoulder-level height (with the gathered edges of the cheesecloth held down by weights or heavy books) works well. Or simply let the yogurt sit in a fine-mesh sieve placed over a deep bowl so it can drain.

Plain full-fat yogurt (with a high fat percentage and a strong sour flavor)	500 grams (heaping 2 cups)
Fine salt	1 heaping teaspoon
Fresh lemon juice	1 teaspoon

1 Whisk the yogurt, salt, and lemon juice together in a bowl. Line a fine-mesh sieve with a large doubled layer of cheesecloth, letting the excess hang over the edges of the sieve (you want quite a bit of extra material so you can gather the ends easily). Pour the yogurt mixture into the cheesecloth and gather the ends, tying them together with a long piece of sturdy kitchen twine. Suspend the yogurt by tying the string to a rod set over the bowl. Remove the sieve and let the yogurt drain into the bowl at cool room temperature, out of the sunlight, for 24 to 36 hours.

2 Untie the string, place the cheesecloth with the drained yogurt in a sieve, and set the sieve and over a bowl. Refrigerate the labne for another 24 hours before using. The labne will keep in an airtight container in the refrigerator for 5 days to 1 week.

Ful

Makes about 2 cups

Tender, herb-infused fava beans are an essential topping to an Egyptian-style hummus "complet." When choosing dried beans, pick ones that are taut, not shriveled. Shriveling means the beans are old, which will affect the cooking time of the beans (they will probably need more than an hour to tenderize), and they won't be as creamy when they are cooked through.

Small dried fava beans	250 grams (8 ounces)
Dried red chile	1
Fresh thyme sprig	1
Fresh sage sprig	1
Garlic clove	1, smashed
Yellow onion	¼ small
Extra-virgin olive oil	45 grams (3 tablespoons)

1 Pick through the dried beans for any small stones or twigs, and then rinse the beans under cold water. Place the beans in a medium bowl and add enough cool water to cover them by 3 inches. Let the beans soak at room temperature for 12 hours, draining and covering with fresh water 2 or 3 times.

2 Drain the beans and pour them into a small saucepan. Add 2½ cups of water, and bring the water to a boil over medium-high heat. Then reduce the heat to a gentle simmer and cook the beans for 30 minutes.

3 Add the chile, thyme, sage, garlic, and onion and cook until the beans are tender, about 30 minutes. Stir in the olive oil. Remove the chile, herb sprigs, garlic clove, and onion before serving.

Preserved Lemons

Makes about 1 quart

Simple and yet with a flavor that completely transcends the humble ingredients of lemons, salt, sugar, and olive oil, preserved lemons add an incredibly complex soft and slightly musky lemon flavor to anything from sandwiches to breads or burekas. I eat them like pickles, and I like adding a few slivers to a Tunisian tuna sandwich—with hard-boiled egg slices, harissa paste, oil-packed tuna, boiled potato slices, and olives, they add a sharp, slightly sour taste that is mildly acidic and briny. They are also excellent in cocktails or in a simple green salad. Preserved lemons will keep for months at room temperature in a cool, dark, dry spot. Always use a very clean spoon to fish one out from the jar so as not to introduce any bacteria that could spoil the whole batch.

Lemons	1 kilo (2¼ pounds), washed well
Diamond Crystal brand kosher salt or coarse sea salt (see Note)	80 grams (½ cup) 80 grams (heaping ⅓ cup)
Granulated sugar	1 teaspoon
Extra-virgin olive oil	500 grams (2 cups)

1 Make 3 lengthwise slits in each lemon, running from top to bottom, cutting through the skin and into the flesh. Place all the lemons in a large airtight container and rub them with the salt and sugar.

2 Close the container tightly and set it aside at room temperature for 3 days, rubbing the lemons with the salt and redistributing them every day.

3 After 3 days, pour the olive oil over the lemons, cover the container, and set it aside for 1 month. After 1 month, the lemons are fully preserved. To use preserved lemons, you can remove the rind and chop it fine, discarding the inside part of the lemon, or you can chop the entire lemon, insides and all (just remember to remove the seeds).

NOTE: AT THE BAKERIES WE USE KOSHER salt. We have found that the brand makes a big difference, especially if you measure in cups rather than with a scale: 1 cup of Diamond Cystal kosher salt is very different from 1 cup of Morton's kosher salt (1 cup of Morton's is nearly double the weight of the Diamond!). So if you're unsure, weigh out the salt rather than scooping and measuring.

THE BAKER'S PANTRY

While all you need is flour, yeast, water, and salt to bake bread, of course it is tastier and easier with the right ingredients and tools on your counter. So here are a couple of lists—first, the ingredients you will find called for throughout the book, and second, the tools that will make baking easier. Read through the description of each item for what you need to know before purchasing.

APRICOT KERNELS AND BITTER ALMONDS

Slightly bitter and with a very specific almond-y flavor, apricot kernels are used in the Moroccan cookies called barouj (page 277). Bitter almonds, which are used in some Middle Eastern and Italian baking recipes, are not available in the United States because they contain cyanide, so many bakers substitute apricot kernels (the inside seed of the apricot) instead; they also have trace amounts of cyanide, but much less in comparison. Apricot kernels have a flavor similar to amaretti cookies and look like small almonds. They can be purchased online and in some health food stores. As a side note, most almond extract is made from bitter almonds, so it can be used—in moderation (a little goes a long way)—instead of apricot kernels if you can't find them.

BUTTER

Use unsalted European-style butter, such as Plugrá, if you can find it. European-style butter has a higher fat percentage than standard supermarket butter, which means that your cakes, cookies, and breads will be even more tender and buttery. It is often made with a culture, similar to yogurt, so the butter has a very nice tangy flavor.

When a recipe calls for cool room-temperature butter, it should be pliable and plastic-y—not so soft that the butter is almost melting and losing its shape. You should be able to bend the butter without it breaking or squishing it into an oily mess. If you let refrigerated butter sit out, unwrapped, at room temperature for about 20 minutes, you can then smash it with your fist a few times, or use a rolling pin to whack the butter to soften it without warming it. The goal is for the fat to stay suspended in the dough, and if the butter is too soft, that won't happen.

CHEESE AND DAIRY

I use a lot of cheese and dairy in my baked goods. For all of the fresh, soft items like sour cream and ricotta, and even the yogurt used to make labne (page 332), look for brands that are thick, with a high fat content. In baking, you don't want a lot of water to leach out from the ricotta in a babka, or from the feta in your bureka. Using thicker, richer, and drier products ensures that your bottom crusts will stay crispy and that the moisture from the dairy item won't adversely affect the final texture of your baked goods.

- **Feta:** I prefer the sharp flavor of sheep's-milk feta cheese to those made with cow's or goat's milk. Taste the feta before adding salt to a recipe; some varieties are quite salty enough on their own, meaning you should omit the extra salt in the recipe.
- **Fresh mozzarella:** It goes without saying that fresh mozzarella should be fresh! Use it within a few days of purchasing for the most buttery taste.
- **Goat's-milk cheese (chèvre):** A fresh and crumbly cheese that can be purchased plain or covered in herbs or peppercorns.
- **Gouda:** Use young Gouda. Aged Gouda is too

dry and crystallized to melt properly for baked goods.

- **Kashkaval:** Made from cow's or sheep's milk, Kashkaval is a hard cheese originating in the Balkans and used throughout the region, from Albania to Turkey and beyond. It has a pungent flavor that is a bit stronger than an Italian Pecorino Romano.
- **Parmigiano-Reggiano:** Buy the best-quality Parmigiano-Reggiano you can find. Save the rind for stock and soup.
- **Ricotta and sour cream:** Choose the highest-fat version you can find with the least amount of water. You don't want the water to leach off during baking.
- **Yogurt:** In general, I prefer a tangy and rich sheep's-milk yogurt. If it is unavailable, then I try to purchase the creamiest and richest cow's- or goat's-milk yogurt I can find.

CHICKPEAS

Buy dried chickpeas at markets with a high turnover. The chickpeas should look clean and not have any dark spots. Use small chickpeas for making hummus and larger ones for making salad. (The big ones absorb more water, which is great for salads but not for hummus, when you want a very creamy, rich, and dense puree.) Many people say the smoothest and silkiest hummus is made with chickpeas grown in Bulgaria—if you see some labeled with that origin, try them out.

CHOCOLATE (AND NUTELLA)

My recipes call for both semisweet and bitter-sweet chocolates. For a good balance of sweetness and acidity, I prefer Valrhona and Callebaut. If a certain percentage of cacao is recommended, it is indicated in the recipe's ingredient list. Generally speaking, the higher the percentage of cacao, the less sweet the chocolate will be.

Nutella is a chocolate spread flavored with hazelnuts. In Israel, I swap Nutella for a kosher chocolate spread made without hazelnuts—use

whichever you prefer. You can even replace Nutella with a homemade chocolate ganache if you like (pour hot cream over chopped bittersweet or semisweet chocolate and whisk until thick and creamy; if it's too thin, add more chocolate; if too thick, add more hot cream; a pat of butter added at the end adds a little extra richness and gloss).

DATES

These are the fruits that grow from date palm trees, which are indigenous to Iraq. My favorite variety is the Medjool date, which is very soft and sticky-sweet. They should look dark and sticky too; if they are dry looking and have crystallized sugar or white spots on the surface, don't buy them. You can find dates sold in bulk or in a brick—just be sure to remove all the pits before using.

FLOUR

These recipes were tested with King Arthur all-purpose flour, which has a protein level of 11.7%. Heckers and Ceresota brand all-purpose flours work well too. Most all-purpose flours have less protein than this, so look at the amount of gluten in your favorite brand before using it. Or look at the other flours available in your supermarket—other brands might come in closer to 11.7%.

Cake flour and pastry flour are typically softer flours with even less protein in them. These flours are good for baking cookies, muffins, and cakes; you get a better crumb. They are NOT for making yeasted cakes. Spelt is a variety of wheat that has never been hybridized, so the flour retains many of its heirloom characteristics like nutritional value and hearty flavor. Whole wheat flour is made by grinding the whole grain of wheat. It typically has a very deep and nutty flavor and will require more water in a bread dough than dough that calls for all-purpose flour typically made from only the endosperm (heart) of the wheat berry.

HALVAH

A fantastic, solid, bricklike confection, halvah is made with sesame paste (tahini) and sugar. Halvah is cooked and formed and can be crumbled, sliced, and sometimes even used as a spread, depending on its consistency. Sometimes the halvah is plain sesame, sometimes pistachios are added, and sometimes it is marbled with chocolate. I think halvah made with some butter in it is best—it has the most pleasant melt-in-your-mouth consistency. One of the best ways to identify well-made halvah is that when you break it, you see thin layers and shards, almost like marbling. You don't want the halvah to be chewy—it should dissolve on the tongue.

LABNE

This thick "yogurt cheese" (page 332) is made by hanging a rich and tangy whole-milk yogurt (usually made from sheep's milk) in a cheesecloth bag and letting the extra liquid drain off over the course of several days so its flavor can sour and concentrate and the texture can become consolidated. The consistency of labne is thick and rich, somewhere between sour cream and crème fraîche, while the flavor is tangy like yogurt. I like labne when it is on the sour side and made from a sheep's-milk yogurt. It can be used as a spread (like on the lachmajun, page 140) or as a dip, drizzled with good olive oil and sprinkled with za'atar.

MARZIPAN

The best and highest-quality marzipan is made with a high percentage of almonds. Some manufacturers include as little as 20% almonds in their marzipan while others have more than 55% almonds (the remainder of the ingredients list includes mostly sugar, water, and glucose). The lesson is to look at the ingredients list on the label before buying, and not to trust the name of the product alone. My favorite marzipan comes from Denmark and Germany. That's not to say you can't find other high-quality marzipan. In my experience, the marzipan/almond paste sold in a can in U.S. supermarkets is too thin to use in my recipes; instead, look for a marzipan packaged as a log. Good marzipan contains a little bitter almond too for a uniquely sharp amaretti cookie flavor (though this can be hard to find since bitter almond is generally unavailable in the United States; see page 336).

NIGELLA

Also called "onion seeds" or "black cumin," nigella is a small, black, sesame-shaped seed that has a fantastic onion-y taste. You'll often see them used as decoration on the top of challahs. You can find them in Indian and Middle Eastern markets. When buying nigella seeds, look into the bag and buy one with less powder at the bottom (who wants to pay good money for seed dust?), and choose the bag with the largest seeds, of course. Like poppy seeds, sesame seeds, and flaxseeds, nigella seeds contain fat and can go rancid, so make sure to look at the sell-by date to ensure you are buying a fresh product.

OLIVES AND OLIVE OIL

Olives are of course a critical component on the Middle Eastern table, whether used in their brined form or as a paste or oil. When buying olive oil, invest in the oil rather than the bottle; choose a brand that sells the oil in a tin (to keep out light and prevent oxidation) rather than a fancy bottle. The oil should be grassy and buttery, a little cloudy, and not too clear or pure. Of course, extra-virgin olive oil has the most flavor and is the best quality to buy.

I love all kinds of olives, but my first pick for black olives is purple-y Kalamatas. For green olives, I love the cracked olives sold in Middle Eastern markets—they are not the most beautiful, but their pungency and bitterness is excellent alongside rich and creamy dishes like babaghanouj, hummus, and labne.

ORANGE BLOSSOM WATER AND ROSE WATER

Orange blossom water is made from a distillation of bitter-orange blossoms. It has a beautiful citrus-flowery fragrance and can be used to add a light floral taste to pastry creams, cookies, cakes, and breads. Similar to orange blossom water, rose water is made by distilling rose petals. Both should be used in moderation; otherwise, your cookies could end up tasting like perfume.

TAHINI

Tahini, a smooth sesame paste, should be made from 100% sesame seeds. Some tahini is very thin and light, some very dark and thick. The best way to find your favorite is to try a few brands and see what you like. Be sure to stir it well after opening the jar to re-homogenize the paste and the oil; most often the two will have separated while the tahini sat in the container. Tahini is an ingredient in babaghanouj and is the basis of tahina, the sauce used on falafel and shawarma. My favorite tahini comes from Israel, where there is endless debate about what to add to it to make the best tahina—some like garlic and lemon juice, others a pinch of parsley. See page 316 for my favorite way (made with ice water for creaminess).

TURKISH DELIGHT

Also called rahat lokum, Turkish delight is a chewy gelled confection that can be flavored with rose water (used in the Rahat Lokum Crescents, page 272) or with pistachios, dates, walnuts, and flavors like lemon and bitter orange. It is usually cut into small cubes and dusted with confectioners' sugar to prevent sticking. Find it in Middle Eastern markets and Indian food shops.

YEAST

I like to use fresh yeast (sometimes called cake yeast because it is sold in a cake-like brick, not because it is used in cake recipes) in my recipes. That said, if you make two breads, one with fresh yeast and another with active dry yeast, I'd

challenge even the most sophisticated palate to tell the difference—because the difference, if there even is one, is slight. Many cooks feel anxious when it comes to baking because they are nervous about dealing with yeast. But yeast is easy to manage if you keep in mind a few simple points:

- When converting the quantity of fresh yeast to instant yeast, simply use 30% of the yeast called for. So if the recipe calls for 30 grams of fresh yeast, use 10 grams of instant yeast instead.
- Keep yeast—whether fresh or dried—in the refrigerator. Write the date you purchased the yeast on the package. If your fresh yeast becomes very dry, cracked, and parched-looking, or is spotty or discolored, discard it. Fresh yeast typically lasts for 2 weeks in the refrigerator; dry yeast will last for several months in the refrigerator.
- Yeast does not like to be covered with salt or sugar or oil or other fat. So keep them separated until it's time to mix.
- Once yeast is incorporated into a dough, it will lose some of its potency if the dough dries out. If your dough is in the rising or proofing stage, always sprinkle it with a little flour and keep it covered with plastic wrap or with a clean kitchen towel. (See page 17 for homemade proof box ideas.)

ZA'ATAR

Za'atar can refer to either a spice blend made with sesame seeds, sumac, and salt, or a wild herb that tastes like a combination of thyme, marjoram, and mint. Za'atar the herb belongs to the oregano family and is a wild grass that is now protected by law in Israel. If you go to a spice shop, you might see many different combinations of spices and herbs labeled "za'atar." Like garam masala or five-spice powder, every spice merchant and family has its own house blend—I like mine with fennel seed. The one must is that za'atar the blend should always include za'atar the herb.

THE BAKER'S TOOLKIT

The only must-haves for making bread are your hands, an oven, and a digital scale. That said, here are some tools that make the process of baking bread cleaner, simpler, and easier.

BENCH SCRAPER

A bench scraper is a rectangular metal piece attached to a wooden or plastic handle. When you scrape your work surface (which bakers call the "bench"), dough—whether it is sticky and tacky or dry and hard—effortlessly comes off. It's the quickest and easiest way to clean a surface (you never want to use water when cleaning a floury surface because you'll just make paste). It's also handy for slicing rounds or coins from a log of dough (like the Parmesan Cookies on page 305) or for dividing bread dough into smaller pieces. It is very inexpensive and can be found in most kitchenware stores.

COUCHE

A couche is a heavy sheet of flax linen cloth used to provide support for soft bread doughs during the proof stage (such as An Everyday Loaf, page 168). Never wash a couche. Instead, brush away the excess flour or bits of dough using a natural-bristle pastry brush.

DIGITAL SCALE

I know Americans like their measuring cups and spoons, but as a baker, the efficiency, speed, and accuracy of measuring by digital scale will always be my go-to. Everyone has a different way of measuring—if you dip and sweep a cupful of flour versus using a spoon to scoop flour and transfer to a measuring cup, you will get a different weight measurement. Additionally, some people sift the flour first with a fork prior to scooping, which aerates the flour and also provides for a different volume measurement. Since accuracy is the key to consistent results in baking, I always measure my ingredients using a digital scale. Don't skimp and buy a cheap scale either—invest in a good-quality one that offers consistency even in small amounts. The accuracy of your scale is important.

DOUGH SCRAPER

This is the best $2 investment you'll ever make. This little piece of flexible plastic has a curved edge that makes removing even the stickiest mass of dough from a bowl incredibly clean and effortless. You can find them at most kitchenware stores.

FOOD PROCESSOR

Generally a great investment for pureeing food, shredding cheese, and making bread crumbs. Buy a food processor with a small bowl insert for small quantities of ingredients as in Kalamata Tapenade (page 328) or z'hug (pages 318–319) (or just use a blender).

HANDHELD TORCH

These small, home-kitchen-friendly butane torches make it extra easy to give eggplant, peppers, or tomatoes a little char. You can purchase one at cookware stores.

KITCHEN TOWELS

Clean kitchen towels—you can never have enough! They are great to drape over rising dough, to clear off a surface, or, when triple-folded, to pull a hot pan from the oven. Be sure to buy towels that won't leave little fuzzy bits of material behind on your dough. Linen or tightly woven cotton towels (often called tea towels) are best.

KUGELHOPF PAN

This narrow, fluted cake pan has a tube in the center, similar to a Bundt pan but with a smaller capacity (7 to 10 cups is typical). It is taller and narrower than a Bundt, which usually has a 12- to 15-cup capacity.

LARGE BINS AND CONTAINERS

For trouble-free measuring, transfer flour and sugar to large containers with airtight lids. Keep a scoop right in the container for easy scooping.

LARGE UNSCENTED CLEAR PLASTIC GARBAGE BAGS

I use unscented garbage bags as homemade proof boxes for dough (see page 17). The plastic creates a humid environment where the dough can rest.

LOAF PANS

A standard-size loaf pan is 8½ by 4½ inches. If you are using higher-end stoneware rather than a metal or glass pan, be sure to measure your pan—it will likely have a different measurement, and you may need to adjust the size that you roll your dough to or change the shape of the loaf to accommodate your pan. If you are using Advanced Babka Dough (page 70) to make the babkas, you will need to buy paper loaf pans that measure 9 by 2¾ by 2 inches (visit bakedeco.com).

METAL SPATULAS

For flipping, turning, and transferring.

MICROPLANE RASP GRATER

For grating citrus zest, finely grating chocolate, or even creating a fine pistachio powder, use a rasp grater. I sometimes like to grate garlic too, but for this, use a separate rasp with a different-colored handle so your lemon zest doesn't taste like garlic.

MIXING BOWLS

Nonreactive metal bowls in all sizes are the most practical.

PARCHMENT PAPER

Parchment paper is endlessly handy for lining baking sheets or holding sifted flour. Pick up the edges and slide the flour right into your bowl—no mess!

PASTRY BRUSH

To egg-wash dough, I like to use natural-bristle brushes. But sometimes they get stiff and can tear the dough, so it's good practice to let the bristles warm up under warm water to soften a bit before applying the egg wash.

RIMMED SHEET PANS

Buy three or four half-sheet pans that measure 13 by 18 inches. A couple of quarter-sheet pans (8¾ by 12¾ inches) will come in handy too.

ROLLING PIN

Forget fancy handles and decorations. All you need is a well-balanced 2- to 3-inch-diameter wooden dowel that is sanded very smooth. A French pin with tapered ends is also a great tool for rolling dough. I prefer a solid piece of wood, tapered or not, to a rolling pin with handles because I often use a rolling pin to soften butter or dough by smacking it with the pin—try doing that with a pin that has handles and see how quickly you break off the handle!

RUBBER SPATULAS

You need this tool for scraping the mixer bowl, folding the dough, and getting all the add-ins out of a measuring cup.

RULER

An old-school ruler is essential for measuring dough after rolling it out. A long ruler or yardstick (3 feet long) comes in handy, but even a standard 12-inch ruler is fine. Plastic rulers work well; the numbers on some metal rulers can wear off with time.

SAUCEPANS

Small, medium, and large saucepans—I use them all. Get one with a tight-fitting lid and a heavy bottom that conducts even heat.

FELT-TIP PERMANENT MARKER AND MASKING TAPE

A permanent marker and a strip of masking tape are useful for labeling bowls of dough with the time at which mixing stopped. You can also mark how many folds the dough has in it if it needs to be refrigerated during the rolling and folding process (as you do with babka dough). If you plan on freezing baked or unbaked shaped bread, always mark the date on the wrapping with a marker; you want to use frozen dough—whether baked or unbaked—within 1 month.

SIEVE

A tamis sieve is a wide, drum-style sieve with a flat bottom (as opposed to a rounded sieve). It's the quickest and easiest way to sift flour to aerate it. However, if you don't have the storage space for a tamis, a rounded fine-mesh sieve with a handle is fine.

SKILLETS

Twelve- to 14-inch skillets are key for making Mofleta (page 152) and Matbucha (page 330). I prefer traditional stainless steel to nonstick because you can heat it at a very high temperature without worrying about ruining the pan (or releasing harmful chemicals into your food or the environment).

STAND MIXER

I'm known to say that all you need to make bread is your hands. Well, it's true . . . but a stand mixer makes the job a lot easier! A large-capacity stand mixer, one with a 5- to 7-quart bowl, generally works best for dough. You'll want to use a heavy-duty or professional mixer too. When handling the dough, you need a mixer with the most power. So while the power difference is noticeable between the small and large mixers, the price difference is negligible. A smaller-capacity bowl is okay—you just may have to stop the mixer occasionally to scrape the dough off the hook.

WIRE COOLING RACKS

Invest in at least two so you can cool multiple loaves or flatbreads at a time.

WORK SURFACE

Use a marble board or a wooden board for kneading bread. For making strudel, and even for making ropes of challah or babka dough, a nice long work surface is helpful. If you don't have a freestanding island or lots of counter space, do what Savta (grandmother) did and use your kitchen table!

ACKNOWLEDGMENTS

A big thank-you to:

The teams at Lehamim Bakery Tel Aviv and Breads Bakery New York, for putting their "true love" into everything they bake and for the hospitality they give to our guests—it's what our work is all about.

Rinat Tzadok, for the inspiration, the support, the recipes, the criticism, and the solutions.

Or Ohana, for so much and for so much more and especially for always looking at the bright side.

Raquel Pelzel, for the hundreds of hours spent together; it was such a pleasure—you are one of a kind.

Lia Ronnen, for your leadership and vision, and for letting me go all the way; you are amazing.

Judy Pray, for being such a pro and seeing all the details.

Michelle Ishay-Cohen, for adding so much color to our breads and pastries.

Con Poulos and Simon Andrews, for the beautiful photos.

Tali and Tal, of Studio Talim Ceramics, for contributing the beautiful ceramic bowls and letting me experiment and bake with them (find them at talim.hoogel.co.pl).

Thanks also to:

Rachel Tzadok	Nora Hussaissy	Yeon Kim
Dor Malka	Gadi Pelg	Toni Tajima
Hila Alpert	Yonatan Floman	Einat Admony
Dolly Haddad	Tamar Heilweil	David Lebovitz
Rafram Boaz Haddad	Adi Barzilay	Joan Nathan
Hedai Offaim	Janine Desiderio	Lior Lev Sercarz
Naa'ma Shefi	Zach Greenwald	Michael Solomonov
Hezi Rotem	Nancy Murray	Mimi Sheraton
Tina Scheftelowitz	Allison McGeehon	
Tova Hallel	Theresa Collier	

And a special thanks to:

Veeresh from the Humaniversity, who was an inspiring teacher of mine.

Margit Scheftelowitz, my creative mother, who taught me to knead, and Moritz Scheftelowitz, my father, who taught me discipline and persistence.

INDEX

Note: Page numbers in *italics* refer to photographs.

CONVERSION CHARTS

Here are rounded-off equivalents between the metric system and the traditional systems that are used in the United States to measure weight and volume.

FRACTIONS	DECIMALS
1/8	.125
1/4	.25
1/3	.33
3/8	.375
1/2	.5
5/8	.625
2/3	.67
3/4	.75
7/8	.875

WEIGHTS

US/UK	METRIC
1/4 oz	7 g
1/2 oz	15 g
1 oz	30 g
2 oz	55 g
3 oz	85 g
4 oz	110 g
5 oz	140 g
6 oz	170 g
7 oz	200 g
8 oz (1/2 lb)	225 g
9 oz	250 g
10 oz	280 g
11 oz	310 g
12 oz	340 g
13 oz	370 g
14 oz	400 g
15 oz	425 g
16 oz (1 lb)	455 g

VOLUME

AMERICAN	IMPERIAL	METRIC
1/4 tsp		1.25 ml
1/2 tsp		2.5 ml
1 tsp		5 ml
1/2 Tbsp (1 1/2 tsp)		7.5 ml
1 Tbsp (3 tsp)		15 ml
1/4 cup (4 Tbsp)	2 fl oz	60 ml
1/3 cup (5 Tbsp)	2 1/2 fl oz	75 ml
1/2 cup (8 Tbsp)	4 fl oz	125 ml
2/3 cup (10 Tbsp)	5 fl oz	150 ml
3/4 cup (12 Tbsp)	6 fl oz	175 ml
1 cup (16 Tbsp)	8 fl oz	250 ml
1 1/4 cups	10 fl oz	300 ml
1 1/2 cups	12 fl oz	350 ml
2 cups (1 pint)	16 fl oz	500 ml
2 1/2 cups	20 fl oz (1 pint)	625 ml
5 cups	40 fl oz (1 qt)	1.25 l

OVEN TEMPERATURES

	°F	°C	GAS MARK
very cool	250–275	130–140	1/2–1
cool	300	148	2
warm	325	163	3
moderate	350	177	4
moderately hot	375–400	190–204	5–6
hot	425	218	7
very hot	450–475	232–245	8–9

°C/F TO °F/C CONVERSION CHART

°C/F	°C	°F	°C/F	°C	°F	°C/F	°C	°F	°C/F	°C	°F
90	32	194	220	104	428	350	177	662	480	249	896
100	38	212	230	110	446	360	182	680	490	254	914
110	43	230	240	116	464	370	188	698	500	260	932
120	49	248	250	121	482	380	193	716	510	266	950
130	54	266	260	127	500	390	199	734	520	271	968
140	60	284	270	132	518	400	204	752	530	277	986
150	66	302	280	138	536	410	210	770	540	282	1,004
160	71	320	290	143	554	420	216	788	550	288	1,022
170	77	338	300	149	572	430	221	806			
180	82	356	310	154	590	440	227	824			
190	88	374	320	160	608	450	232	842			
200	93	392	330	166	626	460	238	860			
210	99	410	340	171	644	470	243	878			

Example: If your temperature is 90°F, your conversion is 32°C; if your temperature is 90°C, your conversion is 194°F.

NOV 2MS

NOV

2M